International Perspectives on Foreign Language Teaching

Edited by Gerard L. Ervin

In Conjunction with the American Council
on the Teaching of
Foreign
Languages

National Textbook Company
a division of *NTC Publishing Group* • Lincolnwood, Illinois USA

Published by National Textbook Company, a division of NTC Publishing Group.
©1991 by NTC Publishing Group, 4255 West Touhy Avenue,
Lincolnwood (Chicago), Illinois 60646-1975 U.S.A.
Manufactured in the United States of America.

1 2 3 4 5 6 7 8 9 VP 9 8 7 6 5 4 3 2 1

Contents

Foreword

This volume was born of a belief that foreign language teachers, although from different countries and concerned with different target languages, nevertheless have much to share with one another. One could argue, for example, that of all professional groups, foreign language educators should be among the most aware of the issues, concerns, practices, and research emphases that our counterparts in other nations are dealing with. After all, we regularly promote our subject matter not only for its direct utilitarian (e.g., foreign languages for careers) and cognitive (e.g., foreign languages as an academic discipline) values, but also for its humanistic values (e.g., foreign languages as a gateway to understanding other peoples and cultures). Moreover, our specialty gives us immediate access to our foreign colleagues and their writings. Yet how much do most of us really know about the foreign language education currents in the country (or countries) where our particular target language is spoken, to say nothing of our knowledge of what is happening in foreign language teaching and second language acquisition elsewhere in the world? How many of us know, for example, what is discussed at foreign language conferences in Europe or Africa? What is published in the foreign language teaching and research journals in the Middle East and the Soviet Union? Where are the major teacher preparation centers in Asia and the South Pacific, and what do we know of their curricula? In fact, what are the names, let alone the concerns and agendas, of the counterpart associations of ACTFL around the world? To the degree that we find it difficult to answer questions such as these, we foreign language teachers may be falling short of our responsibility—which is perhaps greater than that of many other professionals—to be aware of what is happening in our worldwide profession.

That responsibility goes well beyond our profession, of course: Neither the world's transcendent problems (e.g., global warming, environmental pollution, hunger, disease) nor its intermittent crises (wars, natural catastrophes) are restricted to North America and Western Europe and the people who live there. Indeed, as Walker (1991: 145) reminds us, 82 percent of the world's population speaks some language other than English, French, German, or Spanish. The lack of congruence between the numbers of speakers of these languages worldwide and the enrollments in these languages (excluding English) in the United States, as shown on figures F-1 and F-2, is striking.

I am indebted to the following indivuduals, in particular, for their pivotal roles in helping bring this volume to light: Dr. G. Michael Riley, Dean of The Ohio State University College of Humanities, who—in a casual conversation several years ago that he may by now have forgotten—planted an idea that grew into this book; the ACTFL Publications Committee and staff, including in particular Diane Birckbichler, Lynn Sandstedt, and C. Edward Scebold, for their confidence and encouragement in letting me pursue the idea; the contributing authors, who tolerated constant proddings and suggestions as the volume was taking shape; Geof Garvey, the eagle-eyed editor for National Textbook Company, whose incredible attention to matters not only of detail but also of substance have won (again) my most profound admiration (I'll work with you *any* time, on *any* book, Geof!); and my wife, Dr. Bette Ervin, who selflessly played a behind-the-scenes supportive role of inestimable value.

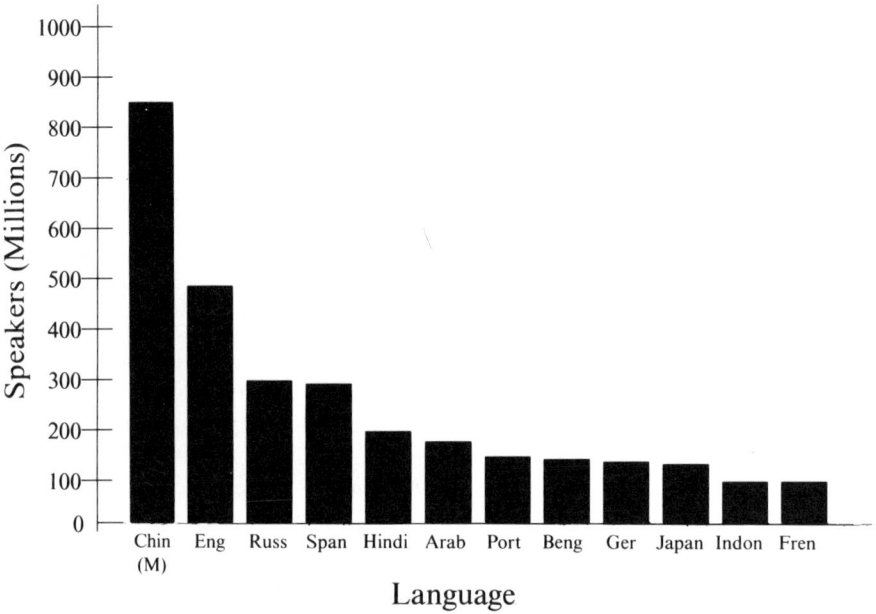

Figure F-1. Distribution of the World's Thirteen Most Common "Languages of Habitual Use"

References, Foreword

Brod, Richard I. 1988. "Foreign Language Enrollments in U.S. Institutions of Higher Education—Fall 1986," *ADFL Bulletin* 19,2: 39–44.

Dandonoli, Patricia. 1987. "Report on Foreign Language Enrollment in Public Secondary Schools, Fall 1985," *Foreign Language Annals* 20,5: 457–70.

Walker, Galal. 1991. "Gaining Place: The Less Commonly Taught Languages in American Schools." *Foreign Language Annals* 24,2: 131–50.

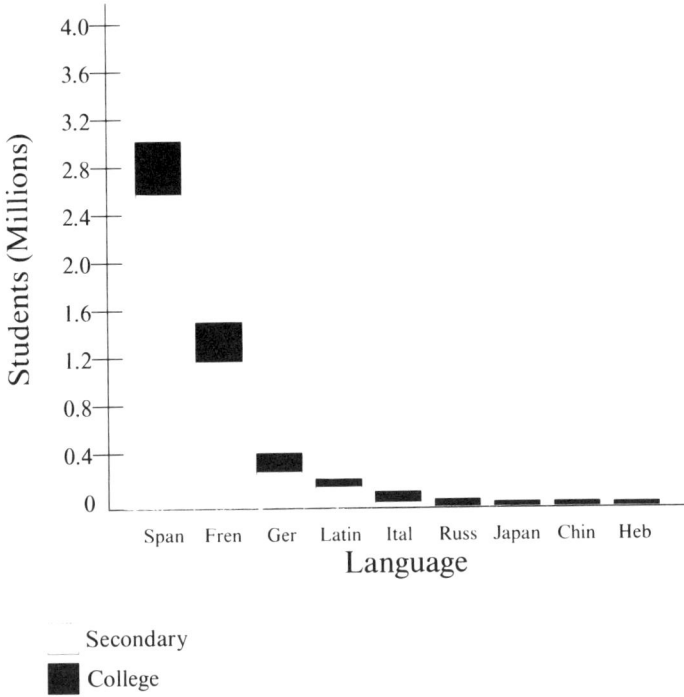

Figure F-2. College and Secondary School Foreign Language Enrollments in the United States (after Brod 1988 and Dandonoli 1987)

International Perspectives on Foreign Language Education: A Synopsis

Gerard L. Ervin
The Ohio State University

No single volume could presume to introduce the worldwide field of foreign language teaching, let alone treat it in depth. Rather, the aim of the present work is to bring before the *ACTFL Review* audience a collection of writings that are intentionally heterogeneous and wide-ranging in scope, with the hope that readers will begin to examine their professional perspectives in light of what they encounter here.

We are fortunate to have as contributors to this volume a distinguished group of authors, many of whom work in foreign language education in other countries and several of whom are appearing for the first time in the pages of this series.

Their chapters are grouped into three sections: Europe 1992, National Foreign Language Policy and Practices, and Emerging Emphases.

Europe 1992

Western Europe as we have known it for generations will undergo dramatic changes in the next few years, brought about by cooperative legislation undertaken by the twelve member states of the European Community. These changes will have the effect of forging from the dozen states a single socioeconomic and political union. Each country will retain its own cultural identity, to be sure, but beyond that a virtual "United States of Europe"—with free migration from one country to another, a single currency, and a total absence

Gerard Ervin is Associate Professor of Slavic Languages at The Ohio State University. He has taught French and Spanish at the secondary school level and Russian, foreign language methods, and ESL at the college level. Founding Director of the Foreign Language Center at The Ohio State University, he has also served as Assistant Dean in the OSU College of Humanities and as Executive Secretary of the Central States Conference on the Teaching of Foreign Languages. He is the author of *Speak and Read Essential Russian* and of many articles and book chapters on language teaching, serves as Associate Editor of *The Modern Language Journal,* and is cofounder and Systems Operator of the Foreign Language Education Forum on CompuServe. He received the ACTFL Florence Steiner Award for Leadership in Foreign Language Education in 1986 and will serve as President of ACTFL in 1992.

of trade barriers—is envisioned. The Council of Europe has recognized that a crucial element in making this new European unit work will be an increase in broad-based language training. Mary Ellen McGoey examines the current linguistic situation in Europe and the steps that have been taken to deal with the linguistic changes that will take place. She shows that the nations affected have established several far-reaching transnational programs by way of response.

One of the cooperative undertakings described by McGoey is the LINGUA program, which is the one perhaps most directly concerned with promoting multilingual skills among the populace of Europe. We are fortunate to be able to include in this volume official documentation about the LINGUA program, with a short introductory commentary by the program's director, Charles Barrière. It is too early yet to assess the effect that the LINGUA program will have in Europe, but there is no question about the clarity of its goal, i.e., to "improve foreign language competence, quantitatively and qualitatively, in order to promote mobility and communication among the citizens of the European Community."

As we watch the changes taking place in Europe, many U.S. foreign language educators (and certainly an even larger proportion of the U.S. public) will have a renewed sense that foreign language teaching there is somehow far ahead of where it is in the United States. Therefore it may come as a surprise to read that many of the same language teaching problems we are debating and wrestling with in the United States are no more resolved in Europe than they are here. François Weiss shows us through the prism of the recent history and current status of FLES in Europe that this promising area (and the issues associated with its inseparable companion, articulation) has gone through, and continues to experience, many of the same ups and downs that FLES practitioners in the United States know only too well. Like his opposite numbers in the United States, Weiss concludes that the potential for FLES is vast, provided that some fundamental issues can be resolved.

To wrap up our focus on the linguistic changes 1992 will bring to Europe, Gerhard Bach, who is familiar with the German as well as the U.S. structure of second language teaching, looks beyond what 1992 means for Europe to consider what it might mean for U.S. foreign language teaching. Recognizing that the education establishment in most countries is typically slow to change, Bach concludes that since most U.S. citizens are afforded little real opportunity to learn a foreign language (in terms of time) in our schools, our methods must be modified. One model he suggests we study is that of the international business community.

National Foreign Language Policy and Practices ⎯⎯⎯⎯⎯

The second section of this volume deals with national foreign language policy; three countries are highlighted. In examining closely the new national foreign language policy (and its derivative educational practices) in the Netherlands, Richard Lambert is the first to admit that the context for foreign language instruction there is far different from that in the United States. He nevertheless brings to our attention some areas worthy of consideration, suggesting that some aspects of a coherent national foreign language policy could, if one could be developed and implemented in America, have unmistakable benefits. "Perhaps," he writes in his conclusion, "our current disaggregated, school-bound, free-choice-driven, unarticulated, low-skill-level-focused, humanities-oriented, European-language-bound system of foreign language instruction is optimal in meeting our national needs in the next century." But then again, perhaps not.

At the time the first Europeans arrived in North America, some 500 Native American languages were spoken here. Today, that number has decreased to just over 200. Whatever the ethics of the past were in dealing with indigenous peoples, the United States and many other countries around the world are now seeking ways to deal positively and fairly with the ethnic and linguistic diversity in their populations. Ann Biersteker and Kimani Njogu examine the roots of Kenyan multilingualism and its history during and after British colonial rule. They then offer a contemporary picture of how multilingualism affects such societal institutions as the media, the legal and political systems, the home and religious practices, and the business and education sectors in Kenya. The clear lesson is that it is possible for two or more language groups to coexist, but that compromise and mutual respect are key to making a multilingual and multicultural society function.

English is surely the most widely studied second/foreign language in the world, and perhaps nowhere is this more evident than in Japan, where both school-based and proprietary English programs flourish. But the combination of the traditional teacher- and subject-centered Japanese educational system and the restraints imposed by Japanese culture on Japanese learners of English have resulted, according to Keiko Samimy and Carl Adams, in largely unsatisfactory English instruction in that country. By way of response, the Japanese educational establishment is seeking to move from teacher-dominated methods to a more learner-centered approach, importing native speakers of English to serve as classroom aides and increasing opportunities for study abroad by Japanese teachers of English.

Emerging Emphases

In the third section of this volume we take up six specific areas of emphasis in foreign language instruction, again seeking to examine them from an international, non-U.S. point of view. Since there may be no more critical area in education than evaluation, we begin with a paper on that topic by Elana Shohamy. Testing and evaluation should touch on virtually everything we and our students do: Only with this kind of feedback can we hope to improve our teaching and learning processes and practices. Indeed, the evaluation and testing processes themselves can surely stand periodic examination and improvement. Shohamy takes the position that the testing done in a country's educational system reflects the underlying values of that society: The manner and extent to which an educational endeavor—in this case, foreign language teaching—is evaluated is indicative of the value that the country places on that endeavor. With this orientation, Shohamy first suggests five areas in which one nation's educational system may differ from that of another. She then compares the Israeli and U.S. systems of foreign language testing as cases in point: Using seven dimensions that describe seven bipolar continua as her criteria for comparison, she concludes that each system has strengths of which the other could well take note.

Despite the virtual certainty shared by many foreign language teachers that foreign language study can and should be as exciting as inventive minds can make it, the field remains characterized in the recollections of many Americans by vocabulary memorization, dialog practice, and grammar drills. Writing from a Canadian perspective, Sally Rehorick tells us that it is not just in the United States that these kinds of classroom activities may still be the norm and draws upon her recent work in creativity to suggest that language teachers might well take a cue from corporate trainers on how to incorporate vivid and stimulating activities into their classrooms.

While it seems likely that U.S. foreign language teaching will remain dominated by the "Big Three" (Spanish, French, and German), exciting things are happening in teaching the so-called less-commonly-taught languages (LCTs). In his paper on the teaching of Arabic, Mahdi Alosh provides a glimpse at the kinds of concerns that teachers of LCTs face. Whereas the tradition of teaching French, German, and Spanish to Westerners is long and the fundamentals have consequently been largely codified, teachers of languages like Arabic, Chinese, and Japanese (to name but a few) in the West are only now beginning to wrestle with fundamental issues such as which variety (or mix of varieties) of their language to teach, what constitute appropriate goals at certain levels of instruction, how and when to introduce the writing system, and so on. It is possible that answers to these questions will be sought from an entirely different orientation from that which exists among teachers of the languages of Western Europe. In so doing, teachers of the LCTs will almost surely add to, even as they profit from, the knowledge base of language teaching that presently constitutes the theoretical foundations of our profession.

That a country's literature is a mirror of its cultural milieu is axiomatic. Judith Muyskens and John Cassini first consider the place of literature in several different societies, noting that countries differ not only in the extent to which literature is a part of the daily lives of a people, but also in the genre(s) of literature that seem to be favored. Against this international backdrop the authors then examine current research and curricular issues in the teaching of literature. They note that for native-speaking anglophone readers, the languages and literatures of some countries are more accessible than others. Similarly, while teachers of language and literature face many common problems of approach and methodology, Muyskens and Cassini point out that teachers of languages and literatures of non-Western cultures face many issues that are quite different from those faced by other language teachers.

Although the phrase "language for special purposes" (LSP) may appear to have entered our professional jargon relatively recently, its reality is very old indeed. Christine Uber Grosse and Geoffrey Kingscott place LSP in its historical and geographical context, then discuss the theoretical as well as the pragmatic reasons behind its developing relationship to the rest of the foreign language teaching field in both the United States and Europe. They show that many of the concerns of foreign language education generally (e.g., communicative language teaching, concerns with proficiency and accountability, the use of authentic materials, application of technology) are clearly reflected in the LSP area, and conclude that LSP is a growth industry that stands to gain from increased contact with and consideration of concerns and solutions being developed in education generally, and in foreign language teaching specifically.

With a land area about the size of the United States but a population less than 8 percent of it, Australia would naturally be keenly interested in distance education. Against this background Roland Sussex describes the establishment and activities of the National Languages Institute of Australia, which seeks to extend the benefits of foreign language study throughout the country. He also looks beyond Australia, to the United States and Europe, to outline recent developments in distance learning and open-access learning, which he views as two constructive responses not only to providing language instruction at far-flung locations, but also to dealing with issues of limited resources. He notes, however, that technology, while offering promise as an instructional support and delivery medium, is probably not the entire answer to guaranteeing access to all who wish to learn: Our ability to make rational use of educational technology is well behind the machines' potential. Moreover, even if that were not the case, the newest technology may be beyond the reach of some educational systems and learners. Therefore, Sussex concludes, imaginative use must be made of existing technologies while newer technological developments (and their practical application to education) are studied and phased into the existing educational framework.

This volume is appearing during the twenty-fifth anniversary year of the founding of ACTFL. It is fitting that as we acknowledge the growth and dynamism of this organization, we look forward to its next quarter-century as one that promises even greater advances in research, professionalism, internationalism, and service.

SECTION I

Europe 1992

1

EC 1992:
Assumptions and Realities[1]

Mary Ellen McGoey
Northeastern Illinois University

The Single European Act, to become effective in January 1992, defines the European Community (EC) as "an area without internal frontiers . . . in which the free movement of goods, persons, services and capital is ensured" (Banks et al. 1989: 1). "In reality," advises J. A. G. Banks of the Cambridge Career Research and Advisory Centre (CRAC),

> 1992 will not herald a set of dramatic overnight changes. Many steps in the direction of the Single Market have already been made. . . . Nonetheless, the symbolism of '1992' has enabled the scale and significance of the changes taking place to penetrate public consciousness both inside and outside Europe. (p. 1)

Inadequate mastery of foreign languages is now recognized as one of the major barriers to European union (Banks et al. 1989: 7). The question for many both within and outside the Community is whether English will become the common denominator, the language that will eventually cement the new European union.

In 1989 *Fortune* magazine reported that many European companies are adopting English as their corporate tongue (Kirkland 1989). Bill Bryson (1990), in his recent book *The Mother Tongue,* concludes that English is fast becoming the dominant world language and points out that it is the language in which two-thirds of European business deals are now conducted. But in the magazine *Europe,* Leif Beck Fallesen (1989) of Copenhagen's *Borsen* newspaper reports that member countries such as France and Spain are fighting the encroachment of English in professional life by instituting measures to promote their national

Mary Ellen McGoey is Assistant Professor of French at Northeastern Illinois University in Chicago. In addition to her ongoing research into teaching and language learning in the European Community, she has presented papers on nineteenth century French art criticism, internships abroad, and the integration of culture into language teaching. She teaches French language, literature, film, and business courses and administers Northeastern's study-abroad programs in France and Belgium.

languages (p. 34). *Industry Week,* in a July 1990 article on the European Community, echoes Fallesen's view and asserts that "None of the countries whose primary language is other than English wants English to become the one language that all must use" (Brodin 1990). Both articles, moreover, caution Americans against thinking they can succeed in nonanglophone countries using English alone.

This is only a small sample of the wealth of contradictory information being reported on the current and future role of English in the European Community. In order to determine if English is indeed becoming the *lingua franca* in the twelve countries[2] comprising the European Community, the present study examines the status of English within the context of second language acquisition both at the elementary and secondary levels of public instruction. We will outline the results of two EC studies done on second language acquisition at these levels in 1979 and 1988 and will then give a brief overview of recent initiatives undertaken by the European Parliament to promote the study of foreign languages in light of the implementation of the Single European Act in January 1992.

The Van Deth Study

In the 1979 study, conducted by Jean-Pierre Van Deth of the Association internationale pour la recherche et la diffusion des méthodes audio-visuelles et structuro-globales, detailed summaries of foreign language instruction are provided for what were then the nine countries[3] of the EC (Van Deth 1979: 11). At the primary level in 1978, the year the data were compiled, only Luxembourg, Belgium (Brussels), and Ireland had programs for second language acquisition. In Luxembourg, where Luxembourgish is spoken in the home, students were introduced to German in the first year of school and French in the second. French remained the second language during the first six years of school, after which it replaced German as the principal language of instruction. Upon entering lower secondary school (age 11), students were required to study English (pp. 63–64, 78). In Belgium in 1978, it was only in Brussels, which is officially bilingual (Dutch/French), that study of one of the national languages was obligatory in the third year of schooling (p. 64). In Ireland, where there are two national languages, English and Irish, the language of instruction depended on the school. The language that was not the language of instruction, usually Irish, was to be taught for one class per day (p. 63). The number of hours devoted to second language acquisition at the primary level in these programs varied from a minimum of three per week to a maximum of nine per week, the amount usually depending on the student's year in school (p. 64). Although at that time there was widespread recognition of the benefits of early foreign language study, only sporadic, experimental programs were actually in operation in France (English/German), Germany (English/French), the United Kingdom (French), and the Netherlands (German, English, French) (pp. 65–68). Poor articulation with the secondary level and scarcity of specially trained elementary language teachers were cited as the principal reasons for the small number of primary programs. The exceptions were Luxembourg and Brussels, where articulation was carefully planned and appropriate teacher training was in place (p. 69).

By the sixth or seventh year of schooling (lower secondary), seven of the nine EC countries required the study of one foreign language, or two in the case of Luxembourg and Brussels. It is impossible to generalize about policies in Britain and Ireland, since both public school systems are completely decentralized, like that of the United States. The requirement was generally maintained through upper secondary school (ages 15 to 18) and in Belgium, Denmark, Luxembourg, and the Netherlands was increased to two foreign languages. The requirement of two foreign languages in other countries depended to a certain extent on the student's chosen discipline: Generally, if a student wished to pursue a university degree or was enrolled in technical programs in tourism and foreign trade, two foreign languages were required. As regards English in particular, Denmark, Luxembourg, and the Netherlands required that students begin studying English by approximately age 11 or at the beginning of lower secondary school. English was the first foreign language chosen in all nonanglophone countries, except Luxembourg and Brussels, followed by French and German. French was the first language of preference in anglophone countries (pp. 70–83). In terms of percentages, English was taken by 79.5 percent of students, French by 54.8 percent, German by 34.6 percent, Spanish by 4.1 percent, and Italian by 0.8 percent (p. 93). The range of languages offered at the secondary level, both lower and upper, was usually restricted to English, French, German, and sometimes Spanish.

A number of reasons were suggested for the predominance of English: (1) the widely held perception by Europeans that it is the most useful and most used language in international technical and commercial communications; (2) the economic dominance of the United States after World War II; (3) the importance of U.S. theories of second language acquisition, especially in the 1960s; (4) the efforts of the British Council to promote the use of English and provide teachers of English after World War II through the 1970s; (5) the preponderance of scientific documents in English; and (6) the influence of U.S. TV and movies (p. 117). French and German, the other two languages with the highest enrollments in the EC in 1978, were the beneficiaries of centuries of political, economic, and cultural dominance in the region.

Because of these factors, teacher training in languages other than English, French, and German in the member countries was virtually nonexistent when Van Deth's study was undertaken. The range of languages taught was a direct reflection of the limited teacher training available.

At the conclusion of his survey, Van Deth observed that member countries who so restricted choices in foreign language were actually undermining Community policies that guaranteed equality of opportunity and freedom of movement (pp. 115–117, 144). The report also cited the fact that foreign language study had actually begun to decline in the EC in the 1970s (p. 145). To counter these trends and nurture real European unity and mobility, it was suggested that students become orally proficient in one European language other than the mother tongue and have a passive knowledge of three or four more (p. 162). Also recommended was an extensive program of country exchanges (scientific, technical, commercial, and cultural) within the Community at all levels and in all disciplines in order to break down linguistic and cultural barriers (p. 10).

The Martin-Bletsas Study

The vital link between foreign language study and EC goals began to receive increased attention in the 1980s. In 1983 the European Council reaffirmed the importance of languages and adopted resolutions on programs to encourage the teaching of foreign languages and foster the diffusion of community languages (Martin-Bletsas 1988: 168). Following a meeting in 1984, the EC Education Ministers agreed that "Member States . . . promote all appropriate measures to enable the maximum number of pupils to acquire, before the end of compulsory education, a practical knowledge of two languages in addition to their mother tongue (Martin-Bletsas 1988: 169). Members also concurred that teacher training and in-service training should include study abroad and that member countries allow younger students "periods of linguistic and cultural study in other Member States" (Martin-Bletsas 1988: 170-171). Finally, the Ministers singled out the importance of teaching foreign languages for special purposes, especially in vocational training (Martin-Bletsas 1988: 171).

There is no doubt that the passage of the Single European Act in 1986 increased the urgency with which the problems outlined in the 1979 study soon were addressed. In March 1988 the Community's Education Information Network, dubbed EURYDICE, prepared a report for the ministers of education, edited by Jean Martin-Bletsas, on the teaching of foreign languages in each member state from primary through secondary school. This was done in anticipation of an important meeting to be held in May of that year to discuss the EC's concerns regarding foreign language and to follow up on measures approved in prior resolution. This report includes data on Greece, Spain, and Portugal, the three countries that were missing from the 1979 survey. No statistics are given, but the report indicates the preference for first, second, and third foreign language, the level at which the language requirement begins, the range of languages offered in each country, the kind of teacher training received, and whether there are pupil/teacher exchanges among member countries, either formal (i.e., state-sponsored) or informal.

By 1988, Denmark and the Netherlands had added obligatory primary programs that required the study of English as the first foreign language. In Denmark instruction begins at the fifth year of schooling for two and a half hours per week, and in the Netherlands at the fourth year for one hour per week (pp. 7, 61). Since 1988, Greece and Italy have also added the compulsory study of a foreign language at the primary level (Révillion 1990). Thus seven of the EC countries now require some instruction of foreign language before lower secondary school. As was the case in 1979, all students in the EC, apart from those in England and Ireland where generalizations are not possible, are required to study at least one foreign language in lower secondary school (sixth or seventh year). English is still the first choice in nonanglophone countries, except in Portugal, where French is the first preference (Martin-Bletsas 1988: viii, 68). Options for the second foreign language now usually include Spanish and Italian in addition to French, German, and English. The number of countries requiring a second foreign language, beginning anywhere from the seventh to the eleventh year of schooling, grew to seven and now includes Belgium, Denmark, Luxembourg, the Netherlands, Germany, and, depending on the course of study, France and Spain. Some countries, notably France, Germany, Denmark, Belgium, and the Netherlands, considerably broadened the curriculum to include languages such as Russian, Chinese, Danish, Dutch, and Portuguese. In addition to these languages France now offers Hebrew, Modern Greek, Arabic, and Polish. To be sure, opportunities to take advantage of these new offerings vary considerably from region to region and even from school to school within the same area. Often they are available only as an optional third foreign language due to teacher scarcity. Class time at both elementary and secondary levels varies from two to six hours per week, with the average being three. In-service training for teachers is often optional, as are student/teacher exchanges. The latter generally occur no earlier than the eleventh or twelfth year of study and are often arranged privately. In sum, although there had been an increase in the number of primary programs since 1979, teacher training was still restricted to a few languages, the number of primary programs remained low, and the range of languages offered, although somewhat broadened, was very unevenly distributed within each country. Finally, there had been very little growth in study abroad or student exchanges.

As if to underscore the lack of movement toward a multilingual Europe, figures were published shortly after the Ministers' meeting in July 1988 indicating that English was the most-spoken language in the EC at 35.5 percent of the total EC population, followed by French (26.5 percent), German (19.3 percent), Italian and Spanish (13.6 percent).[4] Statistics also revealed that the population of the Netherlands, at 44 percent, had the highest rate of plurilingualism, defined for this survey as knowledge of two foreign languages in addition to the native language. After the Netherlands came Northern Belgium and Denmark (31 percent), Southern Belgium (22 percent), France and Germany (7 percent), the United Kingdom, Spain, and Italy (6 percent) (L'Europe 1989: 25). Statistics on unilingualism—no knowledge of a foreign language—showed Italy ranking highest at 76 percent, followed by the United Kingdom (74 percent), Spain (68 percent), France (67 percent), Southern Belgium (56 percent), Flanders (46 percent), Denmark (40 percent), and the Netherlands (28 percent) (L'Europe 1989: 25). Although neither set of data includes all the member states, both demonstrate the extent to which much of the population in the EC remains unilingual even though foreign language study is required by most countries beginning at age 11 and continuing until age 18.

Initiatives to Promote Foreign Language Study _____

Despite the fact that English appears to be the one language spoken by the most EC citizens, the European Commission has embraced multilingualism as its official policy. In its proposal for the LINGUA program, discussed below, the Commission stated it had "deliberately chosen to propose a strategy of action involving the diversification of the foreign languages on offer in education and training programmes, rather than promote one or two priority languages. Conscious of the rich diversity of European linguistic and cultural traditions, the Commission has taken the view that all the official languages of the Community should be more widely spoken" ("The Commission" 1988). Consequently, with the approach of 1992, there is widespread agreement that if the EC is to achieve a truly open employment market based on freedom of movement, its citizens will have to know more languages than just English. Candidates will have to convince the potential employer that their qualifications are better than those of another, even those born, raised, and educated in the local community or region (Banks 1989: 10). "In many cases," says Cambridge's Banks, "this means that they will need to have a sufficiently good knowledge of the local language. A lot of employers are now demanding that applicants for jobs, at least at graduate level, should have a knowledge of one or even two languages other than their own" (p. 10). Those who aspire to maximum mobility will need to know French, English, German, and Spanish (Banks 1989: 10). Particular jobs may even require a knowledge of a minority language (Banks 1989: 10).

In light of findings such as those in the Martin-Bletsas EURYDICE report, the pressing need to prepare students for equal access to the European employment market, and the decision to encourage plurilingualism rather than monolingualism, the Commission of the European Communities has undertaken three major initiatives. The programs funded by the EC are mainly for postsecondary students and teachers, since compulsory education does not lie within the Community's jurisdiction. It is hoped, however, that they will be the catalyst for change in primary and secondary programs in the member countries.

ERASMUS

The oldest of the three is ERASMUS (European Community Action Scheme for the Mobility of University Students). Adopted June 15, 1987, ERASMUS is designed to promote student mobility and cooperation in higher education principally through student and teacher exchanges ("The E.C." 1989: 25–26). It employs three means of achieving its objectives.

The first is the promotion of student mobility through grants for study abroad and formal recognition of studies completed in another Community member state through a program called the ECTS or European Credit Transport System. The ECTS is currently in its pilot stages (1989–95) in 80 of the 3600 institutions of higher learning in the EC. Five areas of concentration were named for the pilot program: management, chemistry, mechanical engineering, medicine, and history (ERASMUS: 11).

The second part of the program funds one-month teaching internships of teaching staff at higher education establishments in other member states and offers resources for the development of joint teaching programs among member countries (Commission 1989: 4).

In its third component, ERASMUS supports short study or teaching visits for staff in higher education in other member countries. The aims of these visits are to promote exploratory contacts, to improve course content, to conduct surveys on higher education, and to encourage intercultural experiences of faculty (Commission 1989: 4).

The ultimate goal of ERASMUS is to ensure that all EC students in higher education, not just those studying foreign language, are able to pursue their degree in another member state for a period of at least three months (Banks 1989: 11). The immediate objective is to raise the percentage of those who do study abroad from the current 2–3 percent of the 6,000,000+ postsecondary students in the EC to 10 percent by 1992 (Banks 1989: 11). Students who are accepted into the ERASMUS program are supported by scholarships that cover travel, living expenses, and money for appropriate language courses (Commission 1989: 5).

The scale of participation in ERASMUS has risen steadily every year since 1987 and the EC has quadrupled its budget for the years 1990–1993. For the years 1987–1989 approximately 16,000 students profited from the program and in 1989–1990 the figure rose to almost 20,000 students. When these numbers are compared to the yearly average of 2500 students who studied abroad before ERASMUS's inception, there can be no doubt that the program has met with success, but it seems unlikely that it will attain its goal of 600,000 participants by 1992. Some problems with ERASMUS have also begun to surface. Member countries have been accused of formulating selection criteria that favor students in university tracks and exclude those who follow shorter programs in technical schools. Consequently, those students for whom ERASMUS scholarships might provide the only means to study abroad are being rejected in favor of those who already have the economic resources to travel and study in other countries (Révillion 1990; "Le brassage" 1989). Individual member countries have also been cited for failure to provide orientation and other services to foreign students, for failing to coordinate requirements between universities, and for inadequate housing. These problems have been especially troublesome in the Mediterranean countries, where traditionally university students obtain information and advice almost entirely within informal networks (Boissonnat 1990).

LINGUA

During the first two years of ERASMUS it was also discovered that many students and teachers participating in the program did not have sufficient linguistic skills to be able to follow a course of study in another country. This in turn led to the adoption of the second EC initiative, the LINGUA program ("Le brassage" 1989). LINGUA, Latin for language, was adopted by the Council of the European Communities on July 28, 1989 (Council 1989). LINGUA's main objective is to foster a quantitative and qualitative improvement in foreign language competence among Community citizens. The languages covered by the program include German, English, Danish, Spanish, French, Greek, Irish, Italian, Luxembourgish, Dutch, and Portuguese—11 languages in all. According to Domenico Lenarduzzi, head of the EC's Division of Cooperation in Education, the LINGUA project is meant not only to encourage foreign language study, but also to encourage students to learn more about other cultures and other ways of living (Simon 1989). Initially, organizers of LINGUA hope to involve 20 percent of EC postsecondary schools and 10 percent of the teaching faculty in its various programs (Simon 1989). The program seeks especially to promote in-service training courses for experienced teachers of foreign languages and to develop and improve the initial training of prospective foreign language teachers (Commission 1989: 8). Grants will be awarded so that foreign language students may spend a portion of their study abroad. Priority for grants will be given to those contemplating a teaching career in foreign languages. Additional priority will be given to those students who specialize in the least widely used and least taught languages of the EC (Council 1989: "Action II"). LINGUA supports exchanges of students in professional, vocational, and technical education programs between the ages of 16 and 25 and seeks to establish an educational visit abroad of at least two weeks as a regular part of the curriculum (Council 1989: "Action IV"). In fact, some ministers in the Commission, led by France's Jacques Delors, hoped to fund exchanges at the lower secondary and even primary levels. Unfortunately, this initiative was voted down when other members demanded strict adherence to the Treaty of Rome, which forbids resolutions in the area of compulsory education (Simon 1989). LINGUA also hopes to further study of foreign languages in the workplace and in economic life through grants for teaching materials, trainers, and exchanges of personnel to small and medium-sized businesses (Council 1989: "Action III").

During 1990 member countries were to establish LINGUA centers to coordinate activities and review applications. By all accounts LINGUA has been greeted enthusiastically by members of the Community and is already having some effect on educational policy within individual countries. The Portuguese Ministry of Education has proposed requiring a foreign language in the fifth year of schooling because of the measures adopted in the LINGUA program (Ministry 1990: 20–21).

TEMPUS

The most recent move in the EC's drive to eliminate language barriers occurred in May 1990 following the historic events in Central Europe. The Council adopted TEMPUS, Trans-European Mobility Programme for University Studies, as a companion program to ERASMUS and LINGUA. TEMPUS is targeted to meet the specific needs of the countries of Central and Eastern Europe. In its pilot phase (three years), it will develop programs with Poland, Hungary, and Czechoslovakia. Three kinds of projects are foreseen:

1. Joint European training projects that link universities and/or enterprises in Eastern European countries with similar bodies in at least two member States
2. Mobility grants for teachers, students, administrative staff, and industry personnel
3. Complementary activities for universities

Joint European project grants will be awarded for the development of curriculum and mobility plans, for continuing education, for retraining for higher education, and for open and distance learning ("Action Phare" 1990). The fields of management, business administration, and modern European languages have been given priority.

It is generally agreed that throughout the 1990s the learning of English will still be considered a necessity, but that an ever-increasing number of EC students and employees will study one other or several other languages as well. This will require a significant investment in initial teacher training for all levels, particularly the primary level, and a reallocation of resources from English, German, and French to other EC languages, including those least commonly taught. Efforts at improved articulation between levels of instruction will have to be intensified and evaluation mechanisms based on proficiency levels will have to be established if the community's goal of real communicative competence is to be reached. Guidance will also be a top priority, since the number of options for students will increase substantially in coming years, as will the requirements for employment.

Conclusion

The assumption underlying initiatives such as ERASMUS, LINGUA, and TEMPUS is that all Community citizens are capable of active mastery of at least one if not several foreign languages. It remains to be seen whether this assumption can be realized: Belgium and the Netherlands have had excellent language programs in place for years and are still struggling with relatively high rates of unilingualism. Will ERASMUS, LINGUA, and TEMPUS truly create a multilingual Community by removing linguistic and cultural barriers? That certainly is the hope, but a great deal depends on the willingness of member countries to comply with the democratic spirit of these initiatives and not favor particular groups or disciplines in the allocation of grants and other resources. Administrative problems will have to be ironed out quickly or students will be reluctant to participate. At this early stage it is virtually impossible to assess their success, but one can say that ERASMUS, LINGUA, and TEMPUS have engendered a great deal of renewed enthusiasm for language study in the EC. The task ahead, fostering European unity while at the same time preserving each country's linguistic heritage, is enormous, but it would be hard to argue that the goals are not worth the effort.

Notes

1. This is a revised version of a paper originally presented at the MLA conference in December 1990.
2. Germany, Belgium, France, Italy, Luxembourg, the Netherlands, Denmark, the United Kingdom, Ireland, Greece, Spain, and Portugal.
3. Greece became a member in 1981 and Spain and Portugal in 1986.
4. *Le Vif-L'Express,* 1 July 1988, quoted in *L'Europe par-dessus le Marché?* 1989: 25.

References, EC 1992: Assumptions and Realities

"Action Phare. Community Adopts Programmes of Higher Education Cooperation with the Countries of Central and Eastern Europe." 1990. (Brussels, Belg.: Spokesman's Service press release, 8 May, IP(90)372).

Banks, J. A. G., et al. 1989. *The Single European Market and Its Implications for Educational and Vocational Guidance Services.* CRAC Occasional Paper. Cambridge, Eng.: Careers Research and Advisory Centre. [ERIC ED315 641]

Boissonnat, Philippe. 1990. "Les plâtres d'"Erasmus'." *La Croix-L'Évènement* [Belg.], 14 February, p. 17.

"Le brassage des étudiants." 1989. *Libre Entreprise* [Belg.], 30 December.

Brodin, James. 1990. "Ciao, Sprechen Sie Français?" *Industry Week,* 16 July, p. 68.

Bryson, Bill. 1990. *The Mother Tongue.* (New York: William Morrow).

Commission of the European Communities Task Force: Human Resources, Education, Training and Youth. 1989. *Guide to the European Community Programmes in the Fields of: Education, Training, Youth.* Brussels, Belg.: EURYDICE European Unit.

"The Commission Proposes the LINGUA Programme: A Better Knowledge of Foreign Languages Is Essential for the Completion of the Internal Market." 1988. (Brussels, Belg.: Spokesman's Service press release, 21 December, P-151).

The Council of the European Communities. 1989. "Council Decision of 28 July 1989 Establishing an Action Programme to Promote Foreign Language Competence in the European Community (Lingua)." *Official Journal of the European Communities* (16 August): L239/24–32.

"The E.C. and Youth." 1989. *Europe,* January/February, 24f.

ERASMUS Bureau. n.d. *ECTS. Système européen d'unités capitalisables transférables dans toute la communauté.* Brussels, Belg.: Commission des Communautés Européenes.

L'Europe par-dessus Le Marché? 1989. Brussels, Belg.: Fondation Roi Baudouin.

Fallesen, Leif Beck. 1989. "Publishing: The Printed Word Seeks a European Audience." *Europe,* June, pp. 32–34.

Kirkland, Richard I., Jr. 1989. "English Spoken Here, There . . ." *Fortune,* 19 June, p. 8.

Martin-Bletsas, Jean, ed. 1988. *The Teaching of Languages in the European Community.* Brussels, Belg.: EURYDICE Central Unit. [ERIC ED317 070]

Ministry of Education of Portugal. 1990. *The Portuguese System of Education—Facts and Trends.*

Révillion, Bertrand. 1990. "L'Europe passe par les études." *La Croix-l'Évènement* [Belg.], 14 February, p. 17.

Simon, Christine. 1989. "L'Objectif de LINGUA: comprendre l'autre en parlant sa langue . . ." *Le soir* [Belg.], 13 June, supplement "Mieux Vivre," p. 11.

Van Deth, Jean-Pierre. 1979. *L'Enseignement scolaire des langues vivantes dans les pays membres de la communauté européenne: bilan, réflexions et propositions (Modern Language Instruction in the Member Countries of the European Community: Evaluation, Reflections, and Proposals)*. Ghent, Belg.: Association internationale pour la recherche et la diffusion des méthodes audio-visuelles et structuro-globales. [ERIC ED279 207]

2

A Linguistic Response to "Europe, 1992": The LINGUA Program

Charles Barrière

Director of the LINGUA Bureau

Education and training in general, and more specifically the teaching and learning of foreign languages, have always been among the main preoccupations of the institutions of the European Community.

The first official and political move toward the improvement of linguistic competence in the twelve member states of the Community was made fifteen years ago, in 1976. On 9 February of that year

> [t]he Council and Ministers of Education meeting within the Council, in adopting . . . a resolution comprising an action programme in the field of education, selected the teaching of foreign languages as an appropriate area for Community activity and . . . they adopted conclusions on this subject at their meeting on 4 June 1984." (*Official Journal* 1989)

Before these conclusions were adopted, the European Council had also,

> [i]n the Solemn Declaration on European Union adopted at its meeting in Stuttgart on 19 June 1983, . . . stressed the importance which must be attached to foreign language teaching and learning within the Community. (*Official Journal* 1989)

Charles Barrière is Director of the LINGUA Bureau, an external unit of the Commission of the European Community. Past positions have included Reader in Linguistics and Director of the Audio-Visual and Computer Department at the Sorbonne, President of the Association of Audio-Visual Specialists in French Higher Education (ARAS), President of the International Center for Audio-Visual in Universities and Higher Education (CIAVU), and member of several advisory boards and expert committees in the French Ministry of Education. His field of research is didactics and new educational technologies.

As a result of this resolution, the Council and the ministers of education in the European Community established EURYDICE, an information network for education.

The Council was so convinced that something had to be done for the promotion of languages in Europe that the matter was taken up again at meetings at Fontainebleau in June 1984 and in Milan in June 1985; there, the ministers emphasized once more the necessity of multilingual communication in Europe.

In February 1989 a proposal from the European Commission, published in the Official Journal of the European Community, suggested the launching of an action program to promote foreign language competence in the twelve member states. This proposal was adopted by the Council on 28 July 1989. This program, named LINGUA, has as its main objective to improve foreign language competence, quantitatively and qualitatively, in order to promote mobility and communication among the citizens of the European Community. Through linguistic communication, LINGUA intends to promote *global* communication among nations and people in the present European Community. Moreover, through the affirmation and implementation of the principle of linguistic and cultural diversification as one of the most important elements in the program, LINGUA will promote communication in a new, extended Europe that may serve as an incentive to the rest of the world.

The following is a description of the LINGUA program taken from a recent official EURYDICE document.[1]

LINGUA

LINGUA is the Community action programme to promote the qualitative and quantitative improvement in foreign language teaching and learning in the European Community. The completion of the internal market in 1993 and the achievement of the free movement of persons and ideas depends on Europe's citizens being able to communicate with each other through an active knowledge of languages other than their mother-tongue.

Knowledge of foreign languages is therefore a key element in the building of Europe.

Foreign Language Teaching: A Longstanding Concern

Since 1976, when the Resolution on the first action programme in the field of education[2] was approved, foreign language teaching has been a central concern of the Ministers for Education.

The Conclusions adopted by the Council and the Ministers for Education in 1984 led to the first guidelines for a general policy to improve foreign language competence in the Community.

The Conclusions of the Ministers gave rise to discussions and exchanges of information which revealed the qualitative and quantitative inadequacies of foreign language teaching and the need to draw up a Community programme in this area.

It was found, for instance, that over the last twenty years, there has been a constant reduction in the range of languages learned in favour of English and, to a lesser extent, French. It was also found that language competence—in many cases the level of competence attained at school—did not enable the individual to hold a conversation, and therefore to communicate, in the language learned.

Language Competence: A Community Priority at All Levels

This awareness of the importance of foreign language teaching very quickly spread beyond the bounds of strictly educational circles to become a central Community concern particularly in connection with the completion of the internal market in 1993. The free movement of persons and ideas will however remain a Utopian concept unless people are really able to *communicate* with each other.

The inability to communicate is not only an obstacle to the mobility of persons, but also a handicap to the development of social, cultural, economic and commercial relations within the Community.

The European Parliament has repeatedly demonstrated the importance it attaches to language teaching. As early as 1983 it adopted a resolution on the teaching of languages in the European Community.[3]

In 1988, the EC Commission proposed a Community programme of specific actions and financial assistance to improve, qualitatively and quantitatively, the teaching and learning of foreign languages.

This programme, entitled LINGUA, was adopted by a Council Decision in July 1989.[4]

Its aim is to support and complement, by Community actions, the Member States' policies and actions in this field.

The LINGUA programme has an estimated budget of ECU 200 million for a five-year period from 1990 to 1994.

The priority accorded to foreign language teaching was set out in the guidelines for the medium term (1989–92) in the field of education and training prepared by the Commission.[5]

The social dialogue which was relaunched in 1989 by Jacques Delors and which brings together employers, trade unions and the Commission, has signalled the crucial importance of improving the teaching of foreign languages.

The "Joint Opinion" of the education and training group[6] delivered in January 1990 states that ". . . initial vocational training should . . . promote the learning of at least one other Community language in addition to the mother tongue . . ." and ". . . the social partners reaffirm their support for the existing Community training programmes relating to the occupational integration of young people (Social Fund and PETRA), language training (LINGUA), training in new information technologies (EUROTECNET) and cooperation between universities and enterprises in the field of initial and continuing training in the technological sphere (COMETT)."

The Priorities of the LINGUA Programme

Improvement in the quality of language teaching and training, diversification, communicative skills, language competence in enterprises and the development of innovative methods are the common themes running through the actions of the LINGUA programme.

Improvement of the Quality of Teaching.   The main aim of the LINGUA programme is to encourage a quantitative and qualitative improvement in foreign language competence in particular by improving the quality of teaching through adaptation of curricula, teacher training, teaching methods and material, etc.

The Diversification of the Range of Languages Taught.   When approving the LINGUA programme, the Council agreed on the need to take account of the role played by the different languages from the cultural, economic and commercial points of view.

Diversifying the range of foreign languages available and giving priority to the least widely used and least taught languages are fundamental principles of the LINGUA programme, which is aimed at preserving Europe's linguistic diversity and cultural wealth.

The languages covered by the programme are: Danish, Dutch, English, French, German, Greek, Irish, Italian, Luxemburgish, Portuguese and Spanish insofar as they are taught as foreign languages.

The Promotion of Communication between European Citizens.   The completion of the internal market will depend on the ability of citizens to communicate with each other and to overcome the language difficulties hindering the free movement of persons, goods, services and capital. Conscious of this reality, the Council decided that in granting financial assistance under the LINGUA programme, priority would be given to projects aimed at promoting the acquisition of communicative skills. This includes, in particular, *practical* foreign-language learning, that is to say, teaching based on everyday realities: how to ask directions, how to ask for information, the organization of public transport, cultural and social customs, etc.

The Promotion of Language Competence in Economic Life.   The shortage of people capable of working through the medium of Community languages other than their own is a fundamental constraint on the completion of the internal market.

Besides the need to widen the range of languages taught so as to preserve Europe's cultural wealth, the Council, when approving the programme, also demonstrated its concern for the promotion of foreign-language teaching in the economic sphere. It agreed that the LINGUA programme should also be aimed at encouraging employers and professional organizations to promote foreign language training for workers. This is to enable them to benefit fully from the opportunities offered by the internal market, particularly in the case of workers in small and medium-sized enterprises (SMEs).

This priority has been reaffirmed in the opinion delivered by the Social Dialogue education and training group organized by the Commission.

The Promotion of Innovation.   Increasing the range of foreign languages taught in the European Community, developing communicative skills and promoting foreign language competence in economic circles are priorities which require the development of effective and innovative teaching methods. This is why the LINGUA programme gives priority to financing projects which contain positive innovation and which also have a multiplier effect. Information and the exchange of experience are therefore central to the organization and operation of the programme and comprise its European "added-value."

Programme Content: The Areas Financed by the Programme

Grants are available for:

1. in-service training of teachers (Action I);
2. foreign language learning in higher education, initial training of teachers (Action II);
3. the promotion of knowledge of foreign languages in work relations and economic life (Action III);
4. exchanges between young people undergoing professional, vocational and technical education (Action IV);
5. the implementation, at Community level, of complementary measures relating to the programme's priorities (Action V).

In-Service Training of Teachers.   The in-service training of teachers is an immediate priority.

The LINGUA programme will finance improvements in teachers' skills, in particular, through the promotion of periods of training and retraining in the country whose language they teach.

Action I of the programme expressly provides for:

1. grants to promote mobility among foreign language teachers and trainers. These grants will assist with training periods of a month, on average, preferably in another Member State.
2. assistance for cooperation programmes organized at European level between in-service training establishments for foreign language teachers. These European Cooperation Programmes (ECPs) will supplement measures taken at national level. Preparation of such programmes will be facilitated by the organization of study visits between the establishments concerned, thereby setting up a genuine cooperation network.

Foreign Language Learning in Higher Education.   The LINGUA programme finances measures which permit foreign language students and, in particular, intending teachers of foreign languages to spend a recognized period of initial training, of not less than three months' duration, in the country whose language they will teach.

The aim is to stimulate the mobility both of students specializing in foreign languages and those who study foreign languages together with another discipline.

This action will complement measures taken under the ERASMUS programme and will be administered in close conjunction with it.

The programme provides for Action II:

1. assistance for inter-university cooperation programmes (ICPs) set up under the ERASMUS programme. It is proposed that within the ERASMUS programme foreign language teaching would be developed at the level of programme content, assessment, examinations, documentation, etc.
2. grants for the mobility of students, in particular intending [future] teachers of foreign languages, in the framework of the ERASMUS European inter-university cooperation network.
3. grants for the mobility and exchange of teaching staff and administrators in higher education in order to support the setting up of cooperation programmes in the area of foreign languages. Such cooperation will include creating appropriate conditions for the exchange of students, exchange of experience concerning teaching methods and the initial training of teachers.

Improvement of Language Competence in Work Relations and Economic Life.   The measures intended to promote foreign language competence in work and economic relations comprise Action III of the programme. Community assistance has been expressly provided for:

1. the development and dissemination of methods for the diagnosis and *analysis of the foreign language needs* of professional or workers' organizations and of enterprises, particularly *SMEs.*
2. the setting-up of pilot projects on the use of *teaching materials* adapted to the needs of each economic sector.
3. the financing of transnational projects leading to the setting up of appropriate structures for language training in economic life. Financial support will be provided for instance for projects using *self-learning methods* in foreign languages and for *multi-media* projects to increase the opportunities for individual training.
4. the organization of a system of *exchanges* between Member States of representatives of enterprises and organizations involved in foreign language training in business relations.
5. the development of appropriate programmes leading to a *system of foreign language diplomas and qualifications for the different professions in the economic sector.*

It should be stressed that this action has NOT been designed for the direct financing of foreign language courses for the staff of individual enterprises. Its aim is rather to provide support for the setting up of appropriate *infrastructures* and strategies for the development of foreign language competence.

Exchanges for Young People Undergoing Professional, Vocational and Technical Education. In order to enhance foreign language learning by young people undergoing professional, vocational and technical education, Action IV of the programme provides for financial assistance for the development of *joint education projects* between the establishments concerned in different Member States and for *exchanges for young people.*

Exchanges and meetings between young people must constitute a natural part of the joint education project, by providing them with the opportunity to use foreign languages as a learning tool and as a means of communicating with their counterparts in the partner establishment.

In the framework of Action IV provision has been made for:

1. grants for the preparatory visits of those responsible for such exchanges in the establishments concerned;
2. grants for exchanges between young people.

The identification of establishments likely to benefit from such financial assistance is the responsibility of the Member States.

The Implementation, at Community Level, of Complementary Measures in Support of the Programme's Objectives. The programme (Action V) provides financial assistance for associations / groups which undertake, at Community level, activities consistent with the programme's objectives.

The activities receiving financial aid must include at least one of the following characteristics:

1. contribute to a *better awareness* of the objectives of the LINGUA programme among education and training policy makers and the general public;
2. set up a *discussion forum* and permit an *exchange of ideas* on issues such as the development of innovative foreign language learning methods;
3. introduce or enhance the *European dimension* in the association / group's activities;
4. *coordinate* at Community level the activities of national associations or groups;
5. launch at Community level an *innovatory activity* relating to the programme's objectives;
6. set up a new association at European level;
7. participate in the development and exchange of teaching materials in the least widely used and least taught languages.

Organization and Implementation of the Programme

The organization and implementation of the programme will be carried out by the following bodies:

The Commission is responsible for the implementation of the LINGUA programme. It is assisted in this task by the LINGUA Bureau, which is a technical assistance unit for the general management of the programme, and by the LINGUA Committee which is made up of two representatives designated by each Member State and is chaired by the Commission representative. The members of the committee may be assisted by experts or advisers.

Coordination and implementation at national level (Actions I and IV) is carried out by one or more national coordination agencies.

These agencies have qualified staff to assign priorities to each "action" of the programme and to keep abreast of the foreign language learning policies applied in the Member States. These national agencies coordinate with agencies responsible for other Community programmes, in particular with the national agencies which administer grants under the ERASMUS programme (Action II).

Programme Evaluation. The Commission and the LINGUA Committee will present an evaluation report at the end of the second year of operation and a final report covering the five-year period of the programme.

LINGUA: A Catalyst for Innovation in the Area of Foreign Language Learning. In general, Community programmes in the field of education and training promote mobility, exchanges and transnational partnerships. The few years' experience of these programmes and the first evaluation reports have revealed that the language obstacle is the major handicap encountered by participants.

The LINGUA programme can therefore be regarded as the linchpin of other Community programmes such as ERASMUS, PETRA, COMETT and YOUTH FOR EUROPE.

LINGUA is obviously not a panacea for the problems encountered in foreign language learning but it may be considered as the catalyst for innovation in this area.

Further information on this programme may be obtained from LINGUA, Place du Luxembourg 2/3, B-1040 Brussels.

Notes

1. EURYDICE Info, Dossier Lingua, n. 9, May 1990.
2. Resolution of the Council and the Ministers for Education meeting within the Council, of 9 February 1976, comprising an action programme in the field of education: Official Journal of the European Communities, No. C 38 19.2, 1976.
3. Official Journal of the European Communities, No. C68, 14.3, 1983.
4. Council Decision of 28 July 1989 establishing an action programme to promote foreign language competence in the European Community (LINGUA); Official Journal of the European Communities, No. L 239, 16.8, 1989, pp. 24–32.
5. Commission communication to the Council on education and training in the European Community Guidelines for the medium term; 1989–92; COM(89)236 final.
6. Joint Opinion concerning education and training; Task Force: Human Resources, Education, Training, Youth: Brussels, 26 January 1990.

Reference, Linguistic Response to "Europe, 1992"

Official Journal of the European Communities. 1989. Council Decision of 28 July 1989, n. L 239/24, 16 June.

3

FLES in Europe: A Revival

François Weiss

Centre International d'Études Pédagogiques

In most European countries the teaching and learning of foreign languages in elementary schools (FLES), after a sharp decline in the mid-1970s, has become a priority. Over the last few years in nearly all twelve member states of the European Economic Community (EEC), FLES will soon be included in the core curriculum of elementary school programs.[1] Italy, by a law implemented in 1985, introduced FLES in the third year of the elementary school for all 8-year-old pupils; Spain, Greece, Portugal, Scotland, and France have followed suit. This trend should be generalized by 1993: All twelve EEC education ministers have made a commitment to it.

For several years interest in FLES was at a low ebb, especially in Great Britain and France, where two rather negative official reports drove it, if not into complete oblivion, at least into a state of hibernation.[2] It has reawakened only in the late 1980s, gathering a new impetus mainly with the acceleration of the creation of a new Europe and with the initiation of new linguistic programs set up by the Council of Europe and by the EEC. At the same time there has been a profound change in national and social attitudes toward the learning of foreign languages and their importance in the daily life of the new European citizen.

The "Single European Act"

The year 1992 will be a most important date in the history of the EEC, as it will be the year of the implementation of the Single European Act. Under the provisions of this act, trade barriers among the twelve member states will be

François Weiss (Ph.D. applied linguistics, University of Nancy) is a teacher trainer at the Centre International d'Études Pédagogiques in Sèvres, France. He also holds a lectureship at the University of Paris III Sorbonne–Nouvelle. He spent twenty years on official assignment for the French government abroad as a linguistic consultant and as a teacher trainer in Australia, Germany, Great Britain, and Greece. He has been closely involved in the language programs of the Council of Europe for over a decade and has run teacher training courses in nearly all European countries as well as in Canada, Costa Rica, Syria, Israel, and Poland. His scholarship has appeared in French, British, German, Australian, and Greek language journals. He is the author or coauthor of several French textbooks and teaching methods volumes.

progressively removed. By 1993 the citizens of the twelve countries will be able to move freely from one country to another to live, find jobs, and establish businesses. In sum, citizens of the member nations will be able to be fully at home in the country of their choice.

For these reasons, 1992 could in fact be viewed by future foreign language educators as having been a turning point, a "founding event" for the renewal of interest in learning foreign languages in Europe. It may well be seen as the year when more appropriate and more realistic objectives than those that prevail today were established, a time that led to a commitment to teaching foreign languages for real communication and better transnational understanding. How might this turnabout take place?

Changes in attitudes toward the learning of foreign languages have mainly been occurring in the larger European countries; in the smaller countries, whose languages are less widely spoken (and therefore less widely taught) such as Greece, Portugal, Denmark, Holland, and Luxembourg, foreign languages— and, in particular, the languages of these countries' larger, more powerful neighbors—have always ranked high in the school curriculum. Languages have also been seen as important in society at large, mainly for economic reasons, i.e., for their utility in trade and tourism. In the smaller countries the learning of two foreign languages either in or outside school has been a general practice, while in the larger and economically stronger countries (such as Great Britain, France, Spain, Italy, and Germany), languages have not enjoyed particularly high social status. They have not been given emphasis equal to that placed on, for example, mathematics and the sciences, which are viewed as keys to higher education and to the better and more prestigious jobs. As a result, in most of these larger countries only one foreign language is offered in most schools.[3] In Great Britain, foreign language as a compulsory subject was introduced into the core curriculum of secondary education only two years ago.[4]

Mentalities in Europe have changed greatly over the last two or three years. As the deadline for the introduction of the Single European Act draws nearer, for example, the "1992 syndrome" is striking more and more people at all levels, political, social, and economic. The emergence of this new order is not viewed as a positive development by all Europeans, however; it even looks threatening to many of them. The "richer," more industrialized countries, for example, fear large-scale invasions by citizens from less wealthy areas. But even in this instance foreign languages will become increasingly important, for they will allow people to cope with the multilingual situations that will inevitably arise.

The development of these multilingual environments implies the teaching and learning of lesser-spoken languages such as Greek, Dutch, Danish, Portuguese, and even Luxembourgish (spoken by only 360,000 people), which is exactly what the EEC's LINGUA program will be promoting: One of the five "actions" of this program is aimed at the development of precisely these languages. This ambitious five-year program, which has solid financial and organizational support from all the EEC countries, will have considerable impact on the field of foreign language teaching and learning, both within and outside of the school setting.[5]

The new interest in foreign languages has been fostered not only by such driving forces as the EEC projects and those of the Council of Europe, but also by long-standing dissatisfaction with the results achieved by students in school foreign language programs. A recent survey done by the Council of Europe found out, for example, that after five to seven years of extensive foreign language study totaling some 700 hours of instruction, the majority of students were still unable to communicate with a native speaker of the target language on topics of common interest (Council of Europe 1988). In Europe, as in the United States, the amount of time spent on foreign language teaching is simply insufficient in the majority of cases to ensure that students will achieve usable levels of proficiency. (There seems to be considerable agreement that in order to achieve this goal, most students need at least 1200 hours of classroom instruction.[6])

S.O.S: FLES

Coping with this overall failure to teach foreign languages in nearly all secondary school settings and meeting the challenge of the emerging multilingual environment in Europe present very real problems. The reintroduction of FLES may offer some solutions, but to make FLES a success after its failures in the 1970s, some basic conditions must be met:

- As a *sine qua non* condition, there must be continuity between elementary and secondary education. A gap of even one year in the learning of foreign languages between the elementary and secondary school systems can result in startlingly high rates of language decay.[7]
- There must be a curriculum for the foreign language taught at the elementary school level followed by a similar curriculum at the secondary level. To make FLES a success, a curriculum covering the whole spectrum of elementary and secondary education should be worked out.
- Developmentally appropriate methodologies, i.e., methodologies suited to the learning styles and learning readiness typical of the specific age group, must be employed.
- FLES teachers, like all other teachers, should have special training that provides them with:
  General professional competence (awareness of trends and developments in education; classroom management skills)
  A high degree of target language competence
  Methodological competence (ability to establish, implement, and evaluate objectives; ability to assess the progress and difficulties of their pupils)

Some countries have tackled the problem of the hiatus between elementary and secondary education by working out a coordinated curriculum for both levels of instruction. Greece, for example, has developed a program that covers the last three years of the elementary school and is followed by a similar program for the next three years in the junior high school, with a similar methodology building on what has been done in the elementary school (Malbosc 1989). France is trying to harmonize FLES with secondary education by involving secondary school language teachers in the language programs of elementary schools: Many secondary school teachers, for example, have spent as much as two years (one year in the elementary school and another year in the junior high school) teaching at these lower levels (Guerin 1990). This practice helps break down barriers between teachers at the two levels.[8] Another way of breaking down barriers is to bring teachers from the various levels together to share information with one another about their programs. A third way is to set up basic and comparable academic qualifications for all teachers.[9]

Even if the desired degree of continuity (program articulation) can be achieved, however, France and other countries will also need to increase the number of instructional classroom hours in order to significantly raise the level of competence in foreign languages typically achieved by students. There should be more intensive instruction right from the beginning of foreign language study, for example, be that at the elementary or the secondary level: Probably the foreign language should be taught at least five hours a week for the first two or three years; thereafter it could be taught on a three-hours-per-week schedule, as it is in most schools now. Ideally, the foreign language being learned should also be used in teaching other subjects, as is done in many European bilingual schools.[10] If foreign languages were first taught as tools for communication and subsequently were "mainstreamed" by being used as a medium for the teaching of other subjects, they would gain substantially in both real and perceived importance. This dual approach would make foreign languages central to the school curriculum.

The Specificity of FLES

There are many reasons for starting children on learning a foreign language at the elementary school level. It is generally accepted, for example, that young children have great powers of imitation for learning new sounds, new rhythms, and new intonations. They have no inhibitions in reproducing strange sounds, words, or sentences. They are keen on new and strange things: their curiosity is always wide awake. They like games, dramatizations, sketches, and role-play. They enjoy the fun and the "strangeness" of the language course.

To capitalize on children's positive predispositions to foreign language learning, teachers must offer them a language menu that exploits the specific characteristics and traits of these eager young learners. This menu should be based on the ingredients of a multidimensional curriculum (Stern 1983) and provide the students with an enjoyable and meaningful learning experience. One such type of learning experience is described as the "progressivist approach" (Clark 1987: 51), the main feature of which is "learner-centeredness." This approach can be summarized as being concerned with:

- Individual growth from within, through interaction with a favorable environment
- Learning through experience
- A speculative view of knowledge
- Exploitation of natural learning processes and stages of development
- Sensitivity to the interests, rhythms, and styles of individuals' learning styles
- The learner as a whole person
- The social nature of the learner and the development of healthy relationships with others in the classroom community
- The promotion of learner responsibility and of learning how to learn

Most of Clark's points are congruent with Bredekamp's (1986) proposals for a developmentally appropriate program; they may also be clearly and convincingly seen in the following adaptation of Bredekamp's "developmentally appropriate practice":

- Accept the principle that a good FLES program is not merely a scaled-down version of a high school program
- Design interactions and activities to develop learners' self-esteem and positive feelings toward the target language
- Provide active learning activities with materials and individuals relevant to the lives of the learners
- Recognize that learners learn from self-directed problem-solving and experimentation
- Accept learners' play and opinions as valuable and contributory to the learning process
- Provide opportunities for aesthetic expression
- Provide opportunity for movement
- Use children's natural curiosity and desire to make sense of their world to motivate them to become involved
- Relate learning experience to the world of children in France, Mexico, Germany, Japan, etc.
- Support learners as they acquire skills; watch to see what learners are trying to do and provide the necessary support to help them accomplish the task
- Respect learners' preferences for activities, songs, topics, stories
- Provide choices (Strupeck and Watson 1990, p. 27)

These recommendations could become the basic guidelines for course designers as well as for teachers in their classrooms.

Cross-Curricular Work

The linking of language study to other subjects has already been mentioned in conjunction with school bilingualism at the secondary school level. It would, of course, be possible to start cross-curricular work with younger children as well. Language work shares many features with other school activities (Halliwell 1991). We should capitalize on these common features to do parts of other lessons in the foreign language and to integrate language work with other subjects. The teacher can, for example, easily exploit shared features such as the following:

- *Responding by doing:* Children can show by physical reactions that they have understood the message. Physical education lessons, for instance, could be done progressively in the foreign language, as could a great number of other physical activities. This approach underlies Asher's "Total Physical Response" method of teaching foreign languages (Asher 1986).
- *Visual understanding:* The success of audiovisual methods has demonstrated the importance of using the medium of sight in teaching and learning foreign languages, especially with younger learners. Reading or telling a story while showing an illustration helps pupils grasp meanings without going into detailed (and tedious) word-by-word comprehension activities.
- *Information gathering from charts or diagrams:* Children can read bus or railway timetables and TV schedules; as they work on questionnaire matrices, town maps, and house plans—all with very limited yet authentic, contextualized, and communicative language—they will be exercising many of the same skills and techniques they need for science or math classes.

Teachers can use work from language lessons as the basis for work on other lessons and can use techniques adapted from other subjects to promote language work. They can even use content from other subjects as the basis for language work and can teach other subjects in the foreign language. This approach promotes integration of languages into the larger curriculum and makes language a part of the daily lives of the young learners.

Conclusion

Much positive thinking about FLES has been done since the 1970s. There is reason to be optimistic, therefore, that FLES will encounter success as it is now being reintroduced in schools in Europe. To be sure, there are many obstacles still standing before it, not all of them merely ones of materials and methods. Perhaps the most difficult and complex issues are curricular in nature. We must find ways to promote cooperation and harmony among the different school levels, from kindergarten through university. As the English saying goes, "Where there's a will, there's a way," and never before in Europe has there been such a keen interest in languages.

It may be, of course, that our school systems alone cannot satisfy the vast linguistic demands that the changing face of Europe will place on our societies; perhaps we will have to find other ways, some of them extracurricular, to meet these demands. FLES can play an important role in the renewal of language learning, however, provided it is not perceived as merely preparation for secondary school foreign language study (where the "serious" language learning will take place), nor as simply an introduction or sensitization to foreign languages. Rather, FLES must be treated as a valuable experience in its own right, providing for young learners a new tool of communication, a taste for languages, an opportunity to enter another world, and preparation to accept cultural differences and develop an awareness of their own language (Hawkins 1987: 4). Ultimately our goal should be that elementary school language study will prepare the students to enter willingly and happily into our emerging multilingual and multicultural European society.

Notes

1. The EEC is also often referred to as "the European Community (EC)," "the European Common Market *(le marché commun),*" and *"l'Europe des 12."*
2. See in particular Claire Burstall, "Primary French in the Balance" (London: NFER, 1974) and the report by Denis Girard, completed in 1974 for the French Ministry of Education (published in condensed form on pp. 209–13 of Christiane Luc, ed., *Les Langues vivantes à l'école élémentaire.* Actes de colloque—juin 1990 (Paris: Institut National de Recherche Pédagogique).
3. One exception to this generalization is France, where two foreign languages are generally available at the high school level. One of these is chosen as the first foreign language, while the other is begun two years later as the second foreign language.
4. See the final report of the National Curriculum Languages Working Group (1990). In the Proposals of the Secretary of State for Education and Science it is specified that "Ten percent of the curriculum time should be allocated to foreign languages, two or three periods out of a four-period week." The report also expresses the hope that "Over the years the monolingual Briton will become an increasingly rare species."
5. When describing the state of the art in foreign language teaching in Europe, special recognition must be given to the outstanding contributions by the Council of Europe. The Council has, for example, developed the concept of "threshold levels" of language competence, and has disseminated the idea of using communicative approaches to teaching, along with all their accompanying positive effects on curricula, course materials, classroom activities, and perhaps most significantly, on teacher training programs. See Council of Europe 1977; 1980; 1981; 1983; 1988.
6. This is one of the conclusions reached by a national study done in Canada. See LeBlanc 1990.
7. This is reportedly the case in Germany, where some French FLES programs have no follow-up at the secondary level because students at this level must learn English as their first foreign language. In such cases, students may not have the opportunity to resume their study of French until three or more years later, when they may choose it as a second foreign language.
8. In many countries of Europe, secondary school teachers seem to have higher social status than do their elementary school counterparts. Having what is perceived to be higher academic qualifications, secondary school teachers tend to look down on their colleagues at the lower level and very often blame them for the poor preparation, and hence low achievement, of their pupils. This happens not only in languages, to be sure, but also in nearly all other school subjects. Indeed, this hierarchical attitude unfortunately seems to exist among teachers from kindergarten to the university level.
9. This is going to happen in France in 1993, when all would-be teachers will need to have completed a B.A. or a B.Sc. degree before entering the new training schools *(Instituts universitaires pour la formation des maîtres).* In these schools the future teachers will be given training specific to the educational level at which they are going to teach: kindergarten, elementary, junior high, high school, or professional schools.
10. There are a sizable number of these schools (and of schools that, though not truly bilingual in nature, otherwise emphasize language programs) in European countries;

they have proven particularly successful in Germany, Hungary, Rumania, and Bulgaria. Unfortunately, these schools are mainly attended by students from privileged socio-economic backgrounds. It has been suggested that European countries make the bilingual model accessible to a greater number of pupils (Dalgalian et al. 1981).

References, FLES in Europe: A Revival

Asher, J. J. 1986. *Learning Another Language through Actions: The Complete Teacher's Guidebook.* 3d ed. Los Gatos, CA: Sky Oaks.

Clark, John. 1987. "Curriculum Renewal in School," in *Foreign Language Learning.* Oxford, Eng.: Oxford Univ. Press.

Council of Europe. 1977. *The Threshold Level for Modern Language Learning in Schools.* London, Eng.: Longman.

_____. 1980. *Approaches to Self-assessment in Foreign Language Learning.* Oxford, Eng.: Pergamon.

_____. 1981. *Autonomy and Foreign Language Learning.* Oxford, Eng.: Pergamon.

_____. 1983. *Case Studies in Identifying Language Needs.* Oxford, Eng.: Pergamon.

_____. 1988. "A Socio-Cultural Framework for Communicative Teaching and Learning of Foreign Languages at the School Level," pp. 10–70 in *Learning and Teaching Modern Languages for Communication: Project No. 12, Education and Culture.* Strasbourg.

Dalgalian, Gilbert, Simonne Lieutaud, and François Weiss. 1981. "Vers un enseignement bilingue," pp. 135–190 in Gilbert Dalgalian, Simonne Lieutaud, and François Weiss, *Pour un nouvelle enseignement des langues et une nouvelles formation des enseignements.* Paris: CLE International.

Guerin, Yves. 1990. "L'Experimentation contrôlée," pp. 185–93 in Christiane Luc, ed., *Les Langues vivantes à l'école élémentaire.* Actes de colloque—juin 1990. Paris: Institut national de recherche pédagogique.

Halliwell, Susan. 1991. *Teaching English in the Primary Classroom.* London, Eng.: Longman.

Hawkins, Eric. 1987. *Awareness of languages: An Introduction.* Rev. ed. Cambridge, Eng.: Cambridge Univ. Press.

LeBlanc, R. 1990. *Étude nationale sur les programmes de français de base.* Rapport synthèse. Ottawa, Ont.: Association canadienne des professeurs de la langue seconde (ACPLS).

Malbosc, Gérard. 1989. "Grèce: le français dès l'école primaire." *Le Français dans le monde* 229 (novembre/décembre): 35–37.

National Curriculum Languages Working Group. 1990. "Modern Foreign Languages for Ages 11–16." *Bilingualism and Languages Network* (Autumn): 1.

Stern, H. H. 1983. "Toward a Multidimensional Foreign Language Curriculum," pp. 120–46 in R. G. Mead, ed., *Foreign Language: Key Links in the Chain of Learning.* Middlebury, VT: Northeast Conference.

Strupeck, Paula K., and Ann P. Watson. 1990. "Integrating a Foreign Language into the Pre-K through Grade 5 Program: The Baker Model," pp. 22–36 in Gerard L. Ervin, ed., *Realizing the Potential of Foreign Language Instruction: Selected Papers from the 1990 Central States Conference.* Lincolnwood, IL: National Textbook Company.

4

Europe after 1992: International Language Needs and U.S. Reform Proposals[1]

Gerhard Bach

Pädagogische Hochschule, Heidelberg, Germany

Early in *The Adventures of Tom Sawyer,* as our hero is struggling with his task of painting the fence, Tom finds out by a combination of observation, intuition, and cunning that his is not such a bad world after all: "He had discovered a great law of human action, without knowing it—namely, that in order to make a man or a boy covet a thing, it is only necessary to make the thing difficult to attain" (Twain 1950: 17). This irony may have worked for Tom to get the fence whitewashed; it will not work in the field of language learning, even though the idea of creating barriers to prevent the attainment of foreign language skills appears to enjoy a continuous tradition in U.S. educational politics. Despite the awareness of the imminent need of reform, the proposals issued by major educational institutions and organizations in the United States, including the MLA, are prone to cement the problem for the coming decade rather than resolve it.

Phyllis Franklin's (1989) editorial column in a recent *MLA Newsletter* is a case in point. In her proposal, which supposedly sums up a three-year discussion among the diverse associations concerned with the learning of languages, Franklin boils down what the MLA's Advisory Committee on Foreign Language Programs has learned about foreign language education reform to three basic demands: study longer; learn more; start earlier. These demands she would like to see enforced in a nationwide foreign language requirement:

Gerhard Bach is Professor of American Studies at the Pädagogische Hochschule (College of Education) in Heidelberg, Germany, and is currently Visiting Professor at Brigham Young University. His publications on foreign language teaching center on aspects of instructional methodology, educational psychology, and the culture curriculum. He is the translator and editor of the German edition of *Gage/Berliner Educational Psychology* (4th ed., 1986). His most recent publication, coauthored with Johannes-Peter Timm, *Englischunterricht* (UTB, 1989), is a task-based emancipatory approach to teaching English as a foreign language.

School foreign language programs could be strengthened if the field provided clearer goals for school districts by redefining the length and nature of the minimum time required for language study, by specifying a minimal number of languages each school system should offer, and by calling for a school foreign language requirement. (p. 3)

Franklin's long-term goal in this is to create a larger supply of American individuals who, apparently for the first time in the country's history, would be able to "participate in [the world's] polyglot life in a sophisticated way" (Franklin 1989: 4).

Presumably Franklin's proposal expresses a sentiment shared by many U.S. foreign language educators and policy makers. Therefore, in this paper I will respond to Franklin's summary account of the U.S. situation from the perspective of a European observer exposed to the everyday linguistic supply-and-demand situations in business, culture, and education. The arguments I am going to present focus on one basic issue: Franklin's proposal may well serve certain limited internal needs for reform, and, in this context, my suggestions may even be considered radical; from an international perspective, however, the proposal is rather tame—it will in no way be sufficient to prepare Americans for the real demands of the global marketplace that increasingly operates on a non-English or not-only-English basis of linguistic and cultural exchange.

The more prominent points in such a discussion are these: (1) "1992" translates into "Now," i.e., a multilingual reality already challenges Europeans today. (2) Meeting that challenge demands asking which directions Europeans are taking in policymaking, industry, and education. (3) U.S. concepts of needs and European and global realities, i.e., language sophistication and linguistic empowerment must be considered. The conclusions to be drawn from this discussion are, as far as my observations on both sides of the Atlantic go, an urgent matter that U.S. educators must address more radically than they are currently prepared to do. It is, in my mind, less an issue of sophisticated participation in the world's polyglot life, as Franklin desires it to be, than a matter of survival.

"1992" Translates "Now"

In 1988, *Time* magazine was first to use the term *zweiundneunzig* [ninety-two] to characterize the changing constellation of the European Common Market situation. In 1992 the contract regulating the unification of the twelve member states of the Common Market will go into effect.[2] At the end of that year, the borders—physical, cultural, and linguistic—will open and in several ways will become obsolete. People will be free to choose where to live and work. The ensuing economic, scientific, and cultural interchange will lead to a greatly intensified mobility and significant increases in communication. Ironically, Europe will, in some ways, actually become what it has been all along for many a U.S. tourist—a conglomerate of interchangeable nationalities and cultures.

The context in which *Time* uses *zweiundneunzig* is much the same: It summarizes the changes of the European marketscape, not only in terms of its economy, but even more importantly in terms of its languages and cultures. For example:

Economy

At present, Americans and Europeans have a common perspective: If there is need to feel a concern with the coming changes at all, this concern addresses the economic changes the EuroMarket is going to effect worldwide. This has been given an added dimension by the recent peaceful revolution in Eastern Europe: The new geographical and political landscape increases the EuroMarket's immediate range of action. Economic strength also is going to propel the European Community politically into the superpower range. Furthermore, active participation in the European economic exchange system is being sought by former Warsaw Pact countries. The Soviet Union's attempt to reshape its self-concept as a European nation lies at the heart of Gorbachev's *perestroika*.

Languages and Cultures

At the same time, Americans and many Europeans alike show little concern for the impact the EuroMarket will have on the linguistic landscape of this conglomerate of nations where presently more than a dozen different languages are spoken and where, politically, eleven of these languages will enjoy equal status.[3] Multilingualism and multiculturalism are still a far cry from a reality in which nationalistic prerogatives condition everyday communication. But then, are we not encouraged in our monolingual shell by our political leaders? The German head of state is unable to speak any of the community's languages but his own; the former British head of state thought it unnecessary and her successor, as it looks, is following suit; and her French counterpart, for all appearances, is unwilling.

Why does *Time* go bilingual with *zweiundneunzig* rather than opting for the monolingual course of "ninety-two"? This question harbors many of the "hot" items presently discussed among the European member states. Is it perhaps the fact that Germany more quickly than the other nations recognizes and assimilates the coming changes? Is it because we need to watch out for a German economic imperialism in the European market and the world? Is it because the other two major economic factors, Great Britain and France, are holding back, for their own individual reasons: Britain, because she may be counting on linguistic leadership—English being Europe's *lingua franca*; France, because the French often appear to go their own way no matter what EuroMarket strategies impose? Whatever the answer(s), the four-digit metaphor is loaded with meaning: No matter which of the market's languages we choose in which to say "1992," the intention is the same: "Be the first to establish your economic

---

Wir warten nicht auf 1992!

Wir sind ein aufstrebendes mittelständisches Unternehmen der Technik-
branche (Ingenieurwesen) in Wiesloch mit Konzernanbindung in der Schweiz
und suchen für unseren europäischen Markt

eine/n Mitarbeiter/in

die/der die deutsche, französische und englische Sprache beherrscht
und kreativ anwenden kann.

Sie sind 25–35 Jahre alt, haben Berufserfahrung im kaufmännischen Bereich und
den Willen, sich "learning by doing" in technische Abläufe einzudenken.
Ihre Aufgabe ist es, selbständig die kaufmännische und technische Korrespondez
zu bearbeiten.

Wir bieten Ihnen eine interessante, vielseitige Tätigkeit im jungen Team
eines innovativen Unternehmens und eine leistungsgerechte Bezahlung
sowie die üblichen Sozialleistungen.

Ihre Bewerbungsunterlagen senden Sie bitte an unser Beratungsnehmen.

PHOENIX Vermögensverwaltung AG

Bahnhofstraße 55–57, 6900 Heidelberg 1

Figure 4-1. Newspaper advertisement for a multilingual staff position

SOURCE: *Rhein Neckar-Zeitung* (Heidelberg, Germany), 15 March 1990.

foothold in the new territory." In other words: *zweiundneunzig* translates "now."
A recent job advertisement expresses this clearly and directly: "We won't wait
for 1992!"

Industry and commerce thus are implementing EuroMarket strategies already
today. Their need for personnel proficient in one or several foreign languages is
an imminent business factor and, in its actuality, must be taken very seriously by
job applicants. The self-confident tone reverberating in the advertisement shown
in figure 4-1 is indicative of the situation in general: "mastering" the foreign
language implies experience, ease, versatility, and creative implementation. More
than simply a skill, language competency is a genuine part of the applicant's
personality, part of her or his professional identity. Achieving this level of
linguistic competence is a challenge indeed, but apparently not an unrealistic
one, considering the frequency of similar job advertisements these days even in
the regional papers. Thus, practical necessity is setting a trend widely recognized—by the individual job-seeker as much as by educational institutions

and educational policy makers. How is the challenge being met, and are there visible results?

Meeting the Challenge

A recent survey on reforms of the foreign language curriculum in Germany has framed this issue of "meeting the challenge of 1992" in its title: "Shakespeare or Foreign Language Correspondent?" is the provocative question (Meyer 1989). The solution suggested by the author is obvious: Given the right training, students can achieve in both sectors, thus serving educational and posteducational needs simultaneously. It is a perspective that until recently had been widely ignored throughout Europe. The emergence of "1992" like a specter on the horizon, however, has imparted an unforeseen momentum to the call for reform, with politics, industry, and education joining the bandwagon. Thus, a partly desolate, partly complacent situation in several of the Community's member nations is suddenly being turned into a challenge. That challenge is visible in a spectrum formed by three distinctly related sectors: political, economic, and educational.

The Political Sector, or: Who Is Going to Speak Which Languages Where, When, and for What Purposes?

Several of the Market's countries are investigating the language requirements they will face in the next decade. Obviously, Portugal and Greece will find themselves in a different position than, say, France and Germany. Great Britain is, or believes it is, in a category by itself. Thus we are looking at a threefold issue: the *lingua franca,* the "major" languages, and the "minor" languages. This relationship is a quantitative one on the surface only. The underlying qualitative issues are, for example: How can Greek, Danish, or Dutch "survive" under the primacy of French, German, or Spanish? Is it necessary or even logical for someone whose home and workplace is in the southwest corner of Germany to learn English as the first foreign language just because it is and will continue to be the "common core" language of the community, when French is so much closer geographically, culturally, and economically? In what ways will the ethnic and cultural constitution of a smaller nation change in view of the necessity to incorporate the major languages into its cultural fold? Are majority languages necessarily priority languages? Is the English language going to effect assimilatory cultural processes throughout Europe, subduing in the process individuality and diversity to a superficial cultural melting-pot of global "McDonaldism"?[4]

The Economic Sector: Language Needs and Language Profiles

Some of these questions relate to the economic sector also; here they appear in sharper focus since international business communication is not new to the individual member states. There is a change, however, in the former consensus about English as the *lingua franca*. The ever-increasing volume of business cooperation at international levels can no longer be accommodated by one "international" language only. Corporate identity today may even forbid that this be so. U.S. and Japanese business operations in Germany and France have started to realize that an essential part of a corporation's identity is its native language and culture. Moreover, the Council of the European Community has made a firm commitment to European multilingualism. Therefore, in all countries of the Community, more than one foreign language will be stipulated in the school curriculum. At the same time, there is mutual agreement that psychological and sociocultural differences will be influential factors in commercial ventures. This extends to the selection and motivation of personnel, management styles, and decision-making processes as much as to safety standards, advertising policies, and honoring terms of payment. None of these factors is culturally "neutral." Therefore it is safe to assume that the best language is that of the customer. This implies that anyone doing business with or within the EEC must, by simple logic, speak three languages: his or her native language, English as the *lingua franca* of international business communication, and the native language of the business partner. "Speaking" these languages implies the strategic skills of versatility and creativeness, exactly those qualities asked for in the advertisement in figure 4-1.

While much investigative groundwork still needs to be done in the area of culture skills, some EEC member states have concentrated on defining specific language needs typical of the individual workplace or interrelated professional areas. Until very recently, the model concept of needs-profiles adhered to what can best be described as the "trunk-and-branches" concept. The trunk was what you had acquired in school, and the branches were what you learned on the job in terms of special field requirements ("Spanish for business adminstration," "French for electrical engineering," etc.). This concept is beginning to fade as language-needs profiles begin to show that, in most cases, we come up with an extremely broad trunk and rather skimpy branches. In other words, *the common core of communication by far outweighs the specialist's further language needs.* These latter needs are primarily lexical, and can be easily acquired on the job, while the semantic and syntactic needs generally cannot.

A few examples may illustrate the issue at hand. Between the early 1970s and the mid-1980s, the London Chamber of Commerce and Industry Examination Board (LCCIEB) carried out several surveys in industrial corporations and firms to find out how foreign languages were used by various types of staff not employed as specialist linguists (such as translators). Several of the member nations participated in this survey. The results were published in 1985 as *The Non-specialist Use of Foreign Languages in Industry and Commerce.* It is a slim booklet that has become a secret classic in the wake of "*zweiundneunzig.*" The individual findings were pooled into language needs profiles that were established for nine different categories of staff:

1. Accounts personnel
2. Advertising / marketing personnel
3. Buying personnel
4. Managers / executives
5. Production personnel
6. Research personnel
7. Secretaries
8. Technical personnel
9. Transport / distribution personnel

Responses were sought for twenty-one language activities, which for the report were grouped into six skill areas:

1. Listening and speaking
2. Speaking
3. Reading
4. Writing
5. Listening and writing
6. Listening

The primary goal of the LCCIEB was to determine to what extent each of these skills were put to use in a nonspecialist business environment. As a secondary goal, the LCCIEB wished to determine the relevance of their own foreign language syllabi in educational curricula.

Two results from this study are important in the present context. Both relate to the question of *stability,* one with respect to *staff categories,* the other with respect to *time.* The first result, about stability and categories of staff, was most surprising to the investigators: They found that "the patterns of foreign language use . . . depict stable and widespread 'profiles' of behaviour" across all nine categories (LCCIEB 1985: 2).

Segmented into "areas of skills," the LCCIEB profile indicates the following relative importance:

Listening and speaking	49 percent
Speaking	4 percent
Reading	19 percent
Writing	17 percent
Listening and writing	3 percent
Listening	8 percent
	100 percent

To put this overall profile into perspective, a comparison between the profiles for managers and secretaries, respectively, is useful:

	Skill Area	Profile for Managers and Executives	Profile for Secretaries
1	Listening and speaking	54.7 percent	35.6 percent
2	Speaking	4.0 percent	1.0 percent
3	Reading	16.6 percent	14.5 percent
4	Writing	14.4 percent	34.5 percent
5	Listening and writing	1.6 percent	11.1 percent
6	Listening	8.7 percent	3.3 percent
		100.0 percent	100.0 percent

Clearly there is a noticeable variance in sectors 1 (listening and speaking) and 4 (writing). This reflects the nature of the professional activities that are characteristic of the two types of staff. The secretarial profile's need for strength in writing skills is exceptional in the overall survey; still, even in this category of staff, "listening and speaking" take up a considerable segment, and "reading" comes close to the average percentage.

The general profile thus may help instructors of foreign languages to fortify (or modify) their tacit assumptions about the practical value of their work and methods. For example, foreign language educators may have anticipated that the "listening/speaking" skill accounts for just about half of all professional communication. On the other hand, "writing," the other productive skill, takes up a greater segment than generally anticipated, especially for types of staff traditionally conceived of as "nonwriting" (i.e., managers). This is true also for the receptive skill of "reading." The importance of writing and reading in professional language usage, however, is perhaps not reflected in foreign language instruction and methodology. Where this is so, a reconsideration and a more even balance may be called for.

The second major result of the LCCIEB study relates to stability and time, and perhaps today bears even greater importance than it did when the study was done five years ago. The report gives evidence that the results of the several surveys made over a span of about fifteen years have proven surprisingly stable: "The information in the report has been continuously updated since 1972 and it appears that there has been little significant change in the patterns of language use since that time. In support of that claim we have included relevant appendices reporting similar work conducted more recently in a number of European countries" (LCCIEB 1985: 3). This sign of stability is reassuring at a time of rapidly changing market and job structures; at the same time, such reassurance should be weighed carefully.

The increased use of computer technologies in international communication may enforce more imminent and noticeable changes in the relationship and importance of individual skills than proposed in the LCCIEB prognosis; this goes especially for oral/aural skills in the business context. The information age already today calls for greater flexibility in communication. For example, information technology is in the process of drastically changing the translator-secretary's workplace, decreasing the need for technical skills (such as typing speed), and increasing the importance of instrumental skills by which information technologies can be put to use conceptionally and creatively (e.g., evaluation and correction of machine translations). At present, estimates predict that in the business sector face-to-face communication will be reduced by 30 percent. A simple but powerful law follows from this: The greater the reduction of social contacts through direct communication, the greater the impact of *le mot juste,* the right word at the right time.

The Educational Sector: Goals, Strategies, Methods

Knowing what the demands of the 1990s on international language needs in Europe are helps us to define the goals, strategies, and methods by which these demands can best be served. At the same time, the strategies and methods chosen will have an impact that is going to reach beyond the borders of a united Europe.

Goals.   Multilingualism is the password for the 1990s, in politics, business, and culture. In most of the EEC member states the educational decision-making processes occur "top down," i.e., by central educational authorities that control curricular developments. In Germany, for example, this control is executed by the individual state departments of education. Thus, curricular changes are rather slow to take effect. Consequently, the time factor becomes a pressing issue: Teachers need to realize that the students they face in the classroom today are the ones that will feel the impact of the new market situation as soon as they finish school. In other words, educational measures cannot wait until the time of market unity has come; they need to be addressed now. "1992" spells "now" in the classroom, too. The major issues here include the following:

- *Lingua franca.* The first issue across national boundaries is the obvious need for a priority language. The idealistic concept of the European Council—to give each of its member languages equal status—has been silently undermined by the realities of the business world: English will remain the Community's *lingua franca,* but as such it will primarily be used in situations where more than two nations and languages are represented in a transnational business venture or cultural exchange.
- *"Starter and offspring."* A second sensitive issue is actually a spinoff from this silent agreement: the question about the new concept of "starter" and "offspring" languages. A starter language is one whose mastery allows us to quickly assimilate a further, etymologically related language, and to do so on our own, with very little formal instruction. From an English or German "home base," then, French would be the starter for Spanish, Portuguese,

and Italian; Russian would serve as a starter for Polish, Czech, or any other of the Slavic languages.

Strategies.   The idea of the "starter/offspring" concept on language learning strategies is going to bring immense changes. Three aspects indicate their impact:

- *Lifelong learning.* Language learning will be functional not only in terms of what we are going to do with the individual language we learn in the context of real or imagined posteducational settings, but also in terms of stressing one's overall ability to learn. Learning to learn, the lifelong learning concept enters the field as a strategy.
- *Languages in the elementary grades.* Foreign language learning will need to begin at an earlier stage than is presently required in most European nations. The earlier students begin to learn a "priority" language, the sooner they can move on to offspring languages, thus ensuring a moderate multilingualism by the end of their formal schooling. There is greater agreement today than there has ever been on the experiments done in the 1960s in Great Britain and Germany about the advantages of language learning in the elementary grades.
- *Controlled diversification.* In combination, these two demands call for a curricular concept of "controlled diversification." This presents such question as: Which languages are to follow the priority languages? How do we diversify and stratify the foreign language curriculum with respect to geographical and social conditions as well as economic and professional needs? "Learning your neighbor's language," a program that debuted in Germany and France more than a decade ago, is only one step in this direction.

Methods.   The needs profiles described above present us with real-life demands that more often than not correlate only marginally with curricular and instructional realities. The traditional approach to teaching languages—with its hazy perspective of what might be needed later in life—must be reconsidered. A few suggestions from the area of skills acquisition may suffice to indicate the directions of change.

- *Productive/receptive skills.* The relationship between productive and receptive skills is currently being redefined to establish a balance that better aligns with posteducational real-life communicative tasks. This is especially true for a balanced mastery of oral and written skills.
- *Skills and tasks.* The relationship between skills and tasks is also being redefined. The traditional instructional approaches give priority to the skills sector. A more immediate and realistic incorporation into real-life tasks will return to the learning process that element that characterizes natural language learning outside the classroom.
- *Culture skills.* In the traditional concept, skills are seen rather exclusively as linguistic skills. Teaching culture skills is equally important if communication is to function properly. This relates not only to the question

of whether in greeting another person it is sufficient to say "hello," or whether it is appropriate to bow, shake hands, kiss, or rub noses. More than that, it addresses the fact that many a commercial venture is agreed upon in the social environment of a business lunch rather than the executive office, and, more often than not, the words used in the one setting will not apply to the other. Culture skills, in such contexts, closely match social skills.

U.S. Needs as Projected by European and Global Realities

Language study in the United States will be affected by the changing European landscape of communication. The reforms presently discussed and implemented in Europe will be felt in this country, and educators and policy makers will (although, as it appears, later rather than sooner) act upon them. The present phase is characterized by awareness mixed with awe: it seems as though, once more, others are getting a head start. To the European observer of these developments, the reform proposals made by U.S. foreign language experts appear to be addressing the real global needs inadequately.[5] First, such proposals are insular, i.e., they take little account of the truly dramatic changes taking place *outside* the United States, changes that, nevertheless, already begin to redefine actual needs for foreign language proficiency inside the United States. Participation in the world's polyglot life is dependent upon the awareness of that world's needs as well as its multilingual progress. There is little actual evidence, for example, in Franklin's proposal that would reflect such an awareness. The reason for this is closely connected with a second issue: U.S. reform proposals generate their goals and their reasoning not from the learners' actual needs but rather from structural givens.

Arguments for entrance age, course integration, language sequencing, minimum requirement, etc., are aligned more to the 6-3-3 structure of the American education system than to evidence of what we know today about intellectual development, language-learning, L1–L2 relationships, affective behavior, motivation, and tomorrow's workplace. To claim, for example, age thirteen as an appropriate developmental stage to begin learning the first foreign language, as Franklin (1989: 4) proposes, is not only uninformed in terms of what we know from developmental psychology; worse than that, it has the effect of self-entrapment in structural prerequisites, curricular conventions, and administrative constraints. Thus, insularity and system entrapment are likely to continue being the major stumbling blocks on the way to curricular reform. Foreign language educators in the United States are still waiting for an answer to why it actually is impossible in this country to enforce an earlier start, i.e., a start in the elementary grades, which would give students a real opportunity to study longer and learn more, with the result of a realistic chance to compete linguistically in the global marketplace.

Conclusion

In summary, since educational politics is slow to effect change, and since, at the same time, students are standing on the threshold of "1992," the only workable solution for U.S. education at this point is to modify existing teaching methods to utilize more fully and effectively the little time most U.S. citizens are afforded to learn a foreign language. Since the problem exists in a similar way for specific educational sectors in several European countries, it is worth looking at recent developments there.

Educators in Britain and Germany, for instance, have begun investigating possibilities of utilizing methods developed by and for those areas of language learning where "languages mean business," i.e., the professional language training institutes. Until recently, such institutions led a marginal existence only, serving mostly the inept student and the occasional traveler or business representative. With *zweiundneunzig* knocking at the door, their methods all of a sudden enjoy center-stage attraction. Their success is measured by the degree to which they manage to align their instruction with ever-increasing and -diversifying posteducational needs. The programs they have designed and the materials they have developed for the adult learner with a specific professional goal in mind can be guidelines for the preprofessional (i.e., academic) foreign language curriculum also.

Students in such programs may not be "laughing their way to 1992," as one language-business venture advertises, but at least they will be able to walk a goals-oriented course to successful international communication. Once they are aware of this potential in the foreign language, they will, as Tom Sawyer knew, "covet the thing," or, in Webster's official terms, they will feel an "inordinate desire for what belongs to another."

Notes

1. This chapter is a revised version of a paper originally presented at the MLA conference in December 1990.
2. The twelve member states of the European Community are Belgium, Denmark, France, Germany, Greece, Ireland, Italy, Luxembourg, the Netherlands, Portugal, Spain, and the United Kingdom.
3. The eleven official languages will be Danish, Dutch, English, French, German, Greek, Irish, Italian, Luxembourgish, Portuguese, and Spanish.
4. These and many other language issues are being addressed through the LINGUA program, which was created by a decision of the Council of the European Community on July 28, 1989.
5. "Language Study in the United States: A Draft Statement" (*MLA Newsletter* 21 [1989]: 16) is a case in point. For a focussed U.S. critique of this statement, consult Dale L. Lange's presentation at the 1990 MLA Convention (Session 221), "A Critical Analysis of the MLA Statement on Foreign Language Study in the United States." Lange strongly advises against adoption of the draft statement as official association policy. For a copy of his paper, write to the author at the College of Education, University of Minnesota, Minneapolis, MN 55455-0211.

References, Europe after 1992

Franklin, Phyllis. 1989. "From the Editor." *MLA Newsletter* 21: 3–4.
London Chamber of Commerce and Industry Examinations Board. 1985. *The Non-specialist Use of Foreign Languages in Industry and Commerce.* London, Eng.: LCCIEB.
Meyer, M. A. 1989. *Shakespeare oder Fremdsprachenkorrespondenz? Zur Reform des Fremdsprachenunterrichts in der Sekundarstufe II.* Wetzlar, Ger.: Büchse der Pandora.
Twain, Mark. 1950. *The Adventures of Tom Sawyer.* New York: Washington Square Press.

SECTION II

National Foreign Language Policy and Practices

5

Implications of the New Dutch National Action Plan for U.S. Foreign Language Policy

Richard D. Lambert

National Foreign Language Center

To many in the United States, to speak of a national policy for foreign language instruction is either an oxymoron or a form of odious heresy. Our foreign language teaching system is not only decentralized but devoutly committed to fragmentation. The closest thing we have to national policy-making lies in existing and proposed federal legislation providing financial support for a few segments of the system. We in the United States have what might be called a "constrained free-market system" of foreign language instruction, that is, as in much of education, one dominated by private choices made by states, school districts, schools, colleges, individual teachers, and students, but anchored firmly in what is already in place. Most foreign language teachers like it that way, and few educational policymakers care enough to debate the virtues of such a system.

I hold no brief for centralized educational policy-making *per se,* nor for a major expansion of the federal or state government's intervention into local educational affairs. This is particularly true when economic policy around the world seems to be backing away from central planning. It does seem appropriate, however, to examine how the aggregate consequences of our *laissez-faire* system in foreign language instruction measure up against what a more carefully crafted, more deliberate policy might accomplish. In doing so, we will want to look at a number of different aspects of foreign language instruction so that we can

Richard D. Lambert is Director of the National Foreign Language Center at The Johns Hopkins University in Washington, D.C., Professor Emeritus of Sociology and South Asian Regional Studies at the University of Pennsylvania, and Editor of *The ANNALS of the American Academy of Political and Social Science.* He is the author of *Points of Leverage: An Agenda for a National Foundation for International Studies, Beyond Growth: The Next Stage in Language and Area Studies,* and *The Transformation of an Indian Labor Market: The Case of Pune.* Dr. Lambert's most recent book, *International Studies and the Undergraduate,* is the result of a massive two-year survey of undergraduate international education in the United States, conducted for the American Council on Education.

discuss in a more informed manner which aspects of our foreign language educational system could benefit from more collective planning and which are better left to the interplay of market forces.

Some insight into this question may be gained by examining a new national plan for foreign language instruction recently prepared for the Dutch government by a committee headed by Professor Theo van Els of Nijmegen University (*Horizon Taal* 1990). There are obvious limitations in using the Dutch example as a basis of comparison. For one thing, it represents a special case even in Europe, as the language instructional systems in other European countries vary considerably on many of the features described below. For another, most U.S. foreign language teachers would sell their souls for some of the features of the Dutch system:

- The high levels of student motivation in language learning found in the Netherlands
- The unquestioned assumption that everybody should receive a great deal of foreign language instruction
- The ability of the Dutch schools to pile on requirements for the lengthy study of two or three foreign languages (only Luxembourg seems able to require its students to devote more time to language learning than do the Dutch)
- The more manageable size and greater homogeneity of the planning unit
- The expectation that a large proportion of the educated elite will in fact use a foreign language in adult life

In the United States, by contrast, we are still debating whether to require a tiny bit of instruction in one language, student motivation is at best uneven, and relatively few Americans have occasion to use their normally very limited foreign language skills as adults.

Even with these important differences of context in mind, however, we can learn a great deal by examining the issues that the Dutch National Action Plan addresses. I do not intend to make one long invidious comparison admiring whatever is found abroad and denigrating our own system. Rather, it is hoped that a review of the Dutch plan will help take the foreign language community in the United States away from total rejection of centralized planning *per se* and suggest that it is time to begin to separate and consider some of the individual issues we must face. What follows, then, is a review of some of the specific issues dealt with in the Dutch plan, and a running commentary on the contrasting U.S. situation and the challenges the issues pose for a planning agenda in the United States.

Centralization and Scope of Policy

The Dutch plan was developed and will be implemented by and large by the national government, a fact that neither surprises nor troubles anyone in the Netherlands. The United States has no equivalent governmental planning mechanism for foreign language instruction. The closest we come are some state- or metropolitan-level officers who hold a foreign language portfolio. The states and metropolitan areas in the United States vary considerably in the amount of attention, direction, and supervision they give to foreign language policy. We can, however, discern that, except for broad requirements for courses and teacher certification, the center of gravity in language policy formulation resides largely in the individual school or teacher. Moreover, what collective planning does take place is confined to the primary and secondary school level of our national foreign language system. Higher education is totally atomized with respect to foreign language policy. Few if any planning mechanisms cross institutional lines in postsecondary education, and within institutions decisions affecting language instruction are normally made by departments and individual teachers. In foreign language instruction we do not even have prestigious national organizations that regularly monitor educational developments and successfully sponsor reform in the teaching in other disciplines. For instance, in disciplines such as physics or mathematics, committees of the National Academy of Sciences or of the relevant professional associations serve as sponsors. We do have major professional membership associations in the various foreign languages that occasionally address issues of national policy in a pursuit of federal funding or in *ad hoc* exercises in discussing national priorities. They have, however, no planning mandate for the field whereby the scattered teachers and programs will follow centrally-arrived-at priorities and agendas even when they are developed. There is no tradition-sanctioned place to stand when debating issues of national policy nor a place to anchor the lever for change once fresh policies have been agreed on.

The arguments for disaggregated decision-making often heard in U.S. foreign language education do not seem to have troubled the Dutch planners very much. Indeed, the new Dutch plan not only assumes a dominant role for centralized planning but also tries to fit all the segments of foreign language instruction into a common framework (except for minority language policy, which in greater part it relegates to another planning division). The various sections of a foreign language instructional system are articulated by deliberately assigning interlocking responsibilities and roles to the different segments, by prescribing in detail the amount of language instruction students must take at various levels, and by attempting to develop what the Dutch call "an autonomous structure" that specifies a grid of language skill levels into which the different parts of the educational system may be expected to fit their foreign language objectives.

I do not mean to imply that all Dutch foreign language instruction, nor that of any other country in Europe, is totally centrally planned and administered. Even in a relatively small country like the Netherlands not all decisions have been made about what will be centrally and what locally governed. In the Netherlands, each school has a fundamental right to decide on its own curriculum, even if it is fully subsidized by the central government; and most schools are run by private foundations, usually denominational. In addition, there is a general move in Dutch education to decentralize control of all education to allow greater local autonomy by providing undifferentiated lump-sum payments to schools. This will loosen even further the control of the specifics of foreign language instruction. And in the Netherlands there are different degrees of centralization in different aspects of language instruction. For instance, even in language testing there is a curious division whereby reading examinations are set and graded centrally while speaking and listening evaluations are done locally. As another example, a central decision has been made that all lower-level schools must teach English to a particular level, but instructional style is determined by the individual school. More generally, centrally developed goals are implemented by the control of funding and testing at the national level and by what the Dutch call "steering," that is, exerting multifaceted influence throughout the system to accomplish centrally determined goals.

The balance between fiat and persuasion is open to continuous negotiation in the Netherlands, as elsewhere. Nonetheless, the notion that the setting of goals and the determination of the architecture of the system as a whole are legitimate functions of the central government is well established in the Netherlands and in many other countries of Europe.

The Choice of Languages

The Dutch plan gives a great deal of attention to deciding which languages will be required or offered in different kinds of institutions, and to differentiating between required and optional languages. There are four basic principles motivating the new Dutch plan: concentration, differentiation by level, adult use, and function.

Unlike the U.S. system, which encourages proliferation, the Dutch decision is to limit the number of languages taught at various levels. The complement of languages offered is constant, based on the argument that education through the secondary school provides a common educational base to all students and the languages studied should be the same for all students. At the primary level instruction is limited to English. In secondary schools, except for minority children who may choose to take instruction in their own language, just three languages are to be offered: English, French, and German. Provided certain conditions have been met, students in the upper secondary school may also take Spanish and possibly also Arabic or Turkish. Barring these exceptions, for most students instruction in all other languages is confined either to the tertiary level or to specialized vocationally oriented schools outside the formal educational system.

In the Dutch plan three rationales govern the choice of languages to be taught. First, the choice of English, French, and German is based upon surveys of actual use of those languages by adults. Second, a conscious decision has been made about where Dutch national interest lies, defined in terms of the demands of international business (both on the world scene and in the coming European market unification in 1992). The third basis of decision is essentially teleological, that is, it is based upon an examination of the ultimate purposes of studying a language and reflects not only *which* but *how* languages are taught. The Dutch distinguish three purposes of language learning:

- The need for communicative skills in that language
- Needs that are linked to the communicative skills, such as familiarity with the culture or literature of another nation
- Needs that are not, or at best are only indirectly, linked to skills in a particular foreign language, e.g., learning to think logically or developing transcultural empathy (van Els 1990: 88)

These three purposes in acquiring foreign language skills are ranked in order of importance. Languages for which only the third need can be argued are not to be offered at the primary or secondary level at all. Those meeting the second need may be considered, but this need is to be met in separate courses dealing with, say, literature, and are not to be confused with communicative language learning.

The Dutch decision to concentrate language instruction through the secondary level in just three languages has its costs. It limits foreign language instruction for all to a single world language—English—and two languages of neighboring countries—French and German. Pressure to expand the number of foreign languages taught in the secondary school is sure to mount. As the unification of the market of the European Community approaches in 1992, there will doubtless be pressure to expand instruction to include other European languages, particularly those of southern Europe that are less frequently studied in northern countries. The proposed Dutch policy also inhibits the growth of instruction in the non-European languages—for instance, Japanese—which may be vital to the Netherlands' future. Even with these drawbacks, however, the decision to concentrate on three languages in the lower levels of the educational system and to limit instruction in other languages to the university, vocational, proprietary, and other private bodies is a rational and carefully thought-out policy. The Dutch believe that thereby a proper and well-balanced division of labor will be developed to meet the need for foreign languages adequately somewhere in the system as a whole. The use of the criteria of actual adult use and strategic national interest in choosing which languages to teach raises interesting questions for U.S. language policy.

In the United States we have no reasoned plan guiding the particular languages that students should be taught.[1] Nor is there any public discussion of the kind reflected in the Dutch plan on what the ideal complement and enrollment profiles in the different languages should be. We cannot, as the Dutch did, use adult usage as the guide to language choice since it would probably make a weak case for the study of foreign languages at all, let alone provide help in determining which ones should be studied. Nor can we argue clear national interest in the choice of language. We might, as the Dutch did, use the geographic propinquity of other countries or the language of our principal ethnic minority—both arguing for Spanish—or commercial importance—arguing for Spanish, German, and Japanese. In point of fact, however, neither adult use nor national interest enters very much into the choice of languages offered or taken in the United States.

One reason for the lack of a discussion about which languages should be offered or studied is that our teleology of language instruction is different from that of the Dutch. Their ranking of languages based on the reasons for studying them—first communication, then cultural knowledge supporting communication, and finally general intellectual development—is not nearly so widely accepted in the United States. Indeed, we tend to turn this list of priorities on its head. The argument so often heard on campuses and in some of the national foreign language associations is that language study is a humanity, and like other humanities, languages should be studied for their mind-broadening effect or for what they teach us about other peoples' cultures. Whatever its intrinsic virtues, giving priority to this function of foreign language learning reverses the Dutch order of priorities. The effect of this reversal is to make it difficult to argue in the United States for any choice of a particular language; the study of almost any language will serve humanistic ends.

More generally, there is little tradition in the United States of making rational decisions about which languages should be offered and taken. Our complement of language courses results from the interaction of three factors: what the individual teachers who are in place are capable of and choose to teach, the nature of foreign language requirements, and student choices. This matrix of institutional constraints and individual student choices constitutes our *de facto* national policy on language selection.

It is interesting to note that in this constrained market economy of language choice the profile of languages offered and taken in the United States has shifted radically over time. Few remember that Latin was the language with the most courses offered and highest enrollments in the United States at the turn of the century. In subsequent decades there was a shift to French, then Spanish as the language with the largest number of students enrolled. German now ranks third, in part because students believe it to be a more difficult language to learn. Other languages are taught at the margin and together account for less than 5 percent of total enrollments. Moreover, since enrollments in these languages are dependent upon ephemeral student preferences, they are subject to rapid expansion and decrease. Russian and Chinese have recently been on a roller coaster in student enrollments, and Japanese instruction is experiencing an extraordinary spurt of growth. Given the zero-sum nature of foreign language enrollments in colleges and high schools, teachers of the other languages see the rapid expansion in Japanese as a possible threat to their own well-being in the academic marketplace. And given the nonfungibility of language competence among teachers, the system as a whole has great difficulty in adjusting to unplanned shifts in student preferences in a situation in which no countervailing rationale guides language choice.

Requirements and Options

Paralleling the lack of a reasoned policy informing the selection of which languages to offer, we in the United States tend to make relatively few other distinctions among languages regarding the proper level at which they should be studied, how long, and by what kind of students. The Dutch plan, on the other hand, makes many such distinctions. First, there are differences by level and by required versus optional languages. English alone is to be studied by all students in primary school. Like most European educational systems, at the secondary level Dutch students are sorted into different curricular tracks according to their presumed occupational interests and their promise of continuing in college. At present, about one-third of the primary school students enter vocational education, although the number has been steadily declining. The others proceed to general secondary education, where students are in turn differentiated into three groups: those who will take four, those who will take five, and those who will take six more years of schooling. Students in the latter group intend to go on to the university level.

Variations in the amount and orientation of secondary education that students take are reflected in differences in foreign language requirements. When the new plan is adopted, English will be mandatory for all students, including vocational students, in the first phase of secondary education. Subsequently, students must choose between French and German. In the second phase of vocational training, the third language may be chosen, but a student need be examined in only two— usually English and German. For students enrolled in general secondary education, English, French, and German are compulsory in the first phase, but after three or four years students may drop two languages. Most drop only one— French more often than German. At the university level, except for students who have special foreign language needs, all language study is optional. It is assumed that all students have the requisite foreign language skills when they enter a university. This is the dream of many university-based teachers of upper-level language and literature courses in the United States.

In addition to differentiating the total amount of foreign language training that various types of students are required to take, the Dutch plan also distinguishes between requirements for language learning in which all four skills (reading, writing, listening, and speaking) are specified and instruction in what are called "partial qualifications," that is, for example, teaching reading skills only. This is particularly true for languages serving the second and third educational purposes: the promotion of cultural understanding or general intellectual improvement.

This highly orchestrated set of foreign language choices and requirements stands in sharp contrast to the essentially *laissez-faire* system in the United States. First, the choice of languages to be studied in the United States is not formally specified, although there is a *de facto* concentration of languages offered in Spanish, French, or German. While there is a greater proliferation of languages at the postsecondary level, it is more the result of historical accident than of planning as in the Dutch case. Moreover, pressure is constantly being exerted to expand the number of languages taught at the level of the high school, or for that matter, the elementary school. Nor do we distinguish between required and optional languages, and "partial qualifications" are viewed as old-fashioned and unacceptable. While some language programs may wind up as *de facto* reading programs, only in Latin, Greek, and in some places Hebrew is the teaching of reading alone viewed as a legitimate enterprise.

In the United States we do not differentiate foreign languages into optional and required categories. For purposes of meeting a language requirement, a language is a language, except for the old Ph.D. requirements that used to specify French and German as the only acceptable languages of scholarship. (Even this restriction is now gone, although in some universities there is a vestigial specification that only "languages of research" or "languages in which there is an extensive scholarly tradition" will qualify.)

The primordial struggle in the United States is not over which languages should be required or optional, as in the Netherlands, but over how to require a minimal amount of study of any language for as many students as possible. The battle over a language requirement is a hardy perennial on many a U.S. campus. In addition, voices at the national level urge the further extension of foreign language requirements. For instance, the Board of Directors of the American Council on Education (ACE), an assembly of college and university presidents, recently declared that every baccalaureate graduate of a U.S. college or university should have a usable level of competency (whatever that means) in a foreign language by the year 2000 (American Council on Education 1989). First, unlike the Dutch plan, the ACE resolution says nothing about which languages should be studied. Second, it relates to all baccalaureate students, undifferentiated by career goals. Third, to accomplish this goal would demand not just a standardization of what is already in place (as in the Dutch plan), but indeed a major expansion in foreign language requirements that would require a curricular revolution.

This *ex cathedra* encyclical provides a further contrast between the U.S. and the Dutch system that is worth noting. In the Netherlands the principal domain of foreign language requirements is the secondary school, while in the United States it is college and university. Some states mandate language requirements for students graduating from high school. More commonly, the college or university sets whatever foreign language requirements there are. The universal foreign language requirement typical of many European countries is uncommon in the United States. In 1987, 13 percent of our four-year colleges had one foreign language requirement for all incoming students and 16 percent for all graduating students. Much more common was the partial language requirement: 52 percent of four-year institutions required some students—usually arts and science students—to have taken foreign language courses in order to graduate (Lambert 1989a).

Very few institutions administer the kind of course-free proficiency examination that would make it possible to determine whether the ACE goal is met. Two-year colleges, where almost half of U.S. college-level students are enrolled, rarely have either an entrance or a graduation foreign language requirement. Moreover, in contrast to the Netherlands, where a *de facto* ten-year requirement of foreign language study is not uncommon, in the United States foreign language requirements, even where they do exist, tend to be quite modest: only one or two semesters of foreign language study satisfy the graduation requirements in 39 percent of all four-year colleges.

Given this rather limited set of foreign language requirements, how much foreign language education do U.S. students get? Curiously, we have no data linking foreign language study in high school with that in college, so we have no idea of how many students take how much language instruction in which languages across the full range of their studies.[2] We do know that about 71 percent of freshmen entering college have had at least two years of foreign language instruction in high school. In top-ranking schools the numbers will be much higher. Unfortunately, when they reach college, students are often put back to a beginning stage. In a recent year, for instance, 98 percent of freshmen entering The Ohio State University had taken three years of a foreign language in high school. Of these, 68 percent who continued studying the same language at the university were placed in the very first semester of instruction in that language upon entering the university (Dihoff 1990).

While we have no data on cumulative foreign language learning across educational levels of the kind that the Dutch system of requirements routinely provides, it is clear that in the United States few students receive anywhere close to the amount of foreign language training that Dutch students of all kinds are exposed to. Half of our four-year college students (52 percent) do not take any foreign language course at all, about 50 percent of the residual students drop out after the first year of collegiate foreign language courses, and another 50 percent drop out after the second year. The average number of foreign language courses taken by those students who get any foreign language instruction at all in college is 1.5 (Lambert 1989a: 66).

This vast difference in the amount of foreign language training for students in the Netherlands versus those in the United States raises fundamental policy questions for us. Given the low demand for and adult utilization of foreign languages, do we want to strive for an immense increase in the number of students who take a limited number of foreign language courses? Do we want to raise all students to a very substantial level of foreign language competence, as the ACE declaration implies? Do we want to accommodate either of these goals by extending universal or selective requirements, as in the Dutch case? Or, given (1) our low starting point in terms of foreign language competency, (2) the U.S. preference for free choice as to whether students take foreign language instruction, and (3) our limited adult use of foreign languages, is the expansion of universal language requirements such as those found in the Netherlands and elsewhere in Europe the only useful policy option? Should we adopt a more targeted, less ambitious language policy, one differentiated more carefully by language, by level, or by type of student? Should we divert some of our national resources into language skill conservation and rejuvenation rather than concentrating them exclusively on first-time learners? Should more resources be put into generating adult use of foreign languages, thereby increasing student demand and inducing students to stay with language instruction until they achieve a genuine communicative competence? Or should we continue to concentrate on expanding the number of students who take a little bit of foreign language training?

Planning for the Whole System

The Dutch national plan incorporates a well-developed occupation- or profession-oriented language instructional system in the same frame of reference as language learning in the formal school system. Most European countries have developed extensive official and proprietary language training facilities for workers in various occupations, and for translators and interpreters. In Finland, for instance, the national government administers a series of training programs and certification examinations. Indeed, the Council of Europe maintains an elaborate network of such governmental facilities. And throughout Europe formal plans usually span both school-based and adult foreign language instruction. In the United States, by contrast, almost all our planning assumes language instruction takes place only in the formal educational system; adult occupational language training is what might be called an unorganized sector. We pay almost no attention to that part of our national language instructional system that serves adults, particularly occupational use (Lambert 1989b). In the main, such instruction is provided within the federal government's own schools or in commercial language schools, and it has almost nothing to do with what takes place in our formal educational system. I know of no planning in the U.S. system that links foreign language instruction for use by government or business employees, or by adults in general, with instruction in our schools and colleges. Yet it is in such use-oriented instruction that we may develop the higher levels of language skills to meet the types of demands that the Europeans take for granted.

Testing

In the Netherlands, foreign language testing is the responsibility of a freestanding organization of the central government that sets and administers examinations and establishes standards for successful completion. In addition, an equivalent organization develops curricula. One of the hallmarks of language instruction in many European countries is the overt link between uniform curricula and tests of student performance, both centrally administered. While there has been some concern about the backwash effect of uniform testing (that is, that classroom teaching is bent toward achieving high ranking on the test), the legitimacy of language tests themselves is not subject to major battles in Europe, as it is in the United States. Indeed, foreign language reform movements in Europe are largely about curriculum and pedagogical style, while in the United States the current dominant reform movement in foreign language education has been centered on testing strategy. (Moreover, the U.S. testing reform movement is moving in a direction opposite to that found in the Netherlands and in much of Europe: We have been seeking to establish criteria for tests of language proficiency that are totally independent of curricular content and style.) Yet in recent years we have been backing away somewhat from this ideology of isolation in a deliberate attempt to promote a test backwash effect that would reshape the U.S. foreign language curriculum to reflect the new conception of foreign language skills embodied in proficiency testing. One of the paradoxes of the U.S. situation is that the movement to induce universal adoption of uniform proficiency standards is severely handicapped by the disaggregated nature of decision making in foreign language education. Except for a few state-level initiatives, such as teacher certification in Texas, every battle for the new testing standards calls for house-to-house combat. It is also curious that in other parts of U.S. education, particularly in mathematics and the sciences, there are strong forces moving toward the kind of national testing procedures and standards found in the Netherlands. Within mathematics there is even a movement toward a uniform national curriculum. In the United States, however, the foreign language profession is curiously almost totally unconnected to such developments.

Conclusion

This review of the issues raised for U.S. foreign language planning by the new Dutch national plan is not meant to be like one long paean of praise for the Dutch system and denigration of our own. The Dutch have their own problems. Indeed, the Dutch plan is an attempt to deal with some of these deficiencies. As I said at the outset, the purpose of this review is not to assess which system of foreign language instruction is better, but to illuminate some of the individual issues we in the United States must face. The fact that the Dutch situation is different from our own does not mean that we need not make more rational decisions on many of these same issues. Perhaps our current disaggregated, school-bound, free-choice-driven, unarticulated, low-skill-level-focused, humanities-oriented, European-language-bound system of foreign language instruction is optimal in meeting our national needs in the next century. In my view, however, some important changes are called for: a vigorous public debate on these and similar issues in our *de facto* national language policy would be very healthy.

Notes

1. Exceptions to this are the various federal funding programs promoting instruction in the less commonly taught languages, particularly the Higher Education Act, Title VI.
2. We know even less about the subsequent language learning careers of students who receive elementary school-level foreign language instruction.

References, Implications of the New Dutch National Action Plan

American Council on Education. 1989. "What We Can't Say Can Hurt Us." Washington, DC: American Council on Education.

Dihoff, Ivan. 1990. Personal telephone communication, January 25.

Horizon Taal. 1990. Nationaal Actieprogramma Moderne Vreemde Talen, Nota van Aanbevelingen. Nijmegen, Neth.: Ministerie van Onderrwijs en Wetenschappen.

Lambert, Richard D. 1989a. *International Studies and the Undergraduate.* Washington, DC: American Council on Education.

————. 1989b. *The National Foreign Language System.* NFLC Position Paper. Washington, DC: National Foreign Language Center.

Van Els, Theo. 1990. "Policy-Making in Foreign Language Teaching." *Toegepaste Taalwetenschap in Artikelen* 36: 88.

6

Multilingualism in Kenya

Ann Biersteker
Kimani Njogu
Yale University

Rũthiomi nĩ rũthiomi. Gũtirĩ rũthiomi atĩ rwega kana rũũru gũkĩra rũria rũũngĩ.
Ũũru no rũthiomi kũhinyĩrĩria iria ingĩ. . . . Kaba Gĩthwaĩri.[1]

In Kenya, as in many other African countries, multilingualism is the norm rather than the exception and current sociolinguistic practice as well as cultural and educational policies reflect this situation. During the final years of the colonial period there were unsuccessful attempts to counteract multilingualism through the imposition of English and the suppression of Kenyan languages. Today multilingualism is not only accepted but encouraged within certain parameters, the boundaries of which are contested and continually being reformulated.

To understand multilingualism in Kenya it is important to understand the sociolinguistic situation and the history of language policies in that country. Various sources provide conflicting information on the number of languages and dialects spoken in Kenya. The estimates range from 58 to 80—Whiteley (1974a) estimates 80; Mann and Dalby (1988), 58 languages plus additional "dialects." There is agreement, however, that languages of three distinct families (Afro-Asiatic, Niger-Kordifanian, and Nilo-Saharan) are spoken within the boundaries

Ann Biersteker is an Assistant Professor in Linguistics and African and African-American Studies at Yale University. She is Director of the Yale Program in African Languages, the author of *Masomo ya Kisasa, Kujibizana: Poetic Dialogue as Political Actions* (forthcoming) and coauthor of *Mashairi ya Vita.* She has also published a series of articles on Kiswahili and Gikuyu literature and was President of the African Language Teachers Association in 1988–89. She has directed four Fulbright-Hays Group Projects Abroad Advanced Intensive Kiswahili programs in Kenya and is currently working on a series of video production projects focused on poetry in Kiswahili. Her Ph.D. from the University of Wisconsin in African Languages and Literature was granted in 1984.

Kimani Njogu is a faculty member in the Department of Kiswahili and African Languages at Kenyatta University and a Ph.D. candidate at Yale. His dissertation is a sociolinguistic study of East African dialogue poetry. He is the author of *Mwongozo wa Kilio cha Haki, Mwongozo wa Mukwava wa Uhehe* and numerous articles on Kiswahili language and literature. He was also the scriptwriter of the prize-winning radio program "Ushikwapo Shikamana."

of Kenya. There has, however, been borrowing of terminology between even the most structurally unrelated languages.

There is little information available on multilingualism before the colonial period in what became Kenya during that time. Given the existence of extensive trade, various types of alliances, intermarriage, and other contact between East African peoples, multilingualism was obviously an important factor in the lives of many people and a topic that merits further research.

A good deal of information on multilingualism in Kenya shortly after independence is found in the *Language in Kenya* study edited by W. H. Whiteley (1974c). In the research for this study conducted during the late 1960s, four studies of language use in Nairobi found high percentages of multilingualism among the populations surveyed. D. J. Parkin's (1974b) study of language use in Bahati housing estate—an area populated by low-income workers 97 percent of whom at the time of the study (1969) identified themselves ethnically as "Kikuyu" (Agĩkũyũ)—indicated that 99.9 percent of the household head speakers of Gĩkũyũ surveyed also knew Kiswahili, 42 percent knew English, and 28 percent knew Kĩkamba. In Kaloleni housing estate (a slightly higher-income and more ethnically mixed, although predominantly Luo, estate) Parkin (1974a) found that 90.9 percent used Kiswahili and 42.3 percent used English with workmates, and that over 35 percent claimed knowledge of at least one language in addition to the language stated to be "mother tongue." In Janet Bujra's (1974) study of Pumwani, a predominantly Muslim housing estate, 64 percent of those surveyed said they spoke Kiswahili fluently, "34.8 per cent said they spoke it moderately well, and 1.2 per cent said they spoke 'only a little.'" (p. 234). Fewer people in Pumwani than in Bahati or Kaloleni claimed useful skills in English (only 5.8 percent claimed fluency), but 69.7 percent claimed knowledge of one or more local languages other than their own.

Whiteley's (1974b) study of rural areas also indicated extensive multilingualism. In three rural areas of Kenya Whiteley found that over 50 percent of the population claimed quadrilingual competence. In six areas he found that over 50 percent of the population claimed trilingual competence. Since these included some of the most densely populated areas in Kenya (Central, Western, and Nyanza Provinces) and since multilingualism is much more prevalent in urban areas, it is reasonable to assume that the majority of the people in Kenya in the 1960s were at least trilingual. There is every reason to assume that during the 1970s and 1980s multilingualism has increased, particularly among young people and women, as school enrollment has increased and urbanization has intensified. With the exception of a few isolated rural areas and among older women in a few other communities, it is rare today to meet a bilingual, much less a monolingual Kenyan.

Two other features of multilingualism in Kenya are code-switching and what is called "Sheng." Multilingual code-switching has become the norm in Kenya especially among the urban middle class in both formal and informal settings. Many young Kenyans today speak Sheng, often described as a "mixture" of languages, but actually a pidgin with a Kiswahili base and Gĩkũyũ, Dholuo, and

English terms. While some writers blame Sheng for low examination results, others claim it should be studied as a school subject.

Colonial Era Language Policies

While there is evidence of multilingualism before the colonial period, the current commitment of Kenyans to multilingualism is explained in part by colonial era language policies. Colonial era language policy in Kenya reflected conflict between colonial government officials, the white settler community, European missionaries in East Africa, and East African political activists. In 1929 then-Governor Sir Mcleay Grigg stated:

> Every encouragement will be given to English which must be the lingua franca of this colony. There shall be no bilingualism in our institutions or courts. (Mkangi 1984: 17)

Grigg's statement suggests that the colonial administration during his administration promoted English for both bureaucratic and nationalistic purposes. This policy was contested by the white settlers of Kenya. For them, English was a political tool that might be used by Africans for liberative objectives. This attitude is well summarized in a 1929 statement by Major Grogan, chairman of the Settlers' Convention of Association:

> Imagine a more desperate happening than that we should introduce the language (English) to large numbers of people . . . whose proper education is to work in the fields. (Gorman 1974: 417)

Missionary groups during the period, as well as some other educational policymakers, promoted the use of Kenyan languages. It was assumed that people in Kenya were monolingual members of "tribes" and that all members of each "tribe" spoke one and only one distinct language. Recent historical studies have demonstrated the ways in which ethnic divisions were created and promoted by these and other colonial policies and practices. For example, Charles Ambler's (1988) research on central Kenyan societies in the nineteenth century demonstrates that

> People identified with others beyond their lineages, neighborhoods, and sections. The movement of commodities, individuals, and ideas broke down insularity, drawing communities into the larger region and beyond. (p. 156)

Ambler does not specifically discuss multilingualism, but it seems logical that multilingualism was involved when Kīkamba-speaking traders bought natron (a form of sodium carbonate) from its Kĩigembe-speaking extractors and sold it to speakers of Kĩembu, Kĩmbeere, and Kĩndia (pp. 90–92). Similarly when Kĩkamba-speaking "refugees fleeing famine in Migwani arrived in Mwimbe" (an area where Kĩmwimbe is spoken) and "were able to invoke a mutually accepted claim of common ancestry" (p. 35), some of the refugees and / or hosts must have been at least bilingual.

For the next two decades no tangible plans were formulated to implement the stated official language policy giving primacy to English in spite of ongoing negotiations. The 1943 Beecher Report recommended that "English take the place of Kiswahili as the colony's lingua franca in as short a time as possible." Practice did not change and another Beecher Committee was set up in 1949. This second committee recommended setting up 340 intermediate schools in which the medium of instruction would be English. In the lower primary school classes the "first language" would be used (Gorman 1974: 429).

This policy reflects the changing world political climate after World War II as various colonies pressed their cases for independence strongly and consistently. Colonial powers had to reconsider their relationships with their colonies. Prior to this period schools were required to apply for a government permit in order to be allowed to teach English. In Kenya there was, and had been, rigorous and insistent articulation of the people's commitment to freedom and liberty expressed in all languages spoken in the colony. With the suppression and banning of publications voicing these commitments and intensified white settler resistance to Kenyan independence, an armed resistance movement took shape in Kenya. As colonial government troops battled the Kenyan Land Freedom Army (the resistance movement called "Mau Mau" by the colonial government) killing thousands and forcing thousands more into detention and concentration camps, English in 1953 was made the compulsory medium of examination in the Kenyan African Preliminary Examination administered at the end of the eighth year of primary schooling. Up until 1952 Kiswahili had been an optional medium for this examination; this option was now removed. Students who had prepared for examinations in Kiswahili were suddenly forced to take them in English.

At this point in time there was also a deliberate shift in colonial discourse on language. English, which had been seen exclusively as the language of the colonizers, was promoted as the language of the colonized as well. Calls for "partnership," such as the following by Sir Philip Mitchell (1954), were typical:

> what we have set ourselves here is the establishment of a civilized state in which the values and standards are to be the values and standards of Britain, in which everyone, whatever his origins, has an interest and a part. The wildest naked man in Turkana has an investment in it, although apart from the security he now enjoys it may be a remotely maturing one. (p. 217)

In the late 1950s the government embarked on a program popularly referred to as the "New Primary Approach" in which the medium of instruction was to be

English throughout. Since it had not been possible to make Kenya "a white man's country," the revised colonial government plan was to make Kenya an English-speaking country. In 1960 the governor of Kenya, Sir Patrick Renison, stated "the most potent force in building a united country is a common language . . . and that language in Kenya must be English" (Mitchell 1954: 2). In the same meeting he emphasized the need for Kenya "to work in partnership" with Britain. The strategy was to "negotiate" for a continuity that accommodated African nationalism. English was to be at the center of that continuity.

Postcolonial Language Tensions

Many thought that Kiswahili would become the language of Kenya when at a mass meeting of the Kenya African National Union (KANU) shortly before independence, Jomo Kenyatta prefaced his switch to Kiswahili by saying:

> Brothers, I think I have spoken enough in this language. It is not my wish that I should be speaking to you in a foreign, and for that matter a colonialist, language. (Kenyatta 1973)

During the postcolonial period in Kenya, however, language policy and practice have been characterized by explicit and ongoing tension between the Pan-Africanist and nationalist appeal and subversive potential of Kiswahili and other Kenyan languages on the one hand, and the range of factors maintaining English on the other. In the dependent capitalist economy of Kenya, U.S. and European tourism has become the primary source of foreign exchange. Similarly Britain and the United States remain the major markets for Kenya's two main export products, coffee and tea. In addition to economic dependence on the United States and Britain, Kenya retains military links with Britain, obtains much of its military hardware from the United States, has granted the U.S. military use of Kenyan port facilities, and has allowed the U.S. army to build a base. All these factors of economic and military dependence maintain English as a language of significance in Kenya.

Yet few in Kenya would today argue that English should be the "national" language. The appellation "national" is reserved for Kiswahili, and English is referred to as "the official language." Kenyans with widely divergent political stances ranging from that of the current president, Daniel Arap Moi, to that of one of the most well known opposition leaders, Ngũgĩ wa Thiong'o, agree on promoting Kiswahili. This agreement is based on East African political history. Nineteenth century East African resistance to Omani rule created a body of poetic texts in Kiswahili that inspired resistance to colonial rule. Harry Thuku published political statements in Kiswahili in newspapers in the 1920s. During the period immediately after World War II, a large number of political newspapers and magazines were published in East Africa in Kiswahili. Kiswahili became the language of the nationalist movement in Tanganyika and upon independence the national language of Tanzania. In April 1965 Kiswahili was declared the national language in Kenya by the Kenyatta government.

As the language of the workers and peasants, the language of socialism in Tanzania, and the language of the Pan-Africanist movement, Kiswahili has become the language of political consciousness in Kenya. Kiswahili is today also an international language enabling communication between the countries of Kenya, Tanzania, Uganda, Zaire, Rwanda, Burundi, and the Comoros. It is also spoken by communities in Somalia, Mozambique, Zambia, Oman, and the Malagasy Republic and is taught in universities in Egypt, Ghana, and the Sudan, as well as in universities in Britain, France, Italy, Germany, Japan, Korea, and over one hundred universities in the United States.

English, of course, remains the language of upward social mobility in Kenya, as in other former British colonies. It is the language of higher education, international business, and the tourist industry. Nor should the localized economic factor in language acquisition be underestimated: among the most multilingual communities in Kenya are hotel and restaurant workers, "beach boys" (tourist hustlers), and prostitutes. Kenyans in these occupations typically speak English, German and/or Italian, Kiswahili, and one or more additional Kenyan languages. Many have also learned French, Japanese, Hebrew, and Scandinavian languages.

Political and social factors should also not be ignored in considering multilingualism in Kenya, which enables horizontal mobility. The hotel worker in Malindi who uses Italian, German, and English to speak to hotel guests and the hotel management uses Kiswahili to speak with other workers and many residents of the city and Kigiriama to speak with other dwellers in the city and surrounding areas. If he is a "Maasai" guard hired by a hotel to wear a red blanket, plait his hair, and carry a long spear to impress tourists, he may speak both Gĩkũyũ and Engkotok ool Maasa: with other "Maasai" guards.

Multilingualism in Modern Kenya

The Media

The media, like other areas of Kenya life, are multilingual. There are three daily newspapers in English and two in Kiswahili. Media efforts to encourage development of language skills include "Lugha Yeta" ("Our Language"), a weekly column in Taifa Leo and a program on Voice of Kenya (VOK), and "Ukumbi wa Kiswahili" ("Kiswahili Forum"), also a program on VOK. The Ministry of Information publishes a series of local newspapers in Kiswahili Sauti ya Kericho, Sauti ya Meru, etc.). Books in Kiswahili and English are easily available in urban book shops, and international magazines are sold in larger urban centers. Most Kenyan magazine publishing is in English.

The Voice of Kenya (VOK) airs radio broadcasts in Kiswahili, English, Gĩkũyũ, Dholuo, Kĩkamba, Oluluyia, Kalenjin, Ekegusii, and Kĩmeru. There is also some broadcasting in Kuria, Af i Rendille, Nga Turkana, Engkotok ool Maasa:, Af Soomaali, and Afaan Oromoo (Mann and Dalby 1988). VOK television service is in Kiswahili and English. Different departments and ministries use the VOK for the promotion of social and cultural projects: between 1987 and 1989, for example, the National Council for Population and Development sponsored the soap operas "Ushikwapo Shikamana" (radio) and "Tushauriane" (television) in the promotion of family planning. In 1990 CNN began broadcasting to Kenya.

Popular music in Kenya is available in a wide range of languages. Music in Kiswahili and American English is perhaps most widely heard, but many Oluluyia, Gĩkũyũ, Kikonog, Lingala, and Dholuo songs are also popular. U.S., European, and Indian films are shown in many areas of Kenya and there are many video shops with films from the same countries. While there have been many U.S. and European films made in Kenya, the Kenyan film industry is concentrated in the production of films for VOK television broadcast.

There was a dramatic increase in publishing in a wide range of Kenyan languages after the 1977 production of *Ngaahika Ndeenda* by the Kamĩrĩĩthu Community Education and Cultural Centre. Licenses for production of the play were withdrawn, the authors were forced into detention (Ngũgĩ wa Thiong'o) and exile (Ngũgĩ wa Mĩriĩ), and the Kamĩrĩĩthu Centre was bulldozed to the ground. The legacy of the production's break with the cultural practice of literary and dramatic production exclusively in English was continued, however, with the publication of Ngũgĩ wa Thiong'o's novels in Gĩkũyũ, *Caitaani Mutharaba-inĩ* (1977) and the *Matigari* (1986).

Other recent controversial literary works in Kenyan languages include Alamin Mazrui's *Kilio cha Haki* and *Chembe cha Moyo*. There have also been a wide range of fictional works published in other Kenyan languages. These include Grace Ogot's *Miaha,* Okoth Okombo's *Masira Kindaki,* and Gakaara wa Wanjaũ's *Hĩngo ya Paawa.* Ngũgĩ, one of Africa's most well known authors, now writes fiction and criticism only in Gĩkũyũ.

The controversy over drama in Kiswahili and Gĩkũyũ continues: In January 1991, licenses were withdrawn for a new production of *Ngaahika Ndeenda* and then for a production of a Kiswahili adaptation of *Shamba la Wanyama,* a Kiswahili adaptation of George Orwell's *Animal Farm* (Wahome 1991).

Parliamentary Practice

In July 1974 the governing council of the ruling party KANU passed a resolution making Kiswahili the language of the National Assembly. This resolution was debated and passed in parliament. Section 53(i) of the constitution was changed to state that the proceedings of the National Assembly were to be conducted in Kiswahili. Later an amendment was passed that required that all bills, memoranda, amendments, and financial resolutions be written in English. Constitutionally English and Kiswahili were set at odds.

The languages are also in competition in terms of the required language skills of parliamentarians. Section 34(c) of the constitution requires that at the time of nomination for election into the National Assembly the candidate "be able to speak and unless incapacitated by blindness or other physical cause to read the English language well enough to take an active part in the proceedings of the National Assembly." Candidates fluent in Kiswahili but incapable of speaking English have legally been barred from contesting elections. In parliament, parliamentarians are allowed to debate in Kiswahili bills drafted in English. These deliberations are then recorded in the official Hansard (published record) in English translation. Obviously a great deal of code-switching takes place in parliament, even though this is a formal setting.

Religious Gatherings

Christianity and Islam are the two main religions in Kenya and multilingualism is central to religious practice in both religions. Islam has a long history in Kenya. Mosques dating to the twelfth century have been studied by archeologists working on the Kenyan coast. The first Christian missions were established in the late nineteenth century at the coast and did not reach many areas of Kenya until later in this century.

Because of Islam, extensive trade with Arabic-speaking countries, and Omani attempts to rule much of the coast, many upper-class men living in coastal areas became bilingual in Arabic and Kiswahili during the eighteenth, nineteenth, and early part of the twentieth century. Classical Arabic has remained the language taught in Koranic schools, but few—except those who travel to Oman and other Arabic-speaking countries and those who study Islam to advanced levels— become fluent in Modern Standard Arabic. Kiswahili has long been the language of greatest significance to East African Muslims. For many, becoming a Muslim in East Africa has meant becoming ethnically identified as "Mswahili" (a Swahili person). East African Islamic communities found in every urban center are Kiswahili-speaking communities where Arabic is the language of prayer, but Kiswahili is the language of daily social as well as religious practice.

Missionary-established churches in Kenya have held and advocated a wide range of language policies. Whiteley's 1968/69 study indicates that Kenyan languages other than Kiswahili were most often used in established churches for the liturgy, preaching, and other purposes, and that Kiswahili generally played a more important role than English (Whiteley 1974b: 337). Whiteley did not discuss simultaneous translation in services: a long-established practice in many urban churches in which the most widely spoken Kenyan language in the area served by the church is the primary language of the service, which is echoed throughout by a simultaneous translation into Kiswahili—or vice-versa. In recent years the use of Kiswahili has increased in established churches in all aspects of church work, although churches serving upper-class and expatriate communities still provide English language services.

African Independent Churches have emphasized the use of Kenyan languages. The Maria Legio Church holds services in Dholuo and Kiswahili, while the

African Israel Church Ninevah holds services in Kiswahili, Oluluyia, and Dholuo. Services of the African Independent Pentecostal Church are predominantly in Gĩkũyũ. As indicated by David Aoko's study Kiswahili has been and remains the primary language of independent churches in Nairobi.

Political Gatherings

Kiswahili is the primary language used in public political discourse today in Kenya. Whether in gatherings of the political and business elite or of the urban poor, the language spoken from the podium is Kiswahili, even if the discussions among those in attendance are conducted primarily in English (by the elite) or Gĩkũyũ, Dholuo, Kĩkamba, Oluluyia, etc. (by the poor). In less multilingual communities a local language is often used with code-switching to Kiswahili. An exception to this general use of Kiswahili is the president's speech on Jamhuri (Independence) Day, an occasion on which it has become almost a tradition for the president's written speech to be delivered in English and then translated to the general public in Kiswahili.

Law Courts

Kenyan law courts use English as the official language of communication between accused individuals and the court. Usually the accused is asked in which language he or she would like to address the court. In urban areas, the less literate members of society often choose to speak in Kiswahili; their utterances are then translated by a court interpreter. In rural areas, any of the other Kenyan languages may be used and then translated into English. Court interpreters are not trained in simultaneous translation and often code-switch when addressing the court. If the accused has some education, he or she would likely choose to address the court in English but would code-switch often to Kiswahili. Evidence from Kenyan linguistic practice in this context, as well as others, suggests that one cannot argue that code-switching is a phenomenon only of informal discourse.

Much dispute resolution that does not reach the law courts takes place in other Kenyan languages. Many disputes are resolved by local "chiefs" or "kadhi" ("judges"), if the case involves Islamic law. These officials generally use Kiswahili or the language(s) most familiar to the disputants.

Commerce

English is the primary language used in international business, the administration of development assistance, and the tourist industry. Kiswahili is the language used in factories and the military and is widely used by workers in commercial agriculture and in much urban trade. It is also the primary language used by the police and in prisons. Kiswahili and Sheng are widely used in public transportation in Nairobi. Other Kenyan languages are used more locally in transportation, agricultural trade, and in the workplace.

The Home and Neighborhood

Language use in Kenyan homes today is often multilingual, particularly in urban areas. Many parents consciously encourage their children to become multilingual by using three or more languages in the home and encouraging reading and writing skills in all languages. In families where one language is less known by one generation than another, it may become a household code language among the generation that knows it better. In that most urban, and many rural, neighborhoods are multiethnic and multilingual, most Kenyans learn at least enough of neighbors' languages to exchange greetings and speak with less multilingual family members.

Language and Educational Policy

Within the recently implemented 8-4-4 system of education (a system based on U.S. models that has replaced the earlier British system), in the first years of schooling (Standards I–III—i.e., the first three years of primary school) the medium of instruction is "mother tongue" or the "language of the school's catchment area," i.e., Kiswahili in urban areas. In theory, reading and writing are initially taught in this language. In practice, of course, this is not the case, as primers are available in fewer than thirty of the languages of Kenya. Many Kenyan children learn a new language when they begin school. For example, a child who speaks Kĩmbeere (and perhaps some Kiswahili, English, Kĩembu, and/or Gĩkũyũ) will begin to read using a primer in Gĩkũyũ, Kĩembu, or Kĩkamba, depending on where in Kĩmbeere-speaking areas the child happens to attend school. If the child also receives Christian religious instruction, reading materials will be in Gĩkũyũ or Kĩkamba or Kiswahili. If the child receives Islamic religious instruction, reading materials will be in Kiswahili and Arabic. In Standards I–III Kiswahili is a required subject alongside English. In Standards IV–VIII English is the medium of instruction and Kiswahili and English are both required subjects. Religious instruction is provided in the schools, and a goal of Islamic religious instruction at this level is that students should "read and write the Quran in its original script," i.e., in Classical Arabic, although this is not stated explicitly (Kenya Institute of Education 1986: 104).

The Kenya Institute of Education and Kenya National Examinations Council are the central institutions in the implementation of language and educational policy. At the secondary level English is the medium of instruction and both English and Kiswahili are compulsory subjects. Students study literatures in other languages (including other Kenyan languages) in English translation as part of their study of "Literature in English." At the end of four years of secondary school, students write parallel examinations in English and Kiswahili. Each exam consists of a language and a literature paper. Each language paper has two parts: a composition section requiring two written essays and a summary, comprehension, and grammar section (Kenya National Examinations Council 1987: 1–5). French and German are optional subjects taught in only a limited number of schools. Unlike the English and Kiswahili examinations, the examinations in these languages include oral sections (Kenya National Examinations Council 1987: 14–15).

At the University of Nairobi the Department of Linguistics and African Languages teaches Kiswahili, German, and Arabic. French is taught in a French department. Literatures in other Kenyan languages are studied in the Department of Literature. Kenyatta, Egerton, and Moi Universities also teach Kiswahili and have departments of literature. Only Kenyatta University teaches French.

Adult education is administered by the Institute of Adult Education at the University of Nairobi Kikuyu Campus. The institute prepares materials in English for advanced classes. However, Kiswahili remains the primary language of current literacy and other adult-education programs in Kenya.

Conclusion

Our consideration of multilingualism in Kenya has both methodological and policy implications. Both sociolinguistic study and language planning efforts typically underestimate the extent of multilingualism in a given society by assuming a monolingual norm. In addition, both also often deny the value of multilingualism for society and the individual. Multilingualism facilitates cross-cultural communication and understanding. It enables people to be effective in social relationships. For a society, multilingualism provides a range of choices in language policy and practice.

Discussion of language issues in the United States often presents multilingualism as an educational problem for the individual and as an obstacle to national integration. The Kenyan situation demonstrates that multilingualism can be both a personal and national resource. It is essential that sociolinguistic study and language policy-making in both countries reexamine assumptions concerning multilingualism and reconsider the actual extent of multilingualism by examining more carefully language use in work, trade, and neighborhoods. Multilingualism has value, not only in fostering international cooperation, but also in enabling national integration.

Note

1. Translation: "Languages are languages. No language is better or worse than another in so far as it does not seek to oppress other nations, nationalities and languages." Ngũgĩ wa Thiong'o 1990): 282.

References, Multilingualism in Kenya

Ambler, Charles. 1988. *Kenyan Communities in the Age of Imperialism.* New Haven, CT: Yale Univ. Press.

Aoko, David. 1974. "Language Use within the African Independent Churches of Nairobi," pp. 253–62 in W. H. Whiteley, ed., *Language in Kenya.* Nairobi: Oxford Univ. Press.

Bujra, Janet. 1974. "Pumwani: Language Usage in an Urban Muslim Community," pp. 217–52 in W. H. Whiteley, ed., *Language in Kenya.* Nairobi: Oxford Univ. Press.

Gorman, T. P. 1974. "The Development of Language Policy in Kenya with Particular Reference to the Educational System," pp. 397–453 in W. H. Whiteley, ed., *Language in Kenya.* Nairobi: Oxford Univ. Press.

Kenya Institute of Education. 1986. *Syllabuses for Kenya Primary Schools,* vols. I, II, III. Nairobi: Jomo Kenyatta Foundation.

Kenya National Examinations Council. 1987. *Kenya Certificate of Secondary Education Regulations and Syllabuses, 1989–1990.* Nairobi: Kenya National Examinations Council.

Kenyatta. 1973. Part III of *The Black Man's Land Trilogy: Images of Colonialism and Independence in Kenya.* London, Eng.: Anthony-David Inc.

Mann, Michael, and David Dalby. 1988. *A Thesaurus of African Languages.* London, Eng.: Hans Zell for the International African Institute.

Mitchell, Sir Philip. 1954. *African Afterthoughts.* London, Eng.: Hutchinson.

Mkangi, K. G. C. 1984. "The Political Economy of Kiswahili: A Kenya–Tanzania Comparison," *Mwamko* 2: 7–25.

Ngũgĩ wa Thiong'o. 1990. "Kĩngeretha Rũthiomi Rwa Thĩ Yoothe? Kaba Gĩthwaĩri." *Yale Journal of Criticism* 4,1: 271–93.

Parkin, D. J. 1974a. "Language Shift and Ethnicity in Nairobi: the Speech Community of Kaloleni," pp. 167–87 in W. H. Whiteley, ed., *Language in Kenya.* Nairobi: Oxford Univ. Press.

————. 1974b. "Status Factors in Language Adding: Bahati Housing Estate in Nairobi," pp. 147–65 in W. H. Whiteley, ed., *Language in Kenya.* Nairobi: Oxford Univ. Press.

Wahome Mutahi. 1991. "This Censorship Smacks of Sanitising Rot in Society." *Daily Nation* (Nairobi), 4 February, p. 4.

Whiteley, W. H. 1974a. "The Classification and Distribution of Kenya's African Language," pp. 13–68 in W. H. Whiteley, ed., *Language in Kenya.* Nairobi: Oxford Univ. Press.

————. 1974b. "Some Patterns of Language Use in Rural Areas of Kenya," pp. 319–96 in W. H. Whiteley, ed., *Language in Kenya.* Nairobi: Oxford Univ. Press.

————, ed. 1974c. *Language in Kenya.* Nairobi: Oxford Univ. Press.

7

Current Perspectives on Japanese English Education

Keiko Samimy
The Ohio State University

Carl Adams
Niigata University

Japan is a big market for English. With constant yearly increases in the numbers of Japanese traveling, working, and studying abroad has come a growing desire for internationalism through the study of English. The mass media constantly churn out various forms of English in FM radio programing, bilingual television programs (e.g., "Sesame Street," "CNN News," English conversation courses, commercials, movies). It is therefore no exaggeration to say that the teaching and learning of English as a foreign language has become a major educational enterprise in Japan. English is a required subject taken by every middle school and high school student. No other foreign languages are taught except at private secondary schools, where about 5 percent of the students take French, German, Spanish, or Korean in addition to English.

According to Koike (1978),

in 1976, 4,700,000 students in junior high schools (middle schools), 4,400,000 in senior high schools, 50,000 in technical colleges, 380,000 in junior colleges and 1,840,000 in universities were studying English. To accommodate this large number of students, 58,000 high school teachers

Keiko Samimy is Assistant Professor in Foreign Language Education at The Ohio State University. Her research interests are affective and sociocultural variables in relation to adult second language acquisition. Currently she is conducting a research project that deals with Japanese sojourners' English acquisition processes.

Carl Adams (M.A.T., School for International Training, Brattleboro, Vermont) is Assistant Professor at the Faculty of Education, Niigata University, where he teaches English as a Foreign Language, communications, and culture. He has taught EFL at the secondary and university levels in Vietnam, Indonesia, and, for the past eighteen years, in Japan. He is a founding member of the Japan Association of Language Teachers (JALT), President of JALT–Niigata, and serves as the National JALT Program Chair for 1991–92.

and 6,000 university and college professors have been trained and are currently teaching. By now, approximately one eleventh of the Japanese population is engaged in the study of English. (p. iv)

Despite the amount of time, money, and energy devoted to the teaching and learning of English in Japan, the outcome has been less than satisfactory. Most Japanese can hardly read or write in English, let alone speak it, after six years of English education. Due to Japanese educational policies, and in particular to the notorious secondary school and college entrance examinations, English education has lagged behind in accommodating the learners' as well as societal needs.

Educational policy is centralized in Japan. The Ministry of Education specifies a detailed curriculum that is implemented in each school. National syllabi and textbooks and a standardized curriculum provide a fairly uniform education for all Japanese students. Textbooks are published by private companies, but they must be approved by the Ministry of Education.

It is obligatory for all school-age children to attend elementary school (6 years) and junior high school (3 years). Entrance to high school and university is determined by scores on nationwide examinations. As students' future careers are closely tied to their educational background, the entrance examinations have an enormous impact on educational practices in elementary and middle school, as well as in high school; even kindergartners are pressured to study hard in preparation for the examinations. Parents often spend between 20 percent and 40 percent of their income on their children's education (including the cost of the JUKU—"after-school" schools—and of the "cram schools" that children attend in preparation for entrance examinations). In urban areas, nearly half of the secondary students attend JUKU.

Students who are actually admitted to universities will almost certainly graduate (the graduation rate in Japanese universities is approximately 95 percent). University credentials practically guarantee initial employment by a desired organization. Thus, the power that the entrance examinations exert on the Japanese curricula is extraordinary. Subject content as well as methodology are often dictated by the examinations. Until recently, English curricula were no exception, offering heavy emphasis on grammar and translation in middle school and high school English classes to better prepare the students for the entrance examinations. Recently, however, the Ministry of Education has been actively engaged in improving the state of English education in Japan. The Ministry is encouraging Japanese English educators now more than ever to incorporate communicative English in the curricula by establishing the Japan Exchange Teachers (JET) and Assistant English Teachers (AET) program. The aim of this program is to address the strong interest in spoken English among Japanese in general, and to promote international understanding through the use of native speakers in secondary English classrooms in Japan.

In this article, the authors will discuss Japanese English education from four perspectives. (1) What is the setting for teaching in Japan? (2) What are some issues related to materials and technology in teaching English in Japan?

(3) What is happening to improve the teaching of English in Japan? and finally
(4) What is the future of Japanese English education?

The Setting for Teaching English in Japan ─────────────

Secondary English Education

The Japanese school system has been described as follows:

> Most Japanese school children live academic lives of order and decorum.
> At school they wear uniforms, are extremely disciplined, and silently listen
> to their teachers. In this way they can quickly digest the Education
> Ministry's nationally standardized curricula. . . . (But) under the Minis-
> try's legally binding guidelines, schools have little latitude in their offer-
> ings. Textbooks are authorized by the Ministry, and teachers who stray
> beyond these guidelines may be sued by the state. . . . Also entrance
> examinations for higher education are tough, and Japanese schools have
> become a place to prepare for tests. (Kambara 1989)

Even at the early stages of foreign languages most lessons are spent on
mechanical drills and memorization of vocabulary and grammatical items,
which therefore become more important to the students than learning the
language for communication purposes. Unlike students in many other countries
where English is learned for practical and conversational purposes, Japanese
students study English only as a tool for access to universities: they must spend
hours studying nationally approved texts and normally attend JUKU (cram
schools) after school and even on Sundays. In a recent letter to the editor of a
newspaper, an 18-year-old high school student wrote:

> I went to the United States for a year to study last year. I felt as if I were a
> child, because I was unable to either understand or speak English for a
> certain period after I arrived. . . . Japan's society, I think, has some
> responsibility for this. It should be blamed for not taking measures to
> prevent the current examination war. As a result, English teaching at the
> secondary school level has become more and more examination oriented.
> (Nakane 1990)

Recently, native English speaking AETs (Assistant English Teachers), hired by
the Ministry of Education under the JET (Japan Exchange and Teaching)
program, have been placed in public secondary schools to "enable students
to practice speaking English in a communicative situation and to develop intercultural communication skills" (Wada 1990). These cultural ambassadors add an
international flavor to the traditional English classes by teaching "dialogs" or
"conversations" once or twice a week in the public schools. (These programs will
be discussed at greater length below.)

Postsecondary English Education

Most foreign English teachers teach oral communication at the postsecondary levels, where students have completed the entrance examinations and have acquired a fair-sized vocabulary and a passive understanding of grammar. As "exam English" has been drilled into their heads, for the most part students can read, translate, analyze, and answer questions; what they cannot do is speak English. They have become "false beginners," i.e., "students who have studied and attained language skills in some areas, but because their instruction was limited in focus, they can function only at a beginning level. . . . Yet to ignore what they have learned is to waste the previous six or more years, and besides, to 'start at the beginning again' would bore and belittle them" (Helgesen forthcoming). So how does one teach communication in Japan?

University Classes—Silent Conversations

Contrary to the stereotypical picture of eager, attentive students that is normally associated with Japan, Japanese university students are generally apathetic and exhibit little motivation to study. Since they have already succeeded in passing the entrance exams, these students look forward to spending the next four years doing part-time jobs and enjoying leisure and club activities. The students seldom give much thought to their future: since university students have already "proven their intelligence and diligence" (Cleaver 1976: 219), prospective employers show little interest in their performance while at the university. Thus, students have little incentive to study or to pursue graduate degrees. Small wonder, then, that statements such as the following can be made: "The fiscal 1990 White Paper on Education compiled by the Education Ministry noted that as many as 43 percent of college students admit they can understand only half of what they are being taught" (Hirezaki 1990).

Most EFL publications emanating from Japan focus on the problems of entrance exams, large classes, lack of motivation, or the invariable passivity of Japanese students. The convergence of these issues is best illustrated in the large English classes offered in the general education courses at the college or university level (and to a lesser extent in business and conversation schools, as we will discuss below). Since most Japanese universities require foreign languages, most freshman and sophomore students elect to retake English. Normally these classes meet once a week for an average of 90 minutes and vary in size from 45 to 65 students per class. In fact, as many as two hundred learners might appear in the classroom on the first day.

Imagine for a moment the students crowding into that first class. To break the ice, the teacher, you, begin by commenting on how nice it is to have such a large, active class and, in hopes of generating some friendly student response, you ask how everyone feels. Total silence. Feeling that the room may be a bit stuffy, you continue, "It is a bit warm in here, isn't it?" and ask if someone would mind opening the window. Again, a hushed silence. No one moves. A few students look down. Now, exasperated at the lack of any oral communication, you take a more traditional tone and say "Okay, let's turn to page one and begin today's lesson, 'Introducing ourselves . . .'"

Finding themselves in such situations, teachers new to Japan need to learn ways of coping with students' silence if they wish to succeed. Japanese students generally are more "hesitant to talk in settings where they will stand out in front of their peers" and so rarely initiate discussion (Anderson forthcoming). Rather, students remain silent, waiting to be called upon instead of volunteering answers; this tactic allows them to save face in case of incorrect answers. Also, students prefer a consensus or 'group mindedness' instead of stating their own individual opinions.

Overall, university teaching positions exhibit both the best and worst aspects of teaching English in Japan. Most universities offer quite good salaries (including annual bonuses), some subsidized housing, and time for research and vacation. Very few full-time tenured positions are available, however, and practically none at all exist at national universities. There are many part-time positions available, but the biggest problem is the number of large classes with low student morale.

Conversation Schools—The Glamorous Life in the Fast Lane

> English Academy is offering fun teaching positions to female native English speakers. Free housing and visa, plus Japanese lessons provided. Part-time 150,000, full-time 250,000.[1]

Amazingly enough, though the number of years spent studying "examination English" have left most Japanese unable to communicate effectively in English, many still seem to harbor the hope of being able to use English with foreigners. With the increase of Japanese traveling, working, and studying abroad, the urgent need for more practical English than that which the school system offers has been keenly recognized among Japanese. This has led to the high demand for private English conversation schools. These are places unlike public schools, where learners hope to practice speaking English in smaller classes with others who share those same interests. For these reasons, in the past fifteen years, the number of private conversation schools in the Tokyo area alone has risen from 700 to more than 9,000—not to mention the informal "conversation salons."

Many conversation schools offer teaching positions to young and attractive teachers who can sell enjoyable English courses to their nondiscriminating clients. Packaging English classes in such glamorous tones does attract unsuspecting learners and teachers. Beneath the wrapping, however, is usually a conversation school or English salon offering poor working conditions with long hours, including Saturdays and Sundays, big classes, and perhaps only six days' vacation per year. In a recent news article one teacher stated, "the conversation schools hire anybody. They take foreigners virtually off the streets, so long as the manager is reasonably convinced that they have degrees. In many cases, of course, the 'teachers' have no degrees, and the schools could not care less . . ." (Waller 1990: 5). Another 'teacher' boasted, "I don't teach language. Japanese hire me by the hour to talk to them" (p. 5). Of course, quite a number of reputable language schools and business colleges, which offer small classes and a full curriculum and hire only qualified EFL teachers, do exist. Most schools, however, are "making a lot of money out of 'teaching' English to the Japanese— billions of yen annually. And to ensure that the cash pours in, they are earnestly aiming to satisfy their students' needs at the expense of good teaching" (Waller 1990: 4). All too frequently, the student–consumers are swayed more by the promises on the package, such as "speak English fluently after only 25 lessons," than the actual contents.

Business

In an effort to internationalize, major Japanese firms offer English courses to their employees either in intensive classes at in-house training centers or in year-round courses at their various factories around the country. In contrast to the students at universities, one cannot help being immediately impressed with the diligence and perseverance shown by most of the student–employees who are being groomed by their companies for international positions abroad. Usually students, eight to sixteen per class, are eager to brush up on practical English in order to apply it to their future work. The salary offered teachers by the company is quite good and contractual arrangements include the usual subsidized accommodations, health and welfare benefits, and biannual bonuses. In return, teachers are expected to work hard and remain loyal to the company, leading occasionally to an inhibiting group-oriented life that assumes foreigners want to live and work happily together. Also, once courses have been established, a tendency to leave them intact without further innovation may occur, a by-product of a widely perceived production line mentality among Japanese managers.

Issues Related to Materials and Technology

Materials

These are exciting times for EFL teachers in Japan, where a wide choice of materials, methods, and resources is available to choose from. Where formerly there was a predominance of British and U.S. English, one now finds a more international flavor, especially with the import of AETs from the Southern Hemisphere. This "internationalism" has helped create a publisher's paradise in which the once popular U.S. or British course books have been supplanted by texts much closer to the Japanese market. International publishers competing for a lucrative share of the commercial market have started producing texts that focus on the needs of false beginners as described above: more listening and communicative activities and less reading and writing.

On the other hand, the imposition of "authorized" materials in the public schools still presents problems. As mentioned before, all elementary and secondary school textbooks must be approved by the Ministry of Education: publishers must meet explicit restrictions on form (the size and number of pages) and content (a certain small number of sentence patterns, vocabulary items, and grammatical constructions) to gain a textbook's approval. From among the approved textbooks, the local boards of education choose the elementary and junior high school texts for their districts. Only senior high schools are allowed to choose authorized textbooks independently. Moreover, teachers are expected to use only the government-approved texts that their schools adopt and are discouraged from supplementing with other texts or materials.

Technology

Japan's technology remains on the cutting edge in the production and development of electronic hardware for use in the language classroom. Educational institutions investing in high-tech language labs are continually provided with the latest in audio, video, and laser-disc equipment. Yet, with the advent of new products and the supercomputers of the future, surprisingly few computers are actually used in language classrooms in Japan. Why? First, despite the fact that the Ministry of Education plans to make computer instruction mandatory in public schools starting in 1993, the Ministry's survey revealed that only 30 percent of public schools have personal computers and, of those computers, 60 percent were being used for clerical and administrative work rather than for teaching students. Also, it found "most teachers are not capable of using the machines themselves" ("Survey" 1989).

A further obstacle for language teachers lies in the incompatibility of most domestic hardware with other systems: NEC equipment, for example, which holds the largest Japanese market share in business and education, is incompatible with equipment from other manufacturers, including IBM and Apple. The biggest problem, however, is the lack of good, user-friendly software available in language education. Some business and technical colleges offer CAI (Computer-Assisted Instruction) and several newly opened colleges are attracting students by offering CALL (Computer-Assisted Language Learning) in the curriculum. Still, the amount of EFL software available in Japan remains sparse, with virtually all audio, visual, CD-ROM, and computer software being imported from the United States or Britain. Lastly, computing can be difficult and time-consuming for the Japanese because of a lack of courses and training in computer use and typing skills. Recently, however, Sony, in cooperation with Dyn Ed (a U.S. software manufacturer), has introduced a multimedia system for learning English, the I.I.C. (Intelligent Interactive Courseware), which may help solve some of the problems with computers in the language class. This computer-controlled "VIEW System" consists of a 16-bit personal computer, a laser disc, and a CD-ROM that allows learners to work at their own pace while interacting with user-friendly software. Learners can stop, repeat, or skip over parts of the program by merely operating the computer mouse, which makes it unnecessary even to touch the keyboard.

New Directions

From Teacher-Centered Approach to Learner-Centered Approach

At present, a central issue in teaching EFL to Japanese students is whether one should continue with a traditional teacher-centered approach or adopt a more learner-centered communicative approach to teaching. In the large classes that are typical of the Japanese educational system, the former top-down approach may be the easier to use, since both teachers and students know and understand their respective roles. The teacher is pivotal in maintaining discipline, controlling student response, and ensuring that students pass examinations. Teachers who expect students to communicate in English in the classroom, however, can anticipate problems, as students who have been trained to conform, keep silent, listen obediently to the teacher, and answer exam-related questions will find it extremely difficult to communicate their own thoughts and opinions aloud in class.

A learner-centered approach takes time and energy as the teacher tries to wean students from their traditional learning habits, but activating students' previously learned English will promote their use of English in a more communicative way. Initial activities, such as listening tasks and information-gap activities (Adams 1986), can be simple approaches that encourage learners to use and develop their existing knowledge of the language. Eventually learners can participate actively in more demanding listening and speaking activities. Learner-centered activities can be quite successful in large classes, too, as their principal focus is on the students and on the students' ability to learn and use the target language rather than on translation or error correction.

Hence, these activities not only maintain students' interest but also encourage individuals to work together in pairs, in groups, and as a whole class. This communication between the teacher and students and among students themselves helps foster greater student interaction, creativity, and expression. Thus, in addition to learning how to use English, students also learn to take initiative and become responsible for their learning, which is not typical in Japanese education.

There are both pros and cons to be considered in adopting a learner-centered approach to teaching English in Japan. For example, "the advantages of using information gap (and communicative) activities are obvious in regard to increased student interaction and communication in the classroom. Since students become involved in using the target language to complete given tasks, motivation is no longer a major factor" (Adams 1986: 36). Though the use of the native language may still appear in the classroom, it normally decreases with increased student involvement in target language activities. Such activities also help students become more independent language learners as they gain confidence in their ability to assert themselves in the target language.

Inexperienced or traditionally oriented teachers, on the other hand, may be disconcerted by the apparent lack of discipline and organization involved in using learner-centered activities. Unless teachers give clear directions, set time limitations, and communicate their expectations explicitly, the class can easily deteriorate into chaos. Although communication activities do require time, patience, and energy both in preparation and retraining learners to think and speak in the target language, they are necessary disciplines to promote communicative competence among Japanese English learners. They should be collaboratively engaged in by both students and the teacher.

AETs (Assistant English Teachers) to Promote Communicative English in Secondary Schools

Since 1987, Japan has been "importing" native speakers of English from the Western nations to "internationalize" the country. The JET (Japan Exchange and Teaching) / AET (Assistant English Teachers) program was initiated by CLAIR (Conference of Local Authorities for International Relations) and three Japanese ministries (Foreign Affairs, Education, and Home Affairs) to "promote mutual understanding between Japan and other countries including the United States, and to foster an international perspective in Japan at the local level by inviting young adults to take a part in international exchange activities and by intensifying foreign language education in Japan" (CLAIR 1990: 1).

Since the inauguration of the program, approximately 2,000 native speakers of English from countries such as the United States, Australia, Britain, New Zealand, and Canada have visited Japan every year to serve as Assistant English Teachers (AETs) in public junior and senior high schools throughout Japan. The program, however, has caused tremendous controversy among Japanese English educators. Some of the controversy seems to stem from vaguely defined program objectives, the rather questionable qualifications of some AETs, and the actual implementation of the program at the local school level. In this section, some of the controversies that are particularly related to the AETs will be discussed in relation to Japanese English education.

What Is an AET?

The main objective of having AETs in Japan is to intensify foreign language education in Japan by increasing communicative activities in English classes, providing opportunities for cross-cultural understanding, and helping Japanese English teachers. The AETs are first screened through their dossier, and the selected candidates proceed to an interview at the Japanese Embassy or a consulate. As the criteria for the application, CLAIR lists the following (CLAIR 1989: 3):

Eligibility Criteria. Applicants must: (1) be under thirty-five years of age; (2) hold at least a Bachelor's degree; (3) have excellent English pronunciation, rhythm, intonation, and voice projection; model standard modern English; have good English writing skills and grammar usage; (4) be interested in Japan; (5) have the ability to adapt oneself to living and working conditions that could be significantly different from those experienced in one's home country; (6) be both mentally and physically healthy; (7) be interested in education and teaching in Japan; (8) enjoy working with children; and finally (9) have qualifications as language teachers, have studied "Teaching English as a Foreign/Second Language," or be motivated to study it.

The selected AETs usually sign a one-year renewable contract. The annual salary is approximately $28,000 and round-trip airfare and transportation in Japan are paid by the ministries.

Duties of Employment.   The main duties of AETs are described (CLAIR 1989) as follows: (1) school visits; (2) assistance in the preparation of teaching materials; (3) assistance in teacher training; (4) providing language information for the Japanese English teachers; and (5) judging English speech contests.

Issues Related to the AET Program

Since the AETs have started coming to Japan, many articles have appeared in Japanese newspapers and professional journals discussing the pros and cons of the program. In the following section, some of the major issues will be discussed.

The Single Visit.   According to one set of statistics (Morinaga 1989), 87.95 percent and 76.32 percent of middle schools and high schools, respectively, have AETs on a single-visit basis. While there are cases where AETs visit schools semi-regularly or regularly, it is predominantly the single visits that occupy most of the AET's time and energy. One of the most frequently voiced concerns with regard to the single visits from the AETs is the lack of time to establish adequate rapport with the Japanese teachers of English (JTE) and the students. One AET, for example, states, "I believe that the system of one-shot English teaching is not productive, and in some cases may even be counterproductive. Often I am asked to play language games and give my self-introduction. . . . [B]y the year's end I will have visited about 37 schools." (CLAIR 1990: 10). Another AET who perceives the single visit as more of a promotional activity than an educational one comments, "I believe that the one-shot visit may be a motivational experience for students and promote an understanding of Western culture, but as far as 'learning' is concerned, a 'full-time' school-based AET can create the most effective curriculum for spoken English" (CLAIR 1990: 10).

It is impossible for any teacher to engage students in a meaningful learning experience without first establishing good rapport. The single-visit system undermines the importance of this factor. Unless this system is improved, the role of the AETs is likely to remain superficial and cosmetic.

Team Teaching. One of the duties that AETs assume is to assist Japanese teachers of English (JTEs) in English classes as a team teacher. According to the Ministry of Education, the purpose of the team teaching between JTEs and AETs is "to create a foreign language classroom in which the students, the JTEs, and the AET are engaged in communicative activities" by joint cooperative lesson planning, class interaction, and joint evaluation of the success and effectiveness of the lesson (CLAIR 1990: 24). Furthermore, it is intended that the JTEs learn innovative approaches to teaching English from the AETs. While there are successful reports about joint enterprises between AETs and JTEs, there are many incidents reported both by AETs and JTEs with regard to the difficulties in actualizing team teaching effectively. The first issue is the lack of a clear and shared definition of team teaching. Neither JTEs nor AETs know what their roles are supposed to be. Some AETs comment that "We hear the vague terms 'team-teaching, teacher competence, and communicative English' without ever being told exactly what the Ministry of Education considers these things to mean. There is still so little guidance in how exactly this team-teaching is to be done" (Ogata 1989: 41).

Secondly, there are conflicts of interest between JTEs and AETs. As long as the same grammar-oriented entrance examinations exist in the Japanese educational system, conscientious teachers will feel obliged to prepare their students for the examination, i.e., to teach them grammar. AETs, on the other hand, feel that the current Japanese English educational approach is outdated and needs to be reformed by introducing more communicative activities into the classroom.[2] Other AETs have expressed their frustrations with their roles in team teaching by saying that they feel as if they are "human tape recorders" for pronunciation practice, or that they are "entertainers" from outer space (Nozawa 1989: 12).

The third important issue is a lack of communication between AETs and JTEs. One obvious reason is the JTEs' lack of communicative proficiency in English, particularly among older JTEs who have never received training in spoken English. Those teachers are most likely to avoid contact with the AETs in order to escape any possible embarrassment in front of their colleagues and students. In defense of their teaching ability, some JTEs contest that AETs tend to assume unjustly that those English teachers who cannot communicate in English are incompetent teachers. They would like to argue that there are more important qualifications for effective English teaching than just being able to speak the language.

The last issue is perhaps the most basic one: How is it possible, some have asked, for the JTEs to learn "innovative approaches" from the AETs when most of the latter have little or no training or practice in ESL or EFL? Do the ministries naively assume that being a native speaker automatically qualifies one as an expert in teaching techniques and methodology? What kinds of qualifications do the AETs bring with them to Japan?

Qualifications of AETs. The list of qualifications the Japanese ministries have outlined are not by any means stringent, considering the duties that the AETs are assigned. Important questions have been raised about how the selection procedure is carried out and who is involved in the process. It has been reported that Japanese ambassadors and/or consuls, not experts in ESL or EFL, have been conducting the interviews with the candidates (Wakabayashi 1989). Furthermore, the criteria used to evaluate the applicants' English have never been publicly reported. In fact, it is public knowledge now that AETs who have no previous teaching experience are currently teaching in Japan. Morinaga (1989) points out that only 10 percent of AETs have studied ESL or EFL for more than six months. Furthermore, those AETs who go to Japan receive only minimal training before they actually start working in local schools. According to Sato (1989), 83 percent of the AETs start teaching within less than a month after their arrival. Some Japanese seriously question the Japanese government for investing such a large amount of money to import untrained native speakers of English. They assert that it would be more cost-effective for Japanese teachers of English to receive training in spoken English in Japan or abroad and to select AETs who have previous experience in teaching EFL or ESL.

Contributions of the AET Program

Despite the above-mentioned problems, there are some positive contributions that the AETs have made to the improvement of Japanese English education. According to a study by the Institute for Research in Language Teaching (1988), favorable motivational and attitudinal changes have been observed among students since the beginning of AETs' school visits. It is reported that not only are the students more willing to speak English with native speakers, but also their enthusiasm for learning English has noticeably increased. As for the JTEs, although there is still some resistance toward AETs and team teaching, an increasing number of them are beginning to see the benefits of having native speakers in their classrooms. According to one survey (Kiyota and Aiga 1990), 90 percent of the senior high school teachers responded that the AETs helped the students' listening comprehension; 86 percent responded that they helped students' speaking skills.

In order to ameliorate the current conditions of team teaching, a pilot study is currently being conducted to better understand the notion of team teaching. The study will involve one school from each prefecture for a period of two years. It will focus on teaching methods, materials, and syllabus design. It is expected that the study will provide pertinent information for both JTEs and AETs about team teaching.

Future: Time for Change ──────────────────────────

In addition to the initiation of the JET / AET program, the Ministry of Education is proposing other innovations in Japanese English education. As of 1994, for example, all the public middle schools and high schools will implement revised English curricula. According to the Ministry of Education, the focus of the revision is to improve students' communicative competence. The new curricula will include new courses in oral communication in addition to reading and writing. In the revised curricula, the number of English classes will be increased from three to four hours per week. It is also reported that the Ministry of Education has been sponsoring overseas programs to send Japanese teachers abroad to improve their English skills. In 1990, approximately 175 teachers studied in the United States and Britain for two months. Currently, the Ministry of Education is negotiating a budget increase with the Ministry of Finance to send more Japanese teachers abroad.

Although the entrance examination remains a complex issue to be examined, if the Japanese government continues to support reform in English education, it may not be a farfetched reality that, in the future, Japanese high schools and universities will start using oral interviews in English as a part of their entrance examinations.

Conclusion ──────────────────────────

One of the strengths of the Japanese as a people is perhaps their amazing dexterity in adopting new things into their culture. Yet Japanese English education has been lagging considerably behind this trend. Large class sizes, the infamous university entrance examination, the Japanese English teachers' lack of oral proficiency, and the students' low motivation are common reasons for the inadequacy of Japanese English education. With the Japanese government taking steps to promote more communicative English in school curricula, and although many issues remain to be solved, programs like the JET / AET program have definitely brought new awareness to students and have challenged English teachers to reevaluate their own communicative competence, syllabus design, and methodology. In addition, if the proposed budget by the Ministry of Education is approved, an increasing number of teachers will be able to go abroad to receive extensive training in oral English as well as in cross-cultural understanding.

While Japanese English teachers are encouraged to improve their oral skills, there should be a more thorough and stringent screening process of native speakers of English, including AETs, before they are hired. Native proficiency in a language does not automatically qualify one to be a teacher of that language.

Finally, Japan seems to be on the right track in reforming English education. The changes will be gradual, yet all indications thus far seem to indicate that they are here to stay.

Notes

1. Want ad, *The Daily Yomiuri,* April 3, 1990.
2. One AET, for example, reported an incident where she was approached by her team-teacher and was told, "When you come, I want you to teach gerunds." When the AET declined, saying that her role was to teach communicative English, the teacher said, "NO, no, that's not important, gerunds are important; I want you to teach gerunds!" (Koller 1990: 9).

References, Current Perspectives on Japanese English Education

Adams, Carl. 1986. "Information Gaps: The Missing Links to Learning." Gaikokugo Kyoiku Ronshu. Foreign Language Center, Tsukuba University, 8:29–42. [EDRS: ED 311 710]

Anderson, Fred. Forthcoming. "The Enigma of the College Classroom: Nails That Don't Stick Up," in Paul Wadden, ed., *Handbook for Teaching English at Japanese Colleges and Universities.* Oxford, Eng.: Oxford Univ. Press.

Cleaver, Charles G. 1976. *Japanese and Americans: Cultural Parallels and Paradoxes.* Tokyo: Charles E. Tuttle.

CLAIR (Conference of Local Authorities for International Relations). 1990. *The JET Program 1990.* Tokyo: CLAIR.

Helgesen, Marc. Forthcoming. "Dismantling a Wall of Silence: The English 'Conversation Class,'" in Paul Wadden, ed., *Handbook for Teaching English at Japanese Colleges and Universities.* Oxford, Eng.: Oxford Univ. Press.

Hirezaki, Ko. 1990. "Lazy College Students Need Jolting," *The Daily Yomiuri,* 21 November, p. 2.

Institute for Research in Language Teaching. 1988. "Research on the Situation of Foreign Teachers of English in Japanese Schools." *IRLT Bulletin* 2:1–108.

Kambara, Keiko. 1989. "Easing Up on Students." *The Daily Yomiuri,* 11 November, p. 7.

Kiyota, M., and Y. Aiga. 1990. "Chuugakkoo Eigo Jugyoo no Kasseika Ni Kansuru Kennkuu." [A Study of the Way of Activating English Classes in Junior High Schools.] *Kanagawa Prefecture Education Center Bulletin* 8:25–32.

Koike, Ikuo. 1978. *The Teaching of English in Japan.* Tokyo: Eichosha.

Koller, Mike. 1990. "AETs Just Doing Time in the Classroom." *JET Journal* (Spring): 8–9.

Morinaga, Makoto. 1989. "Gaikoku-jin Kooshi no Koe." [The Voice of the AETs.] *The English Teachers' Magazine* 13:29–31.

Nakane, Yoshie. 1990. "Studying for Examinations Doesn't Help You Abroad." *The Daily Yomiuri,* 27 December, p. 7.

Nozawa, Soko. 1989. "Gaikoju-jin Kooshi." [AETs.] *The English Teachers' Magazine* 10:8–12.

Ogata, Hisanori. 1989. "AET wa Team-Teaching wo Do Miteiru ka." [How Do the AETs Perceive Team Teaching?] *The English Teachers' Magazine* 10:40–46.

Sato, Hideshi. 1989. "Gaikoku-jin Kooshi Donyu no Mondaiten." [Problems about the AETs.] *The English Teachers' Magazine* 13:17–18.

"Survey: Most Teachers Not Ready for PC Age." 1989. *The Daily Yomiuri,* 19 October, p. 2.

Wada, Minoru. 1990. "1990 Rings Out Year of Initial Reforms," *The Daily Yomiuri,* 27 December, p. 7.

Wakabayashi, T. 1989. "AET Donyu Hantai no Ben." [AETs Are Not Necessary.] *The English Teachers' Magazine.* 13:13–15.

Waller, Adrian. 1990. "The English School Fiasco." *The Japan Times Weekly* 30:4–5.

SECTION III

Emerging Emphases

8

International Perspectives of Foreign Language Testing Systems and Policy

Elana Shohamy
Tel Aviv University

Tests are used for a variety of purposes: to measure students' knowledge in relation to future tasks that they are expected to perform, to place students in appropriate levels of classes, to grant certificates, to determine whether students can continue in future studies, to select those who are most suitable for higher-education institutions, to motivate students to learn and perform well, and to select people for jobs. Because of the strong impact that tests have on the lives of individuals, they have become powerful and authoritative tools, capable of changing the behavior of those who are affected by their results—students, teachers, and administrators. Even central agencies, being aware of this phenomenon, often use tests as effective vehicles to introduce new curricula, new textbooks, and new teaching methods.

One test that has such power, prestige, and authority is the one given in many countries at the end of secondary school, when the test-taker is around 18 years of age. Such tests have particularly strong bearing on the test-takers' lives, as the results can determine who will graduate from high school and who will be allowed to continue at higher-education institutions. Central agencies in some nations, therefore, often use this test as a tool to motivate students to learn (and teachers to teach) the very material that is likely to appear on that test. For example, if a central agency (such as a ministry of education) decides it wants students to master certain material, it can make a decision to include that material as part of the end-of-secondary-school test.

Elana Shohamy (Ph.D., University of Minnesota) is a Professor of Language Education at Tel Aviv University, School of Education. Her main research is in the area of language testing and evaluation. She is the author of numerous articles in this field and of the book *Second Language Research Methods* (coauthored with Herbert Seliger; Oxford Univ. Press, 1989) and of *A Handbook in Language Testing for the Second/Foreign Language Teacher* (Oxford Univ. Press, forthcoming).

In foreign language learning as well, an end-of-secondary-school test can be used as a tool to focus, channel, and motivate learning in certain directions. For example, by deciding to include a certain language skill (for example, speaking) or, alternatively, not to include an area (such as grammar) on the test, there is a high probability that students and teachers will be motivated to practice speaking and will be less motivated to practice grammar.

Differences in Educational Systems

Introducing educational change through tests is a practice used mostly in countries that have centralized educational systems. Such systems are found in, for example, Israel and Finland, while countries such as the United States do not have them. In countries with centralized educational systems, a central body establishes and controls the national curriculum and many other aspects of the educational system; the national tests, especially the end-of-secondary-school test, are one means to enforce that control. Another use of national tests is to provide a national assessment, i.e., to obtain aggregate information on the level of learning in the country. In this way national tests provide information used in making policy decisions.

The degree of centralization is one of the most important, if not the single most important, characteristic that differentiates educational systems around the world from one another. Centralized and decentralized educational systems are based on fundamentally different assumptions: in centralized systems there is a focus on the needs of the society to provide opportunities to those most "deserving" of them, i.e., to those who possess special talents, since in countries with centralized systems there are often economic and social needs for skilled labor. In countries with decentralized educational systems, on the other hand, there is far less selection; in such countries there is often a belief that everyone in the society should have the opportunity to continue to higher education. The two systems can be said to function, therefore, in opposite directions, one being based on "selection" and the other on "democratization." (See figure 8-1.)

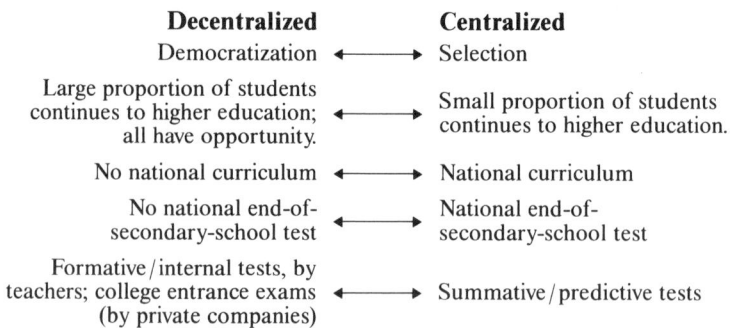

Decentralized	**Centralized**
Democratization ←→	Selection
Large proportion of students continues to higher education; all have opportunity. ←→	Small proportion of students continues to higher education.
No national curriculum ←→	National curriculum
No national end-of-secondary-school test ←→	National end-of-secondary-school test
Formative/internal tests, by teachers; college entrance exams (by private companies) ←→	Summative/predictive tests

Figure 8-1. Features Typical of Centralized vs. Decentralized Educational Systems

National Exams

It is typical of countries where the broader social and political system is based on selection that only a small portion of the population enters higher-education institutions, and that such access is a function of performance on national exams. The exams are usually controlled by a central body such as a testing institute or a ministry of education that is responsible for determining the test content, writing the test, and grading it. On the other hand, in countries where the educational system is based on democratization, i.e., where the opportunity to enter higher-education institutions is open to a large segment of the population, entry to such institutions depends mostly on other factors. In these systems, while there may be general national agreement on the overall goals of education, each school or region determines the specific curriculum. Tests are used mostly as part of the learning process (although there may often be national assessment surveys in subjects that the nation regards as important). Sometimes, as in the United States, private testing companies design and administer tests that supposedly serve as predictors of success in college (rather than as measures of high school achievement), and many colleges and universities use these test results in making admissions decisions.

Even countries that have decentralized educational systems and do not use national tests for selection recognize that tests are efficient devices for affecting motivation, changing curricula, and upgrading student achievement. Such is the case, for example, in the United States and Britain: These countries are now searching for ways to introduce national tests into their educational system despite the fact that having a national testing program is inconsistent, one could argue, with these countries' social and educational philosophy.

The Case of Israel

Israel, India, Scotland, and Finland are examples of countries with centralized educational systems where national end-of-secondary-school tests are administered. In Israel, for example, there is a national end-of-secondary-school test called the "Matriculation Examination," which is written and scored by the national supervisors of the various subject-matter areas on behalf of the Ministry of Education. It is given at the end of twelfth grade to secondary school students, and it serves as an important criterion for graduation as well as for entrance to college. While some weight is given to formative assessment as expressed in "internal" scores assigned by the classroom teacher, these measures are marginal in the general calculation of a student's final ("external") Matriculation Examination score: Whenever large discrepancies between a student's external and internal scores are encountered, the assumption is that the school is not assessing well, and that the external one-shot test is the more reliable and valid measure. In addition to the Matriculation Examination (given in school subjects that are considered to be of high status, such as math, English, Bible literature, and language), there is a college entrance test for higher-educational institutions. This test is administered by a body representing the different universities (not related to the Ministry of Education); it consists of an aptitude and a language component and is considered an important predictor for success in college. The criterion for entering college, then, consists of an average of two scores: those achieved on the Matriculation Examination and on the university aptitude test.

The Case of the United States

The educational system in the United States is an example of a decentralized system in which no national end-of-secondary-school exam is administered by a central body. Each state has autonomy with regard to these tests and in giving out achievement assessments, i.e., grades. The assessment is formative, as grades are given out at various times during, and at the completion of, academic terms. To bring some measure of standardization to the grades and academic requirements in use by local schools, there are a number of criteria used for institutional accreditation.

Relatively speaking, few students fail or do not graduate from the U.S. K–12 school system. The schools are comprehensive in terms of subjects and levels. The grouping of students by ability is not common, although there are honors classes for exceptional students in some secondary school subjects. Selection for admission for college most often takes into account two main criteria: (1) the courses the student has taken and his or her grades in those courses; and (2) scholastic aptitude tests, such as the SAT (Scholastic Aptitude Test), the ACT (American College Testing Assessment), and the College Board exams. Top scores on these exams are often considered essential for admission to prestigious universities. In some individual states (e.g., New York, Michigan) there are centralized systems of examination; but even in these states the tests do not serve as the only criterion for graduation.[1]

Mixed Systems

The centralization/decentralization opposition describes a continuum, not a dichotomy: Around the world there are educational systems that combine features of both decentralized and centralized systems. In the Netherlands, for example, while there is a national curriculum, some components of the school subjects are assessed by the same teacher(s) responsible for writing tests and assigning scores, while the assessment of other components is based on a centralized test that is written, administered, and scored by a national testing body. The student's final grade is an average of the two scores.

▼ United States	Level of Testing Body	Israel ▼
Internal	**Level of Testing Body**	External
Continuous	**Composition of Final Score**	"One-shot"
Comprehensive: All language skills	**Content of Test**	High-status subjects
High	**Proportion of Students Tested**	Low
Formative / summative Achievement	**Purpose of Test**	Summative / predictive Achievement / proficiency
Flexible	**Format of Test**	Uniform
Not known	**Psychometric Accuracy**	Low

Figure 8-2. Summary of Features Typical of the U.S. and Israeli Educational Systems along Seven Dimensions

Dimensions of End-of-Secondary-School Tests in Foreign Languages

In considering typical foreign language tests at the end of secondary school, in educational systems where they exist, we will use seven dimensions proposed by Zack (1982): (1) the level of the testing body; (2) the timing of the test; (3) the content of the test; (4) the proportion of students tested; (5) the purpose of the test; (6) the type of test; and (7) the psychometric accuracy of the test. The focus will be the foreign language tests used in two countries, Israel and the United States, as they may be taken to represent the two extreme points along the continuum of centralization. Figure 8-2 summarizes the features of these seven dimensions as they are represented in the two types of educational systems typified by Israel and the United States.

The Level of the Testing Body

This dimension focuses specifically on who determines what will be tested on the end-of-secondary-school test and who the responsible testing body will be. This dimension is bipolar, ranging from a totally external to a wholly internal testing body: On one end of the continuum the model posits a testing body, testing agency, or ministry of education that develops, administers, and scores the test; at the other extreme may be found an internal testing body such as the school itself, or even a single classroom teacher who determines the content of the test and administers and scores it. Along this continuum there are other points that represent various combinations, such as when parts of the test are determined by an external body while other parts are determined internally by the teacher or the school (e.g., the Netherlands). Note that this dimension relates not only to *who* the testing body is, but also to *aspects of the testing process itself:* what will be tested, who will administer the test, and who will score it. In most cases the body that decides what will be tested also determines how the test will be scored. The question of who the testing body is can also provide a good indicator of the extent to which the educational system trusts the teacher and his or her independence in the educational system. The testing body can therefore be said to reflect the level of democratization of the educational system.

We observe that particularly as concerns foreign languages, the United States, which has a decentralized educational system, represents the 'internal' pole of this dimension. That is, typically most foreign language tests are planned, administered, and scored by the teachers themselves; there is no central body that is responsible for them. To be sure, the past few years have seen growing interest in developing and using external foreign language tests or criteria at the end of secondary school. This shift is evident in the development of the American Council for the Teaching of Foreign Languages (ACTFL) guidelines (1986) and tests such as the Oral Proficiency Interview (OPI) that may serve as external tests and provide a common yardstick to measure the learning of foreign languages at the end of secondary school in the United States (Byrnes 1987; Lowe and Stansfield 1988; Liskin-Gasparro 1983). Both the ACTFL guidelines and the OPI may be viewed as embodying some aspects of external criteria that determine the content and the scoring of language tests. The testing body can also be viewed as external, since the OPI is conducted by testers who must be trained by an external agency, i.e., ACTFL. The use of the OPI and the ACTFL Proficiency Guidelines is becoming increasingly common in the United States.

In Israel, on the other hand, which has a centralized educational system, there are national foreign language end-of-high-school tests (Matriculation Examinations) in all the languages that are taught in secondary school (English, Arabic, and French). These tests are written, administered, and scored by an external agency—the national supervisor of the language in the Ministry of Education, often with the aid of a committee of other local supervisors. The national supervisor often has neither background nor training in language testing, specifically; writing tests is simply included in his or her job description.[2]

There is a provision for the classroom teacher in Israel to assign an internal "end-of-secondary-school score" that is supposed to be a reflection of the student's language performance in school and also is presumably considered in the final matriculation score. But since it is not entirely clear what the role of the internal (school) score is, and since the external Matriculation Examination carries far more authority and prestige than the internal score, the latter becomes essentially an approximation of what the classroom teacher expects the student's score to be on the external Matriculation Examination. In most cases, the internal score is not based on school performance, but on the examinee's performance on a test that is similar in format and content to the external test. When there is a discrepancy between the external and the internal scores, the external score prevails, as the assumption is always that the external score is the more valid and accurate of the two.

The Israeli end-of-secondary-school test consists of five parts: reading, writing, speaking, listening, and grammar. All the parts, including speaking (which is made up of an oral interview, a role play, a reporting task, and a literature test and which is conducted on an individual basis), are conducted by external testers. The listening comprehension part is broadcast over national radio to provide some measure of standardization in the testing conditions. All the parts are given on a specific date determined in advance by the Ministry of Education, and the entire test is scored by external testers. The results are reported to the students by the Ministry of Education about three to five months after the administration.

The Composition of the Final Score

This dimension relates to the extent to which an external test score is obtained from a single, one-time, summative instrument or from formative assessments conducted over a period of time—be that one year or a number of years. Here, too, there are hybrids between the two poles. For example, a final score may be based simply on the results of a number of assessments done throughout one school year or over a number of years. Another possibility is one external test at the end of secondary school along with a number of tests conducted throughout the school year(s); the scores obtained from both sources are combined to render the final score. This dimension is strongly related to the selectivity criterion: highly selective systems tend to assign great importance to single, summative tests. This type of test is often viewed as more objective in comparison to continuous assessments, which are viewed as subjective; the criticism of the latter is that a teacher who knows the student may not be able to provide an objective judgment.[3]

In Israel, the final secondary school foreign language score is based on a one-shot, single, summative test, most often conducted at the end of twelfth grade, on a particular day throughout the country. In the United States, however, there is no single, widely used external foreign language test. Rather, typically the student's scores are formative over each year, based on class performance as evaluated by the classroom teacher. A combination of these two systems can be seen in countries where the external language test is based on continuous assessment done over a period of a number of years; the student's final score consists of the average score over that period, during which the student is constantly aware of his or her status in each subject.

The Content of the Test

This dimension relates to the choice of school subjects that are tested. On one end of the continuum there are the classic subjects such as mathematics, physics, history, and literature; these are often perceived as "high-status" subjects that are considered more important for mastery than other subjects. On the other end of the continuum, all school subjects are perceived to be of equal importance and status and therefore they all need to be tested.

In each country there are discussions and debates over the choice of school subjects that need to be tested, for this dimension is also related to issues of democratization. In most countries the emphasis is on four or five high-status subjects, although in some countries a number of subjects of perceived lesser importance may be tested via one integrated instrument. Including a certain subject in the external end-of-high-school tests reflects an underlying belief that the subject is important to the society. Similarly, when a certain subject is not included on the external exams at the end of secondary school, one may assume that the subject is not viewed as significant by the society.

Relating this "content" dimension to foreign language tests, we observe that, typically, countries that view foreign language learning as an important subject test it on the external examination. Thus, in Israel, where knowing foreign languages (especially English—less so Arabic and French) is viewed by the society as important, these languages are included as part of the end-of-secondary-school tests.[4]

In those places where foreign languages are tested, it is interesting to note what skills are examined, as this provides a good indication of how the society views the purpose of learning the language. In Israel, for example, reading, writing, speaking, and listening are all tested on the national exam, but each receives a different weight: reading, 50 percent; listening, 20 percent; writing, 15 percent; and speaking, 15 percent. These proportions clearly reflect the purpose of teaching English in Israel's schools, to develop reading comprehension. In many locations in the United States, by contrast, speaking is viewed as the most important skill to be tested, while the other skills receive less attention (Liskin-Gasparro 1983).

The Proportion of Students Tested

This dimension relates to the extent to which the end-of-secondary-school test is used for selection. In countries where compulsory education has been extended to age 16 and higher, all students are entitled to graduate from secondary school, and therefore there is no need for a device such as the end-of-secondary-school test to assist in selection for further education. On the other hand, in countries where only a portion of the population is entitled to secondary and post-secondary education, the end-of-secondary-school test serves as the device that is used to decide who will be allowed to continue their studies. In these situations the "threat" of the test as a selection device is often encountered well before the exam is actually taken: A school may in fact accept or reject students based on teachers' assessments of the *likelihood* that the student will be able pass the test.

Thus, in this dimension there is differentiation among slightly, moderately, and highly selective systems that determines the extent to which schools use the end-of-secondary-school test as a criterion for selection. At one end of this continuum we find developing nations such as India and the countries of West Africa, where only a very small proportion of the population is entitled to graduate from secondary school. Next are countries that have a strong tradition of selection such as Austria, Ireland, and Hong Kong. Further along are developed countries that have a trend toward some democratization, such as Scotland, England, and the Netherlands; these countries rely only slightly on the end-of-secondary-school test as a criterion for selection. Finally there are countries with a strong democratization trend (i.e., where a large number of students graduate from high schools), such as the United States, that have no compulsory end-of-secondary-school test.[5]

In Israel, obtaining a high score on the Matriculation Examination in English as a foreign language is one of the most important criteria for both graduation from secondary school and acceptance to college. This exam may even serve as a selection device before secondary school: Students who are not *expected* to obtain a high score may not be accepted to a prestigious secondary school (or at times to *any* secondary school), nor to college.[6] In the United States, by contrast, one's score in foreign languages does not in most cases significantly affect one's chances of being accepted to college.

The Purpose of the Test

This dimension relates to the specific purpose of the end-of-secondary-school test: formative, summative, or predictive (or some combination). *Formative* testing refers to assessment on an ongoing basis, as part of the learning process in the classroom; *summative* testing implies that the purpose of the test is to examine the extent to which the student has acquired the material covered in the entire curriculum covered by the test; *predictive* tests presumably provide information about the probable future performance of the test-taker in college or in some other context.

The terms *achievement* and *proficiency* describe another of the distinctions that can be made in the purposes of testing. With regard to a foreign language curriculum, achievement testing examines a student's mastery of language learned in a specific course of study (most often in school), while proficiency testing seeks to measure the language competence that the student will bring to real life in a specific, future, well-defined context. It is understood that while in some situations these two purposes can overlap, in most situations they do not, as what is learned in school is not necessarily the same as what is needed in real life.

Relating the above purposes to the end-of-secondary-school test in Israel, we find that the test is used for both summative and predictive purposes and as an indicator of both achievement and proficiency; indeed, there is often confusion between the two. Thus, on the test there will be questions based on specific material taken from the curriculum as well as questions that aim at finding out whether the test-taker can function in a future real-life language context, such as reading texts from academic material that will be needed in college. In the United States, where tests are administered by teachers throughout secondary school, the purpose of testing is usually formative. It can also be summative, however, as when a test covers a whole year of material. In either case these examinations are achievement tests, since the language tested is based on what was learned in school. The recent trend toward adopting the ACTFL Proficiency Guidelines and the OPI testing format in secondary schools in the United States signifies, however, a shift from testing for formative purposes to testing for summative and predictive purposes, and from an achievement to a proficiency orientation (Liskin-Gasparro 1983; Byrnes and Canale 1987).

The Format of the Test

This dimension refers to whether the format of the end-of-secondary-school assessment is uniform or flexible. On one end of the continuum are assessments based on tests that are uniform, i.e., similar test formats are given to all test-takers. On the other end of the continuum are flexible assessments that have alternative formats, usually in accordance with the preference of the test-takers and different programs. For example, certain students may be assessed by doing a project that requires application of knowledge to real life. Others may write an essay, some may turn in information on self- or peer-assessment, while still others can prepare a portfolio that includes a variety of documents of language samples such as résumés, letters, revised drafts of written documents, and taped language samples that provide evidence of the student's language proficiency. Such assessments can be done internally or externally. The combinations of the different formats imply that the test-taker's score may be based on a variety of sources of assessment. In the discussions currently taking place in the United States about the format of a new national test at the end of secondary school, there are proposals that the assessment should consist of a number of different components such as portfolios, performance projects, and tests.

Relating this dimension to the United States and Israel, we find that the Matriculation Examination in Israel is uniform: the most common format is a test administered by the Ministry of Education. In the past few years, however, provisions for other formats, such as projects or seminar papers on language and literature, have been introduced. In the United States the teacher can use a large number of options within the classroom for formative assessment procedures.[7] It seems, however, that the most commonly used procedure in the classroom is still the paper-and-pencil test, although there is very little documented evidence for this assertion. It should be noted that increased use of the OPI, which is an interview format, is adding flexibility to the system.

Psychometric Accuracy

This dimension relates to the extent to which the end-of-secondary-school test meets psychometric criteria (such as reliability and validity) and whether the tests go through a careful item analysis in which items are revised and deleted. On one end of the continuum are tests based on standards of accuracy established using empirical psychometric evidence. On the other end are tests constructed without such evidence.

In Israel the external foreign language test that is written by the Ministry of Education and administered throughout the country is not examined for reliability and validity. Nor is an item analysis performed on the test after it has been administered to identify and remove bad items. The national supervisors who write the tests in the various subjects do not have formal training in test construction. In the introduction of the new oral Matriculation Examination, while there was consideration of certain aspects of reliability and validity in the research phases (Shohamy et al. 1986), there has been no subsequent study of these criteria since the tests have been in use. Thus, centralization does not necessarily guarantee psychometric accuracy and high-quality tests.

In the United States there is very little information on the psychometric accuracy of typical classroom tests constructed, administered, and scored by teachers. Evidence from a number of studies (e.g., Hoge and Coladarci 1989), suggests that teacher-made tests are often more valid than one-shot external tests. As for the OPI test, while some aspects of reliability (e.g., inter-rater reliability) have been examined, other types of reliability and validity (e.g., content, construct, and predictive validity; test-retest and parallel forms reliability), need to be examined as well. Also, as in the Israeli case, there is a need to evaluate the psychometric properties of the tests once they are administered on a large scale (van Lier 1989; Shohamy 1990): There is no guarantee that the level of reliability obtained in the experimental phase will be maintained when the tests are administered on a large scale.

Current Trends

A number of emerging phenomena in the Israeli and U.S. educational systems in the past few years suggest that a convergence is taking place: the centralized system in Israel is adopting features of decentralized systems, while the decentralized system in the United States is moving toward centralization.

The Trend toward Decentralization in Israeli Education

Israeli schools are gaining greater autonomy. Currently, for example, a quarter of each school's curriculum can be determined by the school itself, free from the influence of the Ministry of Education. Moreover, a recent project experimented with an alternative model of assessment at the end of the secondary school years. The project, "Alternative Matriculation System: A Feasible Model," took place at Tel Aviv University between the years 1984 and 1988 under the sponsorship of the Ministry of Education.[8] It involved three subject areas—L-1 (Hebrew) writing, math, and English as a foreign language—and was based on the following principles: (1) the student's score at the end of secondary school would be based on the teacher's assessment of classroom performance; (2) the assessment would be continuous, i.e., would cover the student's performance during the final three years of secondary school; (3) all teachers who provided assessments would go through intensive training in using effective testing and assessment procedures; and (4) external tests would be used to calibrate and standardize teachers' scores.

The most important component of this project was the continuous assignment of student scores by well-trained teachers. Whereas under the standard Israeli system the teacher has the responsibility of preparing the students but lacks the authority to assign scores, in the alternative assessment project, the teacher had both the teaching responsibility and the authority to assign the scores. Thus, in terms of the dimensions described earlier, there was a shift (1) from external testing to internal, (2) from one-shot testing to continuous assessment, (3) from a low proportion of students tested to a high one, (4) from summative/predictive testing purposes to formative/summative purposes, (5) from uniform test formats to flexible formats, and (6) from low to high psychometric accuracy. While this experimental program has not been adopted, the fact that it was sponsored by the Ministry of Education may imply that it is at least being considered. In addition, there are a number of ventures by the Ministry to adopt informal nontesting assessment procedures such as portfolios and projects. The Ministry at this point still insists, however, on being the main body to conduct the tests and thus control the national system.

Trends toward Centralization in the United States

In the United States, the trend toward centralization of the testing system can be seen both in general education and in the specific area of foreign language testing. In general education, for example, Madaus (1991) reports a number of indicators, the most salient of which is perhaps the growing number of proposals to introduce a national external end-of-secondary-school test. He indicates that in the last congress, in Public Law 100297, the secretary of education was actually authorized to create a national test to administer to twelfth-graders in certain subject areas and to issue certificates of competence in those areas. The format of the proposed test is not yet clear, but suggestions have been made to incorporate some innovative procedures such as portfolios and other performance-based components.

Another sign of the centralization trend in the United States can be found in the reports of the annual state governors' meetings. Madaus (1991) contends that much of the discussion at these meetings is concerned with how to measure the attainment of skills; substantially less attention is devoted to issues of curriculum, syllabus changes, and how to reach the goals. A third indicator can be seen in the move to develop a test that employers can use to ascertain that prospective employees have the basic skills needed to perform in entry-level positions at the workplace. There is even talk about putting the test results into a national computer database, so that no matter where the person is in the country it will be possible to call his or her scores up. Yet a fourth signal is the current move to develop national centers that will establish standards and create actual tests, and to allow each state to create its own tests that will then be calibrated against this national standard. Madaus cites as the main impetus behind this trend a desire to promote control over the educational system in order to ensure acceptable levels of student achievement.

There are a number of unanswered questions with regard to whether these and other dimensions of centralization will be adopted in the United States. One issue has to do with the relationship between the development of tests and criteria and whether they will lead to a national curriculum. Other issues include whether a national test would be syllabus-driven, subject-matter-specific, or skill-oriented.

While the assessment of foreign language learning has not yet been formally included in discussions about a national testing program, there have been some signs in the past decade that might be taken to suggest interest in just that step. One of the first of these, for example, dates from the release of the Presidential Commission (1979) report on foreign languages and international studies. The appearance of this report led to a recommendation to establish language-proficiency achievement goals for the end of each year of study at all levels, with special attention to speaking proficiency. Liskin-Gasparro (1983) points to a shift in focus from assessing success or failure with the language *in* the classroom to such assessment *outside* the classroom. That is, whereas previously the main criterion for accountability was internal (whether the students measured up to the expectation of the teacher), the ACTFL Guidelines introduced external goals that reflected language proficiency, i.e., the ability to function effectively in real-life contexts.

Liskin-Gasparro (1983), in describing the recommendations emanating from the first meeting of the President's Commission on Foreign Languages and International Studies in October 1978, also reports the establishment of nationally recognized proficiency standards for foreign language study. The report of the Task Force on Institutional Language Policy discussed by Liskin-Gasparro, for example, is a statement of national goals: It states that institutional and state educational systems should be encouraged by the Modern Language Association (MLA) to adopt nationally recognized performance or proficiency standards and to make such standards known widely to students and faculty.

Another recommendation stated that the MLA and ACTFL should secure funding for the revision and redevelopment of tests to measure proficiencies in the four language skills in the most commonly taught and widely used languages. The tests would be developed by committees consisting of both secondary school and college teachers. It called for a "national criteria and assessment program" to develop foreign language proficiency tests to better monitor and assess foreign language teaching. Among the various possible uses of such examinations, it was specified that they could be used in the granting of high school diplomas. Thus, the introduction of the ACTFL Guidelines, the newly established OPI language tests, the convergence of the government and academic educational sectors in this effort, and the need to better monitor achievement and proficiency in the country, are all steps that suggest a trend toward greater centralization of U.S. foreign language teaching.

Conclusion

This chapter has focused on ways that tests, in particular language tests, are used in two different educational systems. Major differences in the existence and use of the end-of-secondary-school tests in centralized and decentralized educational systems have been described. One focus was on the United States, which represents a decentralized and democratic educational system with no national curriculum and no national end-of-secondary-school test. In this system classroom teachers have the responsibility for teaching and the authority to assign grades. The other focus was on the Israeli educational system, which is selective and has a national curriculum and a formal national end-of-secondary-school test that is written, administered, and scored by an external body. This body uses the end-of-secondary-school test as a tool to enforce the curriculum and to provide criteria for selection for further educational opportunities. The fact that the test is controlled by an external body means that much of what happens in the educational system is in effect dictated by that test.

We have seen how tests that have a strong impact on the future of individuals are also used for a variety of other purposes, such as implementing educational policies, imposing curricula, and motivating learning. There are differences in the degrees to which tests are used for these purposes, varying according to the type of educational system(s) in each country. A distinction was made between centralized educational systems, where a central body dictates a uniform curriculum, and decentralized systems, where decisions are made by individual groups or regions with minimal or no intervention on the part of central bodies. It was shown how in centralized systems tests are employed mostly as authoritative tools for imposing curriculum and learning, whereas in decentralized systems tests are used more as sources of information while other devices are used to implement curriculum and improve learning. This distinction was analyzed through specific dimensions that are typical for each system, i.e., whether the tests are external or internal, one-shot or continuous, categorical or comprehensive, predictive or summative, and uniform or flexible, and whether they have accurate psychometric properties.

It is not possible to claim that one system or a certain feature of a particular system is superior to another, as each system is based on and must reflect the beliefs, philosophy, and policies of the society in which it exists. We have seen that some decentralized systems are moving toward greater reliance on tests as devices for implementing policy, while simultaneously some centralized systems are moving toward less reliance on tests for that purpose; that is, some centralized systems are adopting what they view as positive features of decentralized systems while decentralized systems are adopting what they consider to be advantageous features of centralized systems.

It is not clear whether the assumption that national tests *per se* contribute to upgrading the level of student achievement in a meaningful, systematic way is valid. Madaus (1991) contends that there is no guarantee that national tests have this effect, but rather suggests that the main outcome of introducing a national test may simply be that students study harder and teachers work harder. Other scholars are examining the phenomenon as well.[9]

In sum, tests are very powerful tools that can provide meaningful information that can lead in turn to diagnoses of strong and weak areas in the educational system, thence to repair, and ultimately to higher student achievement. It could therefore be advantageous to invest in constructing tests that provide teachers, students, and other decision makers with meaningful information that can help foreign language (and other) learning. This can be done by involving external and internal bodies, teachers, external testers, and students; by utilizing a variety of information sources—not just tests—in a combined effort to improve learning in and out of the classroom; and by combining the formative, summative, and predictive uses of testing.

Various initiatives in this direction have recently been proposed: One of the most noticeable is the notion of systemic validity (Frederiksen and Collins 1989), where tests are viewed not as isolated events, but rather as combined components of the educational system, integrated with instruction and learning. This approach is based on the assumption that a systemic and valid test is one that can show a positive effect on learning. Ultimately it is important to ensure that regardless of the specific characteristics of a country's educational system, the real value of tests—that of providing meaningful information to improve learning—is maximized, while the use of tests as a threatening or power device is minimized.

Notes

1. It is important to note that in recent years there has been a decrease in the status of the SAT as a result of claims that it does not accurately reflect school content. Also, decreases in the level of achievement of U.S. students shown on international surveys is of national concern at this time; proposals are currently being made to introduce a national achievement test in some school subjects (e.g. math) (Madaus 1991). If such tests are introduced, it seems likely that passing them could become a condition for receiving a high school certificate.
2. Perhaps surprisingly, the school language teacher, who may have the appropriate background, is not considered to have the authority to devise the end-of-secondary-school test and is often not even allowed to be present during its administration.
3. The extent to which a score is objective, however, is a psychometric issue that can be addressed by a variety of measurement techniques.
4. In the United States, where there is no national end-of-high-school test, this dimension may not be applicable. There are, however, privately managed national assessments in certain subjects—those considered to be important to U.S. society. The fact that foreign languages are not included on these assessments sends a message. The development of the ACTFL Guidelines and the OPI testing instrument after the

President's Commission (1979) report may, however, be taken to convey the message that U.S. society is indeed beginning to view foreign language as having greater significance.

5. Some of these countries are currently considering the adoption of an end-of-secondary-school test, but for reasons other than for the purpose of selection, e.g., to increase student motivation to study and to upgrade student achievement.

6. Other languages, such as Arabic or French, do not serve as critical areas for selection, as only a small proportion of the population is tested in these subjects and they are not, in any case, compulsory subject-matter areas.

7. See, for example, Shohamy 1991 for a description of such alternatives.

8. See Zack (1982) and Shohamy (1985) for details of this project.

9. For example, Stake (in press) showed that while tests make teachers and students more focused on their learning and the introduction of tests diverts attention to neglected areas, it also tends to narrow the scope of education as teachers and students focus primarily on the test's material.

References, International Perspectives on Foreign Language Testing

ACTFL. 1986. *Proficiency Guidelines.* Hastings-on-Hudson, NY: American Council on the Teaching of Foreign Languages.

Byrnes, Heidi. 1987. "Second Language Acquisition: Insights from a Proficiency Orientation," pp. 107–32 in Heidi Byrnes and Michael Canale, eds., *Defining and Developing Proficiency: Guidelines, Implementations, and Concepts.* ACTFL Foreign Language Education Series, vol. 17. Lincolnwood, IL: National Textbook Company.

_____, and Michael Canale, eds. 1987. *Defining and Developing Proficiency: Guidelines, Implementations, and Concepts.* ACTFL Foreign Language Education Series, vol. 17. Lincolnwood, IL: National Textbook Company.

Frederiksen, John R., and Allan Collins. 1989. "A System Approach to Educational Testing." *Educational Researcher* 18: 27–32.

Hoge, Robert D., and Theodore Coladarci. 1989. "Teacher-Based Judgments of Academic Achievement: A Review of Literature." *Review of Educational Research* 59: 297–313.

Liskin-Gasparro, Judith E. 1983. "The ACTFL Proficiency Guidelines: A Historical Perspective," pp. 11–42 in Theodore V. Higgs, ed., *Teaching for Proficiency, the Organizing Principle.* ACTFL Foreign Language Education Series, vol. 15. Lincolnwood, IL: National Textbook Company.

Lowe, Pardee, Jr., and Charles Stansfield. 1988. *Second Language Proficiency Assessment.* Englewood Cliffs, NJ: Prentice Hall Regents.

Madaus, George. 1991. "Current Trends in Testing in the USA." Paper presented at the conference Testing and Evaluation: Feedback Strategies for Improvement of Foreign Language Learning, February 4–5. Washington, DC: The National Foreign Language Center.

President's Commission on the Teaching of Foreign Languages and International Studies. 1979. *Strength through Wisdom: A Critique of U.S. Capability.* Washington, DC: U.S. Government Printing Office.

Shohamy, Elana. 1985. "An Alternative Model for Assessing Language Proficiency at the End of Secondary School," pp. 149–56 in Viljo Kohonen, Cris Klein Braley, and Hilkka von Essen, eds., *Practice and Problems in Language Testing.* Vol. 8. Tampere, Finland: FinLA (Finnish Association for Applied Linguistics).

_____. 1990. "Language Testing Priorities: A Different Perspective." *Foreign Language Annals* 23: 385–93.

_____. 1991. "Connecting Testing and Learning in the Classroom and on the Program Level," pp. 154–76 in June Phillips, ed., *Building Bridges and Making Connections.* Middlebury, VT: Northeast Conference on the Teaching of Foreign Languages.

_____, Thea Reves, and Yael Bejerano. 1986. "Introducing a New Comprehensive Test of Oral Proficiency." *English Language Teaching Journal* 40: 212–20.

Stake, Robert. In press. *Effects of Changes in Assessment Policy.* Greenwich, CT: JAI Press.

van Lier, Leo. 1989. "Reeling, Writhing, Drawling, Stretching, and Fainting in Coils: Oral Proficiency Interviews as Conversations." *TESOL Quarterly* 23: 489–508.

Zack, Itai. 1982. *Alternative Assessment for the Matriculation Examination: A Feasible Model.* Internal document, School of Education, Tel Aviv University.

9

The New Meaning of Creativity in the Foreign Language Classroom: A Canadian Perspective

Sally Rehorick

University of New Brunswick

The mind is not a vessel to be filled but a fire to be kindled.

(Plutarch, quoted in Carnevale et al. 1990: 191)

A Scenario

During a classroom visit to observe one of my student teachers demonstrate her teaching skills in a practice lesson of French, I was struck with what seemed to me to be a time warp of some twenty-five years. The 45-minute class consisted of the following activities: a 20-minute segment on adjective agreement during which the teacher had students spell (orally) the correct form of the particular adjective used in a series of unrelated sentences; a 10-minute segment consisting of an oral reading by students of isolated words written in phonetic script; and a final 15 minutes of listening to a recorded story that the students followed by reading along in their textbooks. During the entire class period, the student teacher designated which students should speak and in what order, and the students spoke to her only in response to questions she had generated. My

Sally Rehorick is currently Senior Research Associate in the French Second Language Teacher Education Centre at the University of New Brunswick, Canada. Her broad career has spanned French and English as second languages as well as human resource development in environments as diverse as universities, government, and corporations. She has taught at the universities of Alberta and Victoria as well as Harvard University and has degrees from the University of Alberta, the Université de Grenoble, and Harvard University. She is coeditor (with Viviane Edwards) of the *Canadian Modern Language Review*. Her research interests focus on human resource development and teacher education, learning environments in the second language classroom, and testing.

dismay at witnessing this practice lesson was heightened by the satisfaction felt by both the student teacher and the supervising classroom teacher with the outcomes of the lesson. In their view, it had fulfilled the objectives of the oral/ aural curriculum prescribed by the provincial department of education: the students spoke and listened. In addition, discipline and order had been maintained throughout.

As I attempted to come to grips with my feeling of having stepped into a class that did not differ materially from any class of twenty-five or thirty years ago, I began to worry that the communicative and interactive pronouncements and urgings of recent years had been only so much rhetoric and that in reality nothing substantive had changed in classroom practice. The only messages communicated by the students in this class were those that met the isolated single-answer possibility expected by the teacher. What was stressed and rewarded by the indulgent student teacher was the importance of facts, not interchanges of "messages that contain information of interest to speaker and listener in a situation of importance to both" (Rivers 1987: 4). The accumulation of facts— forms of adjectives, phonetic symbols, and sound/letter correspondences—was the principal goal of this lesson. Regrettably I realized that little more than passing homage had been paid to those noble curriculum objectives of oral interaction and communication.

When I broached some of these issues with the student teacher, including the need to give more "air time" to the students, she noted, not overly defensively, that she had permitted the students to "have conversations" in a class two weeks previously.

This experience of classroom observation might lead one to believe that the laments of Hoetker and Ahlbrand (1969) concerning the "remarkable stability of classroom verbal behavior patterns over the last half century" and the notion that "each successive generation of educational thinkers . . . has condemned the rapid-fire, question-answer pattern of instruction" (p. 163) had been published only recently. Hoetker and Ahlbrand proposed the possibility that the persistence of the recitation as a pedagogical tool might simply reflect the overwhelming practical needs of the classroom teacher.

There is no doubt that this reality persists today. A teacher must necessarily consider what is practical for the class of some twenty-five to thirty students. One must also consider, however, the nature of the student participation, since even in a teacher-centered, recitation style of pedagogy students are required to be involved (although not necessarily engaged). Even as Hoetker and Ahlbrand were exposing the results of their classroom observations, other foreign language educators were calling for increased flexibility and creativity in the classroom.

In Canada this call was, in part, answered by the implementation of a large-scale innovation in language learning. The need to find creative and effective ways for children to learn the two official languages (English and French) of the country led to experimentation with immersion classes in which students learn regular subject matter such as mathematics, social studies, and science in their second language. Although not without its critics (see, for example, Hammerly 1989), immersion has been demonstrated to be one of the most successful language-learning innovations in the world today (Allen et al. 1989). This finding notwithstanding, there has been much attention devoted to the need to find better and more creative ways for immersion teachers to develop more effective methods for their classroom, methods that would view language as a means as well as an end (Kiriloff 1990; Bélanger 1990; Lyster 1990). This research has shown that although immersion might be considered an innovation when seen in its totality, individual classroom teachers very often follow the same teaching methods of which they themselves had been victims some twenty years earlier. That some of these teachers are conscious of this was evident at two recent conferences of foreign language teachers in Canada (Canadian Association of Immersion Teachers annual conference, Vancouver 1990; Ontario Modern Language Teachers Association annual conference, Toronto 1991): Three separate sessions on creativity offered by this author were filled to capacity.

This chapter will consider how creativity has been viewed by educators in the past and how one might find evidence of this view in today's classrooms in Canada. In addition, it will examine how the notion of creativity coincides with current theories of second language acquisition. Finally we will determine how the proliferation of creative techniques available in the business world might be transferred to the foreign language classroom, both in Canada and abroad.

Past Views of Creativity in the Foreign Language Classroom

As enthusiasm for the audiolingual approach of the 1950s and 1960s waned, educators paid increasing attention to legitimizing experimentation in the foreign language classroom. The chairman of the 1971 Central States Conference on the Teaching of Foreign Languages (whose theme was "Creativity in the Foreign Language Classroom"), remarked that "in this age of computerized report cards, programmed instruction, mechanistic behavioral objectives, demands for educational accountability and student alienation it seemed appropriate that practitioners of a discipline like foreign languages should not lose sight of the element of personal creativity which must be present in the classroom if instruction is not to fall to the level of mere mental calisthenics" (Grittner 1971).

The occurrence of this conference on creativity makes a rather pointed commentary on the state of affairs in language teaching two decades ago. The keynote speakers (Strasheim 1971; Birkmaier 1971) lamented the lack of flexibility and freedom accorded to foreign language teachers. In an obviously apologetic tone they admonished the rigid tenets of the structuralist approach, which required teachers to "cover" the curriculum. Strasheim (1971) said in this regard that

> we go on calling and crying for creativity, but we always want to impose limits: the teacher may "create" whatever she or he wants so long as it meets next year's syllabus and causes no format problems to Mr. Z who

teaches that part of the sequence; the teacher may "create" whatever he or she wants IF the "creation" includes the attached list of 125 verbs; the teacher may "create" whatever seems to expedite learning BUT the students should be prepared to read these four authors at the end of their experience. (p. 343)

Creativity as a concept was almost an anomaly in the context of the methodologies of the 1960s. If learning a foreign language was a result of habits whose formation was carefully controlled and monitored by the teacher, how could either teacher or students be expected to deviate from this carefully devised prescription without throwing the whole language acquisition process into jeopardy? Even Birkmaier (1971), who admonished foreign language educators for having too long "paid homage to a psychology bound to develop passive robots who accept a predetermined way of performing" (p. 353), was herself caught up in the discourse of audiolingualism, which encouraged "manipulation" of various linguistic elements (p. 347).

Both Strasheim and Birkmaier viewed creativity as an innate personality characteristic. Although creativity could be encouraged or guided in certain individuals, truly creative individuals could only be born, not developed. Thus Birkmaier proposed the development of "performance criteria to predict the innovative skills of the teacher" (p. 353). Prospective teachers would be asked to undergo a series of temperament and personality tests as well as a battery of performance tests to determine their creative potential. Strasheim went so far as to suggest that the language-teaching profession should not place the "burden of 'being creative'" (p. 345) upon teachers because the "truly creative teacher is one in a thousand if not a million" (p. 343). This is not to suggest that Strasheim necessarily considered teachers, as a group, to be singularly *uncreative;* the same statement might well be made about any profession.

The speakers at the 1971 conference seemed unanimous in pointing to the need for teacher recruiters and teacher trainers to locate exceptional individuals to become teachers and to foster an environment of change and flexibility in the schools. This process would pave the way for the development of innovative foreign language programs that would in turn promote better foreign language acquisition among students. The speakers stopped short of making concrete suggestions to begin this process, although Birkmaier (1971: 353) encouraged educators to look to the world of the advertising industry for ideas concerning creative training techniques.

Some Examples of Current Classroom Practices

The fact that creativity in foreign language teaching was raised as an issue more than twenty years ago leads one to wonder to what extent classroom practice has changed as a result of that concern. That creativity is very much on the minds of educators and administrators today is evidenced in very visible ways. A recent job advertisement in Canada's national newspaper, the *Globe and Mail,* called for an adviser of curriculum enrichment who would be capable of "critical thinking, creative thinking and problem solving" (*Globe and Mail* 1990). In the United States, the American Institute for Creative Education offers regular seminars on methods and techniques for the creative teacher (*Bangor Daily News* 1991).

One might be tempted to point to certain methods or technologies as being creative. This approach, however, would fall short of defining the fundamental aspects of creativity. It perhaps makes more sense to introduce a working definition of creativity by first explaining what it is not. To begin with, creativity does not refer to a single philosophy or methodology. While many of the approaches to foreign language teaching and learning developed over the past two or three decades likely could be characterized as creative by virtue of being different from other approaches, none can claim sole ownership of the term. Methods such as Lozanov's Suggestopedia, Curran's Counseling-Learning, or Gattegno's Silent Way (as described in Stevick 1980) could all be classified as creative, in particular because of the manner by which they allow for individuality in learning (although not so much in teaching). In addition, there are frequent reports on innovative techniques to exploit traditional materials such as drama. (See, for example, McNeece 1983; Mueller and Rehorick 1984; Maley and Duff 1978; Fancy 1991.) These reports either describe experiments that have been successful or they present a formula or recipe for the teacher who must continually be concerned with the question of what to do on Monday morning. None of the reports attempted to delineate how the experiments have been successful nor what the underlying characteristics of their successes are.

Can we therefore look for evidence of creativity in the world of technology? One cannot ignore the wealth of recent information about technology and foreign language learning. The emergence of computer technology has had a major impact on the profession, not so much by its widespread use as by the thought that it *should* be used. The existence of the *CALICO Journal,* the regular column entitled "Computers in French Education" in *Contact, Canadian Review for French Teachers,* and similar technology-related publications points to this continuing concern. As Rivers (1990) points out, however, if the courseware and programers behind the technology are found lacking, no amount of dazzling graphics is going to enhance language learning. The computer is simply another tool that, much like its technological predecessor, the language laboratory, can lead to laziness on the part of both teacher and student. In other words, the computer by itself does not ensure creativity; rather it is the *manner in which it is used* that determines how innovative a tool it can be.

The Relationship between Second Language Acquisition and Creativity

Considerable attention has been paid to the efficacy of different kinds of student/teacher interaction patterns in the foreign language classroom; we now know, for example, that participation is not *ipso facto* a route to better second language acquisition (Allwright 1980: 166). Teachers are becoming aware of the negotiated process of participation and of the difference between "habitual and skilful performance" (Rivers 1991: 261). We also know that language is not acquired in linear fashion, but rather that the brain organizes information in an associative network, changing and adapting according to the situation. Rivers (1991) states that "as circumstances and purposes change, we, as thinking beings, need to be able to contemplate our performance even in the act of executing a routine procedure, so as to continue comparing and matching with information from the ever-active associative networks" (p. 261).

According to current theory, language acquisition is an individual and creative activity in which each learner, in an effort to communicate his or her own sense of the world and to understand others' understanding of their world, expresses his or her own individuality in a unique way. Thus, far from viewing creativity as a personality trait as did Birkmaier (1971), we now can envision creativity as an integral component of the process of second language acquisition. (How this view of creativity can be incorporated into a foreign language pedagogy will be treated later on in this chapter.)

Creativity and the World of Business

Let us now examine some of the trends that have occurred recently in the business world, which can possibly influence how foreign language teachers might approach their work in a different way.

Creativity and innovation have been buzzwords in the world of business for some years. Ever since Peters and Waterman (1982) documented the characteristics of the most successful companies in the United States, researchers have been attempting to describe the characteristics of individuals who contribute the most to their companies' successes. Innes and Southwick-Trask (1989), for example, studied ten Canadian companies that turned their fortunes around by implementing innovative practices.

Whenever such research reveals potentially marketable trends, management consultants and human-resource developers scramble to provide a plethora of tools, techniques, and training programs through which companies can be assured of duplicating the same successes. Many of the resulting products reveal nothing more than a comical attempt to profit quickly from a vulnerable market. Witness, for example, the Idea Volley Bulb. The developers, Creative Learning International (Organizational Learning Resources 1990: 36), urge clients to "energize your meetings. Think on your feet. Bounce ideas off your boardroom walls." The Idea Volley Bulb, a large inflatable light bulb, "promotes creative thinking and team building" by being tossed among team members "who must quickly develop an idea." Somewhat less absurd, although no less humorous, is the "Pocket Innovator," which is a "hand-held creativity tool that quickly helps you brainstorm, solve problems, and develop high-quality ideas" (Organizational Learning Resources 1990: 36). Its color-coded cards contain words designed to stimulate creative thinking on cue at any time of day.

Although these items can be considered mostly as gimmicks, they are reflections of a concern in the business world that individuals within organizations become more creative in approaching their work. Along with the gimmicks is a wealth of excellent products and services that are widely used in training programs. Many of these products and services are grounded in the belief that a person's individual thinking style affects greatly how he or she will solve problems. While there is no single *personality type* that can be said to be more creative than another, there are numerous *thinking style inventories* that can assist individuals to determine their own particular approaches to problem-solving (see, for example, Kolb 1975; Grossman et al. 1988; Hogan and Champagne 1990; Honey and Mumford 1990). In addition to these inventories, there are books and manuals that delineate an array of techniques that can be used either in training programs or by managers to help employees solve problems and find creative solutions (Biondi and Parnes 1976; Grossman et al. 1988; Feingold 1989; Nierenberg 1982; von Oech 1983). It is from these aspects of creativity in the business world that teachers of foreign languages can learn much.

Some examples of creativity techniques from the business world follow.

Brainstorming

One of the oldest and most dependable of creativity techniques is brainstorming. Birkmaier (1971) mentioned this as one of the possible avenues for foreign language teachers to explore during the 1971 conference on creativity. The fundamental principle behind this technique is that the whole is greater than the sum of its parts. That is, by taking advantage of a certain collective creative energy of the group, when people hear the idea of another person, they are apt to think of other ideas on their own, which in turns leads to more ideas.

Brainstorming can help to accomplish a number of goals. It can be used as an icebreaker, as a way to introduce a new topic, and as a way to generate several possible avenues of action concerning a particular problem to be solved. It is often a subtechnique used as part of other techniques, some of which appear below. Brainstorming is not, however, simply an undirected free-for-all. Specific guidelines have been offered for brainstorming (Renner 1983: 47) and a knowledgeable facilitator can help the group come to a consensus once a number of alternatives have been generated.

Forcing Relationships

A second technique for developing creative thinking is called "forcing relationships." Developed by Grossman et al. (1988), it involves "the ability to connect two or more apparently different ideas, concepts, or things which have been previously unrelated" (p. 26). This technique incorporates brainstorming and endeavors to solve real problems by forcing participants to view the problem from a completely different, and very often comical, perspective.

The process involves generating a list of ideas or characteristics about something unrelated to the problem at hand. For example, a group might be trying to solve the problem of how to increase interaction in the foreign language classroom. Before dealing specifically with this, however, the group generates characteristics of, say, a good party. On this "key" list might appear such items as "attractive invitations," "warn the neighbors," "good food, drinks, and music," and "interesting and diverse guests." Once this process is complete, a series of "insights" is generated concerning the problem at hand. These insights are inspired by, but not limited to, the items appearing on the key list. Some of the possibilities concerning increasing interaction in the foreign language classroom might be as follows: "a nonthreatening atmosphere," "a letter to students before school begins," "warn teachers in neighboring classes that the language class might be noisy," and "make the most of the different backgrounds of students."

Becoming the Angel's Advocate

This technique, also developed by Grossman et al. (1988), is based on a corollary of the statement that not all ideas are good ideas: "Not all bad ideas are useless ideas" (p. 31). This means that, in the process of brainstorming or forcing relationships, a few ideas might surface that are discarded as impractical or nonsensical. When one becomes the angel's advocate, the task is to look at "a partially successful solution and separate the part that is useful from the part that is not" (p. 31). Ideas are rated on a scale of 100 according to how useful they are. By combining the "forcing relationships" technique with the "angel's advocate," members of a group can explore the usefulness of some seemingly useless ideas. For example, the following statement might be generated in response to a problem-solving session concerned with how to conduct professional development sessions for Spanish teachers: "To become better Spanish teachers, everyone should visit the zoo once a week." The first step is to develop a key list of ideas about visiting the zoo. The next step is to take from these ideas everything that is useful for solving the problem of how to conduct professional development sessions for Spanish teachers. The following list might thus be generated:

Key Column	Insight Column
Visiting the Zoo	Developing Spanish Teachers
Zoos have many animals.	We may learn about different teachers by watching different animals.
Many children go to the zoo.	We want our teachers to be as enthusiastic as children at the zoo.
The zoo is usually in a park setting.	We can learn more about the effect of our teaching environment on students.

| Animals come from all over. | Different approaches might be useful for teachers of different backgrounds. |
| Animals are fed in public. | We can ask teachers to eat their lunches with their students. |

(list adapted from Grossman et al. 1988: 33)

Once a list is generated, group members choose the seemingly worst of the ideas and try to list ten useful things about it. From the above list we might choose the last idea, since most teachers would not relish giving up their lunch hour to spend it with their students. Some of the useful aspects of this "bad" idea might be as follows: (1) students can get to know their teachers better; (2) teachers can talk about Spanish food customs; (3) students can practice their Spanish outside the classroom; (4) teachers could make the students responsible for organizing the meal; (5) students could order a Spanish film; (6) students could organize a Spanish club; (7) students could meet after school or on weekends. From an idea that, at the outset, seemed to represent an unwelcome intrusion into a teacher's private time, we can see the development of a Spanish club for which the students carry the major responsibility.

Unlocking Mental Locks

One of the greatest barriers to creativity is human reluctance to think something different. Von Oech points out that much of the educational system "is geared toward teaching people the *one right answer* [and that this] 'right answer' approach becomes deeply ingrained in our thinking" (1983: 21). People become reluctant to think in a manner different from the expected approach and thus a series of "mental locks" (p. 8) prevents creativity.

Von Oech proposes a number of techniques for unlocking the mental locks. One of the mental locks he describes is a person's propensity to "be practical" (p. 53). He notes that as people get older "they become prisoners of familiarity" (p. 60) and they need help in unlocking the barrier. To do this, he advises using the "what if" technique that involves asking a question about a situation that does not currently exist in reality. These questions might run something like this: "What if we had seven fingers on each hand?" or "What if animals became more intelligent than people?" (p. 55). Through a process of free association, group members generate some possible as well as some improbable and impractical answers to these questions. In a foreign language setting, a teacher might use this technique to help students learn about dinosaurs, which in Canada are an important part of the primary school French as a second language curriculum. If a lesson objective concerns dinosaurs, the question posed could be: "What if a family of dinosaurs moved to Toronto?" The students might generate a list of free associative statements and more questions, which would lead them to discover at least some of the characteristics of dinosaurs. The process might look something like this:

- What if a family of dinosaurs moved to Toronto?

- Would they be able to walk down the streets without bumping into buildings? What would the people in the buildings do when they saw a dinosaur coming through the walls? If they bumped into a furniture store, would they want to buy a bed to sleep on? What would a dinosaur bed look like?
- If they're tired, it must mean that they're hungry too. How would grocery stores have to change what they sell to accommodate the dinosaur's appetite? Would that mean that everyone else would have to go hungry? They're probably cold too, since it's winter in Toronto and the dinosaurs have come from the south. How can they stay warm? What would a dinosaur sweater look like?

The results of such an activity could engender others that can include playful speculation or more serious content. In either event, students will have had an opportunity to acquire and use new vocabulary and structures in a stimulating and enjoyable way.

Futuristic Exercises

Many of the think tanks that operate in the business world use "futuring" to generate ideas for how their businesses can cope in an ever-changing and ever-shrinking global economy. Many of these exercises provide fertile ground for the foreign language teacher and learner. The topic of the future is inherently of interest to students, since most students will spend over three-quarters of their lives in the future. By attempting to predict and describe the world as it will be, students engage themselves in the fundamental choice "between being completely surprised by the future and wholly subject to the control of external forces or, alternatively, having some basis of knowledge about what is possible so that [they] can attempt to shape the future in accordance with [their] own desires" (Ferkiss 1977: 10).

Studying the future can be done through many different avenues. One of these is "genius forecasting," which involves "leaping to a date" sometime in the future (Haas 1988: 41) and attempting to depict either what the world will be like, or how a particular scientific discovery or technological creation will affect life. One such exercise is described by Feingold (1989: 29):

In a future society on earth, everyone remains healthy, emotionally and physically, to age 200. Moreover, everyone has an IQ of at least 200. A few people produce all the food needed. Everyone has all the material possessions he or she wants. What will this society do?

This exercise could easily be adapted to the foreign language classroom. Students could develop an entire project that might involve describing the physical features of a person 200 years old, inventing a new sport that would appeal to a 150-year-old, and speculating on how people in this society would make a living.

Other techniques for probing the future include "trend extrapolation," which is the extension of historical and current patterns into the future; constructing a future history by either "postulating a future event and then flashing back to the present or recent past to trace the sequence from past to present to future" or by "beginning in the past or present and 'playing out' a plausible future" (Haas 1988: 43); "decision trees," which are visual representations of the potential effects of various alternatives to a problem; and simulations and games, such as role playing (see Rockler 1988 for a comprehensive listing). Most of these would be directly applicable to the foreign language classroom.

Conclusion: Chrysalis and Other Goddesses of Classroom Creativity

The underlying theme of this chapter is that the theories and strategies considered here can play a central role in the development of more creative foreign language classrooms. Foreign language educators might at first shy away from some of the suggestions, surmising perhaps that the techniques are too difficult or not relevant for their students (e.g., "Where does teaching verbs fit in?"). However, we would do well to remember some of the basic tenets of the interactive approach to language learning: to wit, the premise that languages are learned best when students are truly engaged in exchanging messages about something of real concern to them (Rivers 1987). Content-based foreign language instruction should not be limited to situations of total or partial immersion. In a content-based model of foreign language instruction, the language teacher decides to concentrate on selected topics or themes such as advertising, ecology, or gun control (Brinton et al. 1989). Within these topics many of the techniques described in this chapter can easily be used and adapted.

It is clear that, in the Canadian context, foreign language educators are ready to implement these innovative techniques. Immersion as a large-scale innovation has been successful, but questions are being asked about how immersion teaching can become more relevant and creative. School boards are sending specific messages in their recruitment of consultants who are conversant with such techniques. In addition, it is evident that experienced teachers are themselves anxious to be a part of this movement and are flocking to conference sessions that deal with individual creativity.

How easy is it to implement the techniques described in this chapter? As with any change process, true innovations are not discrete or describable entities so much as they are gradual and wide-ranging processes that require time to steep. Much depends on the organizational climate in which the teacher is working, and one must be prepared at times for an inhospitable reaction to changes of a major scale. These reactions might come from the students, the institution, or the teachers themselves. The nurturing of a creative environment in the foreign language classroom can perhaps be likened to the metamorphosis of a butterfly whose less beautiful, more vulnerable state is protected by a chrysalis within which the transformation occurs (McKisson 1981). Once the initial transformation is complete, the newly formed butterfly can continue what will now have become a tradition of creativity.

References, The New Meaning of Creativity in the Foreign Language Classroom

Allen, J. P. B., J. Cummins, R. Mougeon, and M. Swain. 1989. *Report of the Development of Bilingual Proficiency Project.* Toronto: Ontario Institute for Studies in Education.

Allwright, R. L. 1980. "Turns, Topics, and Tasks: Patterns of Participation in Language Learning and Teaching," pp. 165–87 in Diane Larsen-Freeman, ed., *Discourse Analysis in Second Language Research.* New York: Newbury House.

Bangor Daily News. 1991. "Creative Education Seminars Slated." February 23–24, p. 20.

Bélanger, Claire. 1990. "Whole Language in the French Immersion Classroom." *Le Journal de l'ACPI* 14,1: 10–12, 25.

Biondi, Angelo M., and Sidney J. Parnes. 1976. *Assessing Creative Growth.* Buffalo, NY: Bearly.

Birkmaier, Emma M. 1971. "The Meaning of Creativity in Foreign Language Teaching." *Modern Language Journal* 55: 345–53.

Brinton, Donna M., Marguerite Ann Snow, and Marjorie Bingham Wesche. 1989. *Content-Based Second Language Instruction.* New York: Newbury House.

Carnevale, Anthony P., Leila J. Gainer, and Ann S. Meltzer. 1990. *Workplace Basics Training Manual.* San Francisco: Jossey-Bass.

Fancy, Alex. 1991. "Didactique du français langue seconde, dramatisation et théâtre." *Canadian Modern Language Review/Revue canadienne des langues vivantes* 47: 341–50.

Feingold, S. Norman. 1989. *Futuristic Exercises: A Workbook on Emerging Lifestyles and Careers in the 21st Century and Beyond.* Garrett Park, MD: Garrett Park Press.

Ferkiss, V. C. 1977. *Futurology: Promise, Performance, Prospects.* Beverly Hills, CA: Sage.

Globe and Mail. 1990. "Working for Learning." Job advertisement for adviser of curriculum enrichment, School District No. 57, Prince George, B.C., November 10, p. 36.

Grittner, Frank. 1971. "Foreword." *Modern Language Journal* 55: 339.

Grossman, Stephen R., Bruce E. Rodgers, and Beverley R. Moore. 1988. *Innovation, Inc.: Unlocking Creativity in the Workplace.* Plano, TX: Wordware.

Haas, John D. 1988. *Future Studies in the K–12 Curriculum.* Boulder, CO: Social Science Education Consortium.

Hammerly, Hector. 1989. *French Immersion: Myths and Reality.* Calgary, Alta.: Detselig.

Hoetker, James, and William P. Ahlbrand, Jr. 1969. "The Persistence of the Recitation." *The American Educational Research Journal* 6: 145–67.

Hogan, R. Craig, and David W. Champagne. 1990. "Personal Style Inventory," p. 11 in *Organizational Learning Resources, Creative Human Resource Development Materials.* Don Mills, Ont: Organization Design and Development, Inc.

Honey, Peter, and Alan Mumford. 1990. "Learning Styles Questionnaire," p. 39 in *Organizational Learning Resources, Creative Human Resource Development Materials.* Don Mills, Ont.: Organization Design and Development, Inc.

Innes, Eva, and Leslie Southwick-Trask. 1989. *Turning It Around: How Ten Canadian Organizations Changed Their Fortunes.* Toronto, Ont.: Random House.

Kiriloff, Olga. 1990. "Whole Language—une réflexion." *Le Journal de l'ACPI* 14,1: 5–8.

Kolb, David. 1975. *The Learning Style Inventory.* Boston: McBer.

Lyster, Roy. 1990. "The Role of Analytic Language Teaching in French Immersion Programs." *Canadian Modern Language Review/Revue canadienne des langues vivantes* 47,1: 159–76.

Maley, Alan, and Alan Duff. 1978. *Drama Techniques in Language Learning.* Cambridge, Eng.: Cambridge Univ. Press.

McKisson, Micki. 1981. *Chrysalis: Nurturing Creative and Independent Thought in Children, Grades 4–12.* Tucson, AZ: Zephyr Press Learning Materials.

McNeece, Lucy Stone. 1983. "The Uses of Improvisation: Drama in the Foreign Language Classroom." *French Review* 56: 829–39.

Mueller, Marlies, and Sally Rehorick. 1984. "Reaching for Caligula's Moon: Teaching Modern Drama in Advanced Language Classes." *French Review* 57: 475–84.

Nierenberg, Gerard I. 1982. *The Art of Creative Thinking*. New York: Simon & Schuster.

Organizational Learning Resources. 1990. *Creative Human Resource Development Materials*. Don Mills, Ont.: Organization Design and Development, Inc.

Peters, T. J., and Waterman, R. H. 1982. *In Search of Excellence: Lessons from America's Best-Run Companies*. New York: Harper and Row.

Renner, Peter Franz. 1983. *The Instructor's Survival Kit: A Handbook for Teachers of Adults*. 2nd ed. Vancouver, B.C.: Training Associates.

Rivers, Wilga M. 1987. "Interaction as the Key to Teaching Language for Communication," pp. 3–16 in Wilga Rivers, ed., *Interactive Language Teaching*. Cambridge, Eng.: Cambridge Univ. Press.

————. 1990. "Interaction and Communication in the Language Class in an Age of Technology." *Canadian Modern Language Review/Revue canadienne des langues vivantes* 46: 271–83.

————. 1991. "Mental Representations and Language in Action." *Canadian Modern Language Review/Revue canadienne des langues vivantes* 47: 249–65.

Rockler, Michael J. 1988. *Innovative Teaching Strategies: Games, Simulations, Creative Exercises, Future Studies*. Scottsdale, AZ: Gorsuch Scarisbrick.

Stevick, Earl W. 1980. *Teaching Languages: A Way and Ways*. New York: Newbury House.

Strasheim, Lorraine A. 1971. "'Creativity' Lies Trippingly on the Tongue." *Modern Language Journal* 55: 339–45.

von Oech, Roger. 1983. *A Whack on the Side of the Head: How to Unlock Your Mind for Innovation*. New York: Warner.

10

Arabic Diglossia and Its Impact on Teaching Arabic as a Foreign Language

Mahdi Alosh
The Ohio State University

Traditionally, academic institutions in the United States and elsewhere in North America, Europe, and even in the Arab world (in the case of Arabic for foreigners) have taught mainly the standard variety of Arabic (or more precisely, the written form of the language) with no or very little attention to the oral aspect. Only lately have some Arabic programs paid attention to the need for developing oral competence in the language. This movement is clearly toward communication and meaning and away from a purely grammatically based approach. Nevertheless, in most of these newer programs oral interaction in the classroom is carried out in Modern Standard Arabic (MSA), a variety of Arabic not commonly used for oral communication by native speakers of the language. For that purpose, native speakers use different colloquial varieties ("C" in contrast to "MSA")—one or more in each speech community, and the varieties vary from one geographical area to another. The rationale for incorporating an oral component in language classes is that students should first develop limited oral proficiency as a skill, regardless of which code (MSA or C) is being used in class, before doing any reading and writing, which are viewed as reinforcement of what has been learned orally. Though this change is taking hold only slowly, it has satisfied to some extent the advocates of teaching all four language skills (including the oral one, which has been grossly neglected).

Mahdi Alosh is Assistant Professor in the Department of Judaic and Near Eastern Languages and Literatures at The Ohio State University, where he teaches Arabic at all levels. His research interests are in second language acquisition, curriculum design, and foreign language instructional methodology. He was part of a team that adapted some 260 episodes of "Sesame Street" for use in Arabic-speaking countries. He is an ACTFL-certified oral proficiency tester of Arabic and has developed proficiency-oriented materials for first- and second-year Arabic under two grants from the U.S. Department of Education. He is codirector of a project for computer-assisted language learning and is also codirector of the Arabic Language and Culture Summer Institute funded by the National Endowment for the Humanities.

Had this major transformation taken place in a field such as French, Spanish, or even Japanese, it probably would have been considered the end of the controversy. In Arabic, however, the change has triggered heated debates and disputes in the profession (al-Batal, forthcoming). The problem emanates from the very criterion against which proficiency in a language is measured, i.e., the construct of the "educated native speaker." It is not that the construct itself is inherently problematic; rather, the difficulty lies in the curricular and pedagogical demands incurred by the special nature of the language skills an educated native speaker of Arabic possesses, i.e., facility in the use of two seemingly separate codes.[1] Thus, in light of the push toward developing proficiency of the sort native speakers possess, Arabic instruction, particularly in the United States, is now facing a new challenge: developing oral proficiency that resembles to a certain degree the proficiency of an educated native speaker. Debate has ensued regarding which Arabic variety or varieties to teach in a given Arabic program so that learners can function in a manner similar to native speakers, albeit in a limited way. The challenge stems not from the difficulty of choice among Arabic varieties, but rather, as noted above, from the pedagogical limitations imposed by the diglossic situation that characterizes the Arabic language.[2] In order to put this matter in perspective, a brief description of diglossia, particularly the diglossic situation in the Arab world, is in order.

Diglossia

Diglossia has been defined as the existence of two varieties of the same language side-by-side in a speech community, each variety having a specialized function.[3] In Arabic, one variety (a certain regional dialect) is used for everyday, informal oral interaction. These regional dialects are collectively known as Colloquial Arabic (C, henceforth). They are largely mutually intelligible, but they do vary from one speech community to another. (The degree of variation usually runs parallel to geographical proximity. Indeed, in one speech community there may be more than one dialect.) The other variety existing alongside the spoken dialects is superposed, mostly written, and it has limited oral use (restricted mainly to highly formal situations).[4] This variety is called Modern Standard Arabic, and it is more or less invariable throughout the Arab world.

The term *diglossia* was first introduced by the German linguist Karl Krumbacher in 1902 and later used by the French linguist William Marçais (Zughoul 1980). Both linguists used the term with reference to the dichotomous linguistic situation in the Arab world. More recently, Ferguson (1959), in a seminal, often-quoted article, described the phenomenon as follows:

> Diglossia is a relatively stable situation in which, in addition to the primary dialects of the language (which may include a standard or regional standards), there is a very divergent, highly codified (often grammatically more complex) superimposed variety, the vehicle of a large and respected body

of written literature . . . which is learned largely by formal education and used for most written and formal spoken purposes but not used by any sector of the community for ordinary conversation. (p. 336)

In his brief yet apt description, Ferguson touches on the major characteristics of this unusual sociolinguistic situation. His model highlights the aspect of *specialization of function* of the two norms used in a given speech community. Although the distinction may sound much like a matter of register, in fact the difference involves substantial lexical, morphological, and syntactic variations. Figure 10-1 reflects Ferguson's conception of Arabic diglossia.

Ferguson's definition seems to make certain assumptions about the linguistic norms, or language varieties, used in the Arabic diglossic situation. The first assumption posits that diglossia is stable. Temporally, this may be the case, since as far as we know Arabic diglossia has been around for as long as Arabic has existed. With regard to distribution of function, however, diglossia may have become less stable with the massive spread of education, particularly in the second half of this century. The more educated a speaker is, the more opportunity there is for him or her to use MSA forms as opposed to C forms in speech: forms that once were exclusively MSA have become part of the spoken repertoire of many educated Arabic speakers. This phenomenon may be a new one, and may be limited mostly to the lexicon, but it serves as an indication of where future developments might lead.

Secondly, Ferguson's model gives the impression that the Arabic diglossic situation is strictly dichotomous and static, and that the choice between norms is binary. In fact, the situation is a highly dynamic one, in which a number of sociolinguistic variables come into play, causing speakers to switch from one norm to another or to mix codes. These variables include, but are not limited to,

Situational Context	MSA	C
Sermon in church or mosque	X	
Instructions to servants, waiters, workmen, clerks		X
Personal letter	X	
Speech in parliament, political speech	X	
University lecture	X	
Conversation with family, friends, colleagues		X
News broadcast	X	
Radio "soap opera"		X
Newspaper editorial, news story, caption on picture	X	
Caption on political cartoon		X
Poetry	X	
Folk literature		X

Figure 10-1. Ferguson's Model of Diglossia

age, sex, education, formality, status, topic, and context of situation (e.g., public, private, familiar). The question thus becomes not *which* variety should be used in a given situation, but rather *how much* of each variety should appropriately be used. It is a matter of appropriateness of use determined by contextual and social factors, not merely by linguistic choice. This characteristic, appropriateness of use, raises the issue of whether rules of use should be formulated and taught alongside morphological and syntactic rules (Johnson 1982: 22).

A Model of Arabic Diglossia

The model proposed below as an alternative to that of Ferguson suggests eight possible combinations, each one representing interaction among three different variables: situation, occasion, and setting (see figure 10-2). The situation can be either formal or familiar. The occasion in a formal situation may be public (e.g., many people involved, as in a ceremony), or private (e.g., two department heads having a meeting). In a familiar situation, the occasion can be either public (e.g., a party) or intimate (e.g., two close friends, man and wife). The setting can be local or nonlocal (local being within the dialectal speech community of the interlocutors).

According to the model, speech is conditioned by these three variables, resulting in output that ranges from pure MSA to pure C, occurring at some point on the continuum. In real life, however, language performance is affected not only by the three named variables, but also by a host of others not included in the model. As one adds other variables, such as age, status, and gender, to the equation, the distinctions of the MSA / C "mix" grow finer and finer. Obviously, therefore, the situation is certainly neither simple nor static.

These rough descriptions of the Arabic diglossic situation will help later to evaluate proposed models of curriculum design for Arabic as a foreign language, with a proficiency orientation that incorporates a sociolinguistic perspective.

A third assumption underlying Ferguson's model suggests that the varieties of Arabic must be genetically related. This is of course true of Arabic, as can be attested at least by the perception of the native speakers themselves about their language. Regardless of claims separating the two varieties on the grounds of C being well-defined and MSA ill-defined (Kaye 1970), Arabic speakers perceive a dichotomy of use; but they generally view the C form they use for informal oral interaction as inferior to or a deformed form of MSA (Mubarak 1970: 41–44). Some Arab writers have an even harsher characterization of C as a "protégé of ignorance and imperialism" (Nasif 1957: 49) or as a form "unworthy of being called a language" (Hussein 1944: 236). These are certainly extreme views. On the other hand, most Arabs treat MSA with reverence and consider it beautiful and appropriate for literary expression and other modes of writing. Nonetheless, whatever their views of the relative "status" of C versus MSA might be, Arabic speakers perceive the two varieties as being two extremes on one language continuum.

Language Interaction

Situation	Formal	Familiar
Occasion	Public Private	Public Intimate
Setting	Nonlocal Local Nonlocal Local	Nonlocal Local Nonlocal Local

Language Continuum   MSA . . . . Colloquial

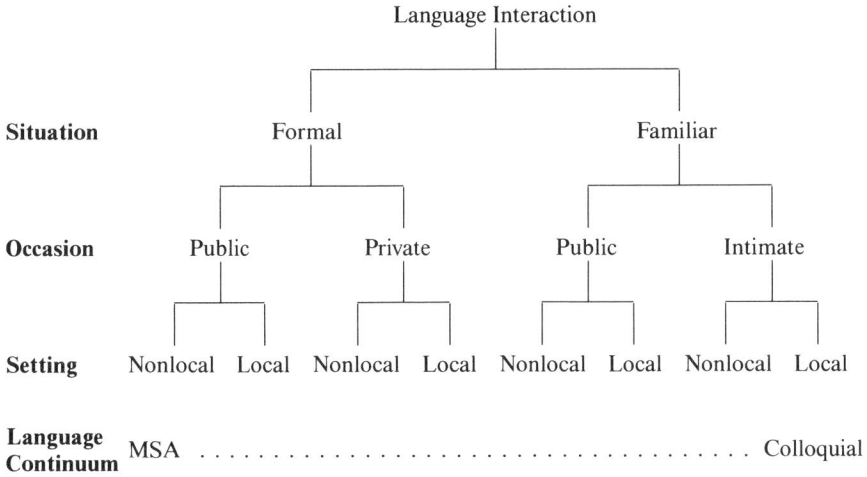

Figure 10-2. Model of the Arabic Language Continuum

Fourth, it appears that Ferguson assumes MSA to be a superposed, highly codified variety of Arabic. It is considered superposed mainly because Arabic speakers learn it through formal instruction, unlike C, which is acquired as a first language. Nevertheless, even many functionally illiterate Arabs have at least a minimal receptive mastery of MSA. Those who are literate have learned to read and write MSA at school, the same way as English speakers learn to write English (Wexler 1971: 335). Ferguson's model treats MSA as not being the native language of anyone in the speech community, which he considers distinctive of diglossia.[5]

Fifth, in Ferguson's model MSA and C are presented as if in complementary distribution, i.e., they are used for different purposes. As one can infer from the model of the Arabic language continuum presented in figure 10-2, however, this is the case only at the extremes of the continuum. More typically, a native speaker uses speech that has elements from both "norms," and that choice depends on many variables. Apart from the extreme situations, no single norm is exclusively used in a given situation, but rather both of them are in a state of dynamic interaction, where the contribution of each norm to oral discourse fluctuates constantly in response to the sociolinguistic variables of the context of the speech act.[6]

Arabic Instruction in the United States

Arabic instruction in the United States may be divided into categories on the basis of the purpose of instruction, the variety of Arabic used as the medium or subject of instruction, and the pedagogical methodology employed.

Classified according to the purpose of instruction, Arabic programs and approaches to teaching fall into two categories: general purpose Arabic programs

(GPA) and programs that teach Arabic for specific purposes (ASP). The first category, GPA, includes most university Arabic programs, since they train students in several language skills (reading, writing, listening, and speaking) and to do many things in and with the language (e.g., describe activities, express emotions and opinion, seek and provide information). Even those programs that teach students a single skill, for example, reading, can still be considered to focus on GPA, for what the language students learn is not restricted in any way. Genres, aims, and topics of the written discourse they read may vary considerably.

The other category includes Arabic programs that have narrow, well-defined goals. At the Foreign Service Institute or at a university involved in training professionals, for instance, the aim is clear-cut, and consequently the objectives, the curriculum, and the instructional materials are designed with that aim in mind. In the introduction to *Formal Spoken Arabic* (Ryding 1990), the author specifies the aim of the course as training Foreign Service officers in "communicative skills to serve them in a variety of posts in the Arab world." She even roughly describes the variety of Arabic that will be taught as one that is "colloquial enough not to sound pedantic and flexible enough to be of use throughout the Arab East" (p. xv). The goal implied in this statement is specific enough to allow program directors or pedagogues to formulate course objectives for an identifiable clientele, taking into account the actual needs of this particular group of learners. Once learner characteristics are described, the needs can be identified, and on this basis the curriculum can be designed, the instructional materials developed, and the methodology specified. Ryding's textbook is a good example of this process. All four elements (needs, design, materials, and methodology) are geared toward the main goal of the program, i.e., to accommodate the needs of foreign-service officers serving in the eastern part of the Arab world.

Al-Batal (forthcoming), lumping categories based on the variety of Arabic and on pedagogical methodology, identifies five approaches that have been used or are currently in use in the United States for teaching Arabic as a foreign language. He reviews them as summarized below, evaluating the worth of each one from a pedagogical perspective.

The Classical Arabic Approach[7]

This approach dates back to the late eighteenth century (McCarus 1987: 13) and is concerned mainly with classical and medieval texts. It uses the Grammar-Translation method of instruction; its objective is clearly to develop a single language skill, reading, which lies in the realm of MSA or Classical Arabic. Thus, given the objective of the classical approach, no diglossic problem arises.

The MSA Approach

The vast majority of Arabic programs in the United States and elsewhere today use MSA as the subject and / or (in some intensive and advanced programs) the medium of instruction. Teaching via the MSA approach flourished after the Second World War thanks to federal and other sources of support. Several textbooks were produced in the 1950s and 1960s, many of them showing little pedagogical expertise, and almost all of them grammar-based. A departure from this practice was *Elementary Modern Standard Arabic* (Abboud et al. 1983)—written in the 1960s—for which the authors enlisted the advice of a pedagogical specialist. On the other hand, given the fact that it was produced in the heyday of the audiolingual approach, it has many of that approach's characteristics and drawbacks.[8]

With the push toward communication and with the advent of the proficiency movement, there was a need for textbooks that presented the language from a functional viewpoint and gave precedence to meaning over form. Two textbooks were produced in the late 1980s and early 1990s with support from the U.S. Department of Education.[9] A second-year Arabic text is currently being developed, also with federal support.[10] These three most recent textbooks subscribe to a proficiency-oriented approach and emphasize promoting all four language skills, but they share the limitation of not dealing with the diglossic situation effectively.[11] Oral interaction in the classroom is done in MSA, not in C, even with topics and in contexts that would normally suggest or require the use of C.

The rationale for not incorporating a C component is threefold.

First, the MSA content of the course is presented not with the assumption that the student will have to use the same MSA items in communicative situations, but rather to help students develop strategies of oral communication. Having first developed the oral skill using MSA, such students can use it later as a springboard to acquire a specific dialect in the social context where the dialect is spoken.[12] Second, the use of MSA in an academic setting, such as a university classroom, is perfectly appropriate from the sociolinguistic point of view, though not appropriate for all topics that might come up within that classroom. Third, at advanced levels of instruction (Intermediate and beyond), students are expected to perform at higher levels of abstraction, which makes the use of MSA appropriate, both in speaking and reading.

The rationale for excluding a C component, however compelling, does not relieve Arabic programs from the responsibility of finding the means to deal with the subtleties of the Arabic diglossic situation. Much research and experimentation are needed to develop a curriculum design that can satisfy the needs of most Arabic programs as well as those of their students.

The Colloquial Approach

Government language schools and a handful of universities teach specific regional Arabic dialects. The textbooks used for instruction in these schools use transliteration instead of Arabic script, and teach no literacy skills. In view of many relatively recent developments in the field toward developing overall (four-skill) proficiency, these "C-only" programs are in a precarious situation. If the proficiency movement maintains its momentum and Arabic textbooks integrate a C component with the MSA material, "C-only" programs are bound to disappear.

Al-Batal provides two cogent arguments in this direction. First, he refers to a survey conducted by Belnap (1987), which has indicated that most students of Arabic are interested in developing overall proficiency. This implies that there is a clear need for including MSA in any course of instruction, at least for developing the literacy skills. Second, he concurs with Allen et al. (1987), who maintain that no colloquial program is likely to take learners beyond the Advanced level (i.e., ILR-3). Also, Allen et al. (1989), in the revised Arabic Proficiency Guidelines, state that proficiency in Arabic at the Advanced level requires knowledge of MSA and of at least one dialect.

The Middle Language Approach

At a number of government language schools and at the School of Advanced International Studies of Johns Hopkins University, Arabic instruction is based on an intermediate variety of the language called Educated Spoken Arabic (ESA). This variety has been identified and recognized by a number of Arabic scholars. The main characteristic of ESA, as the name indicates, is that it is used by educated speakers who mix MSA forms with C forms, using a mixture of C and MSA lexical, morphological, and syntactic elements. Two textbooks have already appeared that use ESA;[13] they represent an attempt to resolve the diglossia problem for learners of Arabic.

There are, however, drawbacks involved in basing instruction solely on ESA. As noted earlier, the language norms used along the continuum, including ESA (if it exists independently at all), are never static except at the two extremes. These norms change with conditions that obtain during a given speech event. At least one of the textbooks with which the present writer is familiar, however, presents the language as a static system, assuming that the conditions governing language use remain unchanged.[14] In order to make language use appropriate and lifelike, rules of use in addition to grammatical rules should be formulated and taught either directly or indirectly. In addition, al-Batal (forthcoming) believes that ESA is still a vaguely defined variety and should not be used as the basis of instruction. He also maintains that using ESA alone will not produce truly proficient speakers and writers.

The Simultaneous Approach

This approach represents another attempt to address the Arabic diglossic situation. It is used at two government language schools, the Foreign Service Institute and the Defense Language Institute. In this approach, instruction begins with an Arabic dialect and continues for a specific period of time, while MSA is incorporated gradually. The only criticism al-Batal has for this approach is that it is structurally based with little attention to context and situation.

Seeking Other Alternatives

The existing Arabic programs along with their curricula and methodologies seem clearly not to respond adequately to student needs, nor do they produce learners who have attained a level of overall proficiency in Arabic that reflects the characteristics of native speaker proficiency. In this section, two new curriculum designs aiming at closing the diglossic gap in Arabic instruction are described. Both proposals have more or less similar goals, but they differ in the approach and design used to attain these goals.

The Alternative Approach[15]

Al-Batal (forthcoming) proposes an orientation based on the "simultaneous approach" described above, which is intended to "cope with the diglossic problem in our classrooms and . . . at the same time help our efforts to make our programs truly proficiency-oriented." He proceeds to describe his alternative approach with a clear understanding of the linguistic situation, giving far less weight to the choice of the C variety to be used than to the appropriateness of language use and specialization of function (e.g., a hotel situation in which C is used to ask for a room and MSA is needed to fill out a registration form). The alternative approach deals with the diglossic situation in a manner consistent with the linguistic behavior of native speakers of Arabic. From the description of the approach, a number of general goals, specific objectives, and a methodology can be distinguished, although they are not operationalized enough to serve as a basis for an Arabic curriculum. The boundaries between goals and objectives seem to be obscure, perhaps due to the expository nature of the description and because the aims are not stated in a formal fashion. Below is a listing of goals/ objectives as they can be identified in the order in which they occur in al- Batal's paper:

1. Coping with the diglossic situation in the Arabic classroom
2. Making Arabic programs truly proficiency-oriented
3. Reflecting in the classroom the diglossic situation as it exists in the Arab world today
4. Introducing MSA as a variety that is mainly written, but also spoken in a multitude of situations
5. Introducing an Arabic dialect (i.e., C) as a variety that is used for everyday communication and also as a vehicle for some forms of literary expression
6. Introducing a third Arabic variety that is a mixture of MSA and C

7. Introducing situations in which different varieties are used
8. Introducing grammar as a complement to situations and functions
9. Offering authentic language
10. Providing a well-rounded program that fulfills most student needs

Implied also in the description is the goal of producing "learners who can function in the language the same way a native speaker does" by achieving "full proficiency" (al-Batal forthcoming). This is certainly a highly ambitious aim, one that cannot realistically be attained in the classroom setting; it constitutes one of the differences between this approach and the one proposed below. Another criticism is the way some goals are stated. Although they are worthy, some of them seem to have little relevance to the main components of a language curriculum (e.g., the processes of learning, teaching, evaluation, and assessment) nor to language (e.g., items 1, 2, 3, and 10 above). This criticism, however, does not detract from the overall importance of the approach as a move in the right direction, for these goals can be recast in a more precise form without changing the general orientation significantly. They simply need to be more operational and concrete. For instance, the role of grammar as a "complement to situations and functions" is vague, although concrete examples are provided. Perhaps it is more useful to specify whether grammatical complexity, for example, is controlled, or if there is any correspondence between the type of grammatical categories and the level of abstraction expected in the discourse of speakers at certain levels of proficiency.

Despite the reservations expressed here, it is easy, by looking at the goals proposed by al-Batal, to envision the general purpose of his alternative approach, which is to teach a form (or forms) of Arabic to the students in appropriate settings so that they can function reasonably well in various situations and at different levels of proficiency in a context where Arabic is spoken. This is exactly what most Arabic programs aspire to achieve.

The Integrated Approach

This approach is called integrated because it is based on a proficiency-oriented, functionally based (POFB) approach for the teaching of MSA as a foreign language (Alosh forthcoming b).[16] In brief, course materials based on the POFB approach are organized around language functions typical of the performance of speakers at particular levels of proficiency as described by the ACTFL Guidelines (1982). The materials seek to place these functions in appropriate contexts and to select relevant MSA items as exponents of these functions. The POFB approach is highly communicative and appears to have stimulated student interest. Nevertheless, the POFB approach suffers from a serious sociolinguistic limitation: the inability of learners to vary their speech within changing situations. To address this deficiency, the integrated approach has been developed. It draws heavily on the strengths of the original POFB approach and integrates with the MSA content a C component that is deemed to render the students' oral performance sociolinguistically more appropriate. Hence the designation "integrated."

The integrated approach is based on a number of assumptions, some of them not present in the parent POFB approach. These assumptions pertain to curriculum design, language acquisition, pedagogy, assessment of learning, and the language system. While the assumptions affect the design of the curriculum and, consequently, the way the content of the language course is selected and sequenced, the curriculum design indicates the interaction and interrelationships between the main components of the curriculum, including goals, objectives, evaluation, methodology, assessment, and outcomes. The following is a selective list of these assumptions:

Proficiency Is a Byproduct of Learning, Not a Direct Consequence of It.   In light of the distinction between proficiency and achievement in testing, this assumption is of critical importance to curriculum design. Lowe (1986) defines the nature of proficiency as "achievement *plus functional evidence* of internalized strategies for creativity" (p. 16, emphasis added). He stresses this distinction and warns that the confusion between the two "must be avoided at all costs" (p. 17). The best way to do this is to specify the curriculum goals in a way that avoids such confusion. Obviously, specification of goals requires understanding of the nature of both concepts. In short, proficiency signifies the ability to perform in the language in various situations, whereas achievement involves knowledge about a specific body of information to be learned.[17]

The Processes of Learning and Teaching Should Be Reflected by a Rigorous Methodology.   In order to develop in learners the ability to function in the language, a set of techniques should be described with reference to what we know today about learning styles and teaching techniques. Left to whim and experimentation, course materials that are designed supposedly according to proficiency principles might in fact be reduced to achievement-oriented materials.

Teaching Rules of Use Is as Crucial as Teaching Rules of Grammar.   Very early in instruction, students must be aware of when and how elements of C and MSA are used and how and why they alternate and vary. These rules of use range from the lower-level pronunciation rules that are used subconsciously to the higher-level rules that involve comprehension of discourse beyond the sentence level. They generally relate to sociolinguistic appropriateness of use. In Arabic diglossia, however, they also involve the ability to switch and mix codes appropriately.

A Foreign Language Course in an Academic Institution Should Not Be Designed with the Purpose of Turning Out Near-Native Speakers.   Research has shown that college foreign language majors who do not spend time in a country where the target language is spoken rarely exceed the ILR 2+ level.[18] In light of this fact, foreign language programs should set realistic and feasible goals pertinent to the desired levels of proficiency.[19]

The Classroom Is Not the Right Setting to Replicate the Process of First Language Acquisition.   This assumption raises the questions of whether the process of first language acquisition is replicable at all, and if so, whether the classroom is the right place for it. I believe neither can be answered in the affirmative. Many variables in both contexts, including the context of learning, cognitive maturity, and length of time, to name but a few, differ so significantly that the claim of resemblance between the two is rendered untenable. The native-speaker language development process in Arabic normally starts with acquiring C first and then learning MSA initially through exposure to it during the preschool period and later through formal instruction. In the academic setting, however, several considerations, including learner variables, program requirements, end goals, and assessment argue against teaching only C at first and then MSA.[20]

Grammatical Knowledge Is Not Equivalent Nor Transferrable to the Ability to Use the Language Functionally.   Much research has been devoted to the role and status of grammar in learning a foreign language, resulting in mixed or conflicting messages to the course designer and the teacher. Part of the problem stems from disagreement on a definition of *grammar.* It seems that there should be two distinct grammars: one that relates to a set of arbitrary, normative rules of correctness that describe the linguistic system and is taught formally and explicitly (usually in the native language of the learners), and another that represents the processes or abilities involved in using the system and in decoding and encoding meaning.[21] Many language programs are moving away from using syllabi based on the former type.[22]

The Level of Grammatical Complexity Should Be Commensurate with the Level of Abstraction Typical of a Particular Level of Proficiency.   This assumption conforms to the ACTFL Proficiency Guidelines, as it takes into account the level of abstraction in the linguistic output of speakers at particular levels. It helps course designers avoid introducing grammatical concepts at inappropriate levels. Unlike the grammar-based approach, where selection and sequencing of grammatical categories is usually done according to preconceived, arbitrary plans based on criteria such as complexity of structures and frequency of occurrence (with little attention to the learning process), selection of language content in an approach that takes this assumption into consideration would be based on what learners can do at particular levels of proficiency, as described in the ACTFL/ILR Guidelines (1982). These language abilities can then be translated into instances of the language, using functional, notional, and situational criteria.

The Concept of Authenticity Is Interpreted Not Only as Authenticity of Product, but Also as Authenticity of Process.   There is general agreement in the field that for instructional materials to be truly proficiency-oriented they must be authentic. In practice, particularly at the elementary level, insistence on using authentic materials may have caused more problems than it solved, despite innovative means to integrate and use them. The trouble again, as in the case of grammar, is a matter of definition. Generally, authenticity is interpreted as the language produced *by* native speakers *for* native speakers to achieve some communicative end. Obviously, this definition refers to the linguistic output, the product. Since the focus in a proficiency orientation is on the process, however, rather than the product, authenticity should be interpreted also in relation to function and to the communicative activity performed by the user. Widdowson (1983) reserves the term *authenticity* for this latter definition, and calls the former *genuine,* referring to "attested instances of the language" (p. 30). He maintains that using "genuine" materials does not guarantee "authentic" student performance in the form of appropriate language use.[23]

Arabic Language Varieties Should Not Be Taught as Discrete Systems. The Arabic diglossia model presented in figure 10-2 represents the perception of the native Arabic speaker of the diglossic situation. It suggests that all Arabic varieties, which are varying "mixtures" of MSA and C, operate on a continuum. This perception should be reflected in the design and implementation of Arabic materials that integrate MSA and C. Learners should understand from the beginning that the MSA and C forms they learn are not separate; rather, only the manner and the contexts in which they are used are different.

Learning a Colloquial Variety Is Limited to the Oral Skill Only. In keeping with the role and function of C, which is confined to everyday oral interaction, teaching this variety should also be restricted to the oral skill. Therefore, language training, practice, and assessment of the use of C should be conducted in the oral domain. Similarly, MSA should be used mainly for the literacy skills. (It may, however, be used orally in formal situations that call for its use.)

In an Arabic Program That Integrates MSA and C, Neither Language Variety Should Infringe on the Other. In other words, there should be a separation between the two forms based on specialization of function to preclude any conflict between the objectives specific to MSA (i.e., reading and writing) and those common to both (i.e., listening and speaking). The C component would serve a double purpose, to reinforce the oral skill and to enrich the Arabic learning process by providing a long-missing dimension. Nevertheless, classroom interaction in C should never take class time originally allotted for the literacy skills, which are in the realm of MSA. This is because the long-range purpose of most Arabic programs is to enable students to deal with written discourse effectively, both in a receptive and a productive manner. The oral part with a C component would complement the learners' overall proficiency and provide them with a sense of confidence derived from the ability to perform in the language with a certain amount of facility at most levels of proficiency, using all language skills.

Conclusion

To summarize, Arabic diglossia is perhaps not as intractable a problem for instruction in Arabic as a foreign language as it has traditionally been viewed to be. The situation should be approached from a sociolinguistic perspective that takes into account the linguistic performance of native speakers in situational contexts. What should be emphasized in an Arabic curriculum is not the distinctiveness of MSA and C, but rather their specialization of function and the rules of use that govern their use. The task of the learner of Arabic then becomes one of adjusting one's choice of the elements of phonology, lexicon, morphology, and syntax to the sociolinguistic context of the speech event than of making a binary choice, as it has been characterized elsewhere.

The most recent approaches to Arabic instruction, influenced by the proficiency movement, are taking into account the need to teach not only the linguistic elements (e.g., vocabulary and grammar), but also a sensitivity to the sociolinguistic contexts that native speakers use as determinants when selecting the "blend" of MSA and C to use in a given situation.

Notes

1. To nonnative learners of Arabic, MSA and C may seem to be two separate codes. Native speakers, however, perceive the two varieties as two levels of use on a single continuum.
2. Arabic is not unique in having a dichotomy between the spoken and written forms. Other examples include Swiss German, Chinese, Haitian Creole, and Greek, though the latter may be moving away from this situation.
3. The term *diglossia* is but one term of several that refer to a similar linguistic situation. Other terms include *koiné, lingua franca, trade jargon, Habsprachen, patois,* and even *multilingualism.*
4. In fact, MSA is gaining in prestige and in opportunity for oral use. Many television and radio programs that used to be in the domain of C are now produced in MSA. The Arabic adaptation of "Sesame Street" is a case in point (Alosh 1984). It scored considerable success in the Arab world, triggering an influx of programs, both for children and adults, that are produced in MSA.
5. Furthermore, MSA has a codified grammar that is more complex than that of C. Perhaps codification is one of the major factors that have perpetuated the diglossic situation by preserving the morphological and syntactic purity of the standard form, while C forms, which are more receptive to influence from foreign languages and other Arabic dialects, have continued to evolve and change.
6. It should be noted, however, that linguists have posited a number of intermediate varieties of Arabic with distinct characteristics that have emerged as a result of the spread of education. Some of these intermediate varieties of Arabic include Educated Spoken Arabic (Ferguson 1959; Blanc 1960; El-Hassan 1977; Mitchell 1978) and Oral Literary Arabic (Meiseles 1980). Both of these varieties are based on a modified C morphology and syntax and exhibit heavy lexical borrowing from MSA.
7. Classical Arabic is the language of ancient and medieval texts, including pre-Islamic poetry, the Qurʔan (the holy book of Muslims), and a vast body of Islamic literary, intellectual, and scientific writing. Classical Arabic shares with MSA the same syntax and morphology and a substantial part of the lexicon. Like MSA, it enjoys considerable prestige.
8. A review of *Elementary Modern Standard Arabic* is found in Alosh 1987.
9. These are *Let's Learn Arabic* by Allen and Allouche (1986), and *Ahlan wa Sahlan* by Alosh (1990).
10. *Our Living Language* by Alosh (1991).
11. An attempt to incorporate a colloquial component in the first course of *Ahlan wa Sahlan* is currently under way at The Ohio State University. The purpose of this effort is to investigate ways and means to equip students early on with the skill of switching between or mixing the C and MSA codes appropriately. If the endeavor is successful, the claim made by these materials to a proficiency orientation would become more credible.

12. The classroom is not seen as an effective environment in which to produce proficient speakers. It is generally accepted that students who wish to acquire Arabic language skills similar to those possessed by an educated native speaker must travel to the target country.

13. See Haddad and Haddad 1984 and Ryding 1990.

14. See a review of Ryding's *Formal Spoken Arabic* in Alosh (forthcoming a).

15. The term *alternative* is not clearly defined. It may be interpreted as meaning that this approach is an alternative to the previous approaches that it is trying to replace. It may also be interpreted as referring to the sequence of presenting the language, where the two varieties alternate in particular situations (Batal forthcoming).

16. This proficiency-oriented approach was developed and implemented by the present writer at The Ohio State University in 1987–88. Instructional materials based on this approach were developed for first-year Arabic under a grant from the U.S. Department of Education. Second-year materials are currently under development through another grant from the same source. The materials are still under evaluation.

17. Any approach that claims a proficiency orientation must have goals that reflect this distinction. The goals cannot be specified in terms of lexical items and grammatical categories to be covered during a course of study, as is done in many textbooks, for these items and the grammatical categories would constitute the bulk of the language material the student is expected to learn, or achieve, by the end of the course. (This is, in fact, a fundamental contradiction with the concept of proficiency.) Rather, goals should be specified as categories of functional abilities to be developed by learners for use during instruction and after it ends. Widdowson (1984) classifies curriculum designs into two categories, product-oriented and process-oriented (p. 178). The latter design has close affinity with the proficiency orientation. He maintains that the aim of instruction is to "develop a capacity to learn" and to provide the learner with the potential for the realization of what has been learned during a course of study (p. 182).

18. See Carroll (1967) and Higgs and Clifford (1982) for a more detailed discussion of this phenomenon.

19. This assumption touches on the question of how much language training is acceptable in an academic setting. Clearly, in foreign language courses, in addition to the long-range educational aim, there is always a measure of language training, normally heavy at the elementary level. A good program strikes a balance between the two, providing the learners with the skills and the ability to use the language, and gradually steering them in the direction of their various disciplines.

20. Most college-level programs are not designed primarily for language training, but rather for language, literature, and other disciplines. Thus, learning Arabic is regarded from this perspective as a means to an end, the end most often being the ability to read and comprehend a literary text. There is, however, a problem with this view, having to do with the ends of instruction. As Widdowson argues, a goal-oriented curriculum is "related to terminal behavior, the ends of learning" (1984: 178). In this orientation, it is the goals that determine the curriculum design (i.e., the content), requiring specifications that match the desired ends. These may be lexical and grammatical items to be mastered by the end of the course. In a curriculum of this sort, attention is directed toward achieving a level of mastery of the content, whereas a process-oriented curriculum is based on an understanding of how people learn and on a description of the learning process (Widdowson 1984: 183). Widdowson maintains that this conception of curriculum design will require taking methodological means into account (p. 83). Needless to say, a proficiency orientation would require the use of a process-oriented curriculum.

21. For a more detailed discussion, see Alosh (forthcoming b).

22. Higgs (1985) recognizes both types and rejects using the explicit grammar in favor of the one that converts "meaning into language" (p. 289). The latter type of grammar is implicit and is acquired by learners in an idiosyncratic manner through performing

well-designed language activities and tasks. It befits the proficiency orientation better than the explicit type, since it develops in learners the ability to use the language and promotes the process of learning, while the other one provides the learners with a body of knowledge to be learned as an abstract subject.

23. This does not mean, however, that "genuine" instances of the language should be avoided or relegated to a secondary position. Rather, they should be incorporated whenever they are called for to promote language use, for there are certain lower-level habitual skills, such as the ability to discriminate and distinguish elements of the phonology and the script of the language, which need attention, but do not relate to authenticity.

References, Arabic Diglossia and Its Impact on Teaching Arabic

Abboud, Peter, et al. 1983. *Elementary Modern Standard Arabic.* New York: Cambridge Univ. Press.

ACTFL. 1982. *Provisional Proficiency Guidelines.* Hastings-on-Hudson, NY: American Council on the Teaching of Foreign Languages.

Allen, Roger, and Adel Allouche. 1986. *Let's Learn Arabic: A Proficiency Based Syllabus for Modern Standard Arabic.* (Unpublished manuscript).

————, et al. 1987. "The Arabic Guidelines: Where Now?" pp. 168–76 in Charles Stansfield and Chip Harman, eds., *ACTFL Proficiency Guidelines for the Less Commonly Taught Languages.* Washington, DC: The Center for Applied Linguistics and the American Council on the Teaching of Foreign Languages.

————, et al. 1989. "Arabic ACTFL Proficiency Guidelines." *Foreign Language Annals* 22: 313–29.

Alosh, Mahdi. 1984. "Implications of the Use of Modern Standard Arabic in the Arabic Adaptation of 'Sesame Street.'" Unpublished master's thesis, Ohio University, Athens, Ohio.

————. 1987. Review of *Elementary Modern Standard Arabic* by P. Abboud et al. *Modern Language Journal* 71,4: 440–42

————. 1990. *Ahlan wa Sahlan,* Parts I–III. Columbus, OH: Ohio State Univ. Foreign Language Publications.

————. 1991a. *Lughatuna al-Hayya (Our Living Language).* Columbus, OH: Ohio State Univ. Foreign Language Publications.

————. Forthcoming a. Review of *Formal Spoken Arabic* by Karin C. Ryding. *Al-ᶜArabiyya* 24.

————. Forthcoming b. "Designing a Proficiency-Oriented Syllabus for Modern Standard Arabic as a Foreign Language," in Aliya Rouchdy, ed., *The Arabic Language in the U.S.* Detroit: Wayne State Univ. Press.

Al-Batal, Mahmoud. Forthcoming. "Diglossia, Proficiency, and the Teaching of Arabic in the U.S.: The Need for an Alternative Approach," in Aliya Rouchdy, ed., *The Arabic Language in the U.S.* Detroit: Wayne State Univ. Press.

Belnap, R. Kirk. 1987. "Who's Taking Arabic and What on Earth for? A Survey of Students in Arabic Language Programs." *Al-ᶜArabiyya* 20: 29–42.

Blanc, Haim. 1960. "Stylistic Variation in Spoken Arabic: A Sample of Interdialectal Educated Conversation," in Charles Ferguson, ed., *Contributions to Arabic Linguistics.* Cambridge, MA: Harvard Univ. Press.

Carroll, John B. 1967. *The Foreign Language Attainment of Language Majors in the Senior Year: A Survey Conducted in U.S. Colleges and Universities.* Cambridge, MA: Graduate School of Education, Harvard University.

Ferguson, Charles A. 1959. "Diglossia." *Word* 15: 325–40.

Haddad, Soraya, and Ayed Haddad. 1984. *Formal Spoken Arabic.* Self-published. (Authors can be contacted at The Johns Hopkins University, 1740 Massachusetts Ave. NW, Washington, DC 20036.)

El-Hassan, S. A. 1977. "Educated Spoken Arabic in Egypt and the Levant: A Critical Review of Diglossia and Related Matters." *Archivum Linguisticum* 8: 112–32.

Higgs, Theodore V. 1985. "Teaching Grammar for Proficiency." *Foreign Language Annals* 18: 289–96.

————, and Ray Clifford. 1982. "The Push toward Communication," pp. 57–79 in Theodore V. Higgs, ed., *Curriculum, Competence, and the Foreign Language Teacher.* ACTFL Foreign Language Education Series, vol. 13. Lincolnwood, IL: National Textbook Company.

Hussein, Taha. 1944. *Mustaqbalu al-Thaqafati fi Misr.* Cairo, Egypt.

Johnson, Keith. 1982. *Communicative Syllabus Design and Methodology.* Oxford, Eng.: Pergamon.

Kaye, Alan S. 1970. "Modern Standard Arabic and the Colloquials." *Lingua* 24: 374–91.

Lowe, Pardee, Jr. 1986. "The ILR Proficiency Scale as a Synthesizing Research Principle: The View from the Mountain," pp. 9–53 in C. J. James, ed., *Foreign Language Proficiency in the Classroom and Beyond.* ACTFL Foreign Language Education Series, vol. 16. Lincolnwood, IL: National Textbook Company.

McCarus, Ernest. 1987. "The Study of Arabic in the United States: A History of Its Development." *Al-ᶜArabiyya* 20: 13–28.

Meiseles, Gustav. 1980. "Educated Spoken Arabic and the Language Continuum." *Archivum Linguisticum* 11: 118–48.

Mitchell, T. F. 1978. "Dimensions of Style in a Grammar of Educated Spoken Arabic." *Archivum Linguisticum* 9:89–105.

Mubarak, Mazen. 1970. *Nahwa Waᶜyin Lughawiyy (Toward Linguistic Awareness).* Damascus, Syria.

Nasif, Ali. 1957. *Min Qadaya al-Lugati wa al-Nahuw (Issues in Language and Syntax).* Cairo, Egypt.

Ryding, Karin C. 1990. *Formal Spoken Arabic: Basic Course.* Washington, DC: Georgetown Univ. Press.

Wexler, Paul. 1971. "Diglossia, Language Standardization and Purism." *Lingua* 27: 330–54.

Widdowson, Henry G. 1983. *Learning Purpose and Language Use.* Oxford, Eng.: Oxford Univ. Press.

————. 1984. *Explorations in Applied Linguistics 2.* Oxford, Eng.: Oxford Univ. Press.

Zughoul, Muhammad Raji. 1980. "Diglossia in Arabic: Investigating Solutions." *Anthropological Linguistics* 22,5: 201–17.

11

Literature in the Foreign Language: A Comparative Study

Judith A. Muyskens
University of Cincinnati
with John Cassini
Université d'Angers

Introduction: Literature in Society

Literature is part of our everyday lives to varying degrees, depending on our culture and educational background.[1] Some of us may encounter literature almost daily in the form of poetry, history, short stories, novels, essays, and diaries; others have little contact with any type of literary work. Many social stereotypes exist about literature, such as what literature one should read to reflect one's educational background or social standing. That a National Football League coach enjoys reading books that don't contain pictures, for instance, is newsworthy in the United States (Berkow 1991). By contrast, perhaps because of their concepts of status, many teachers may claim to do only "serious" reading. Recently, for example, the Library Guild at the University of Cincinnati asked faculty and employees to name their favorite book for a display in the library. No one mentioned the works of Robert Ludlum or Jacqueline Suzanne. Instead,

Judith A. Muyskens (Ph.D., The Ohio State University) is Associate Professor of French at the University of Cincinnati, where she chairs the Department of Romance Languages and Literatures and the Faculty Board of the Charles Phelps Taft Memorial Fund. She supervises teaching assistants in French and team-teaches a methodology course for them. She has published in the areas of teacher education, French civilization, and teaching foreign literatures and has coauthored several college French textbooks.

John Cassini (*doctorat de troisième cycle,* Paris III) has been *maître des conférences* at the Université d'Angers since 1989, where he teaches American studies, especially courses on the history of political science and American literature. Previously he taught English as a second language at the École nationale supérieure des arts et métiers in Angers and was an adjunct instructor at the Université d'Angers. He has presented teaching seminars in Africa and Madagascar for the U.S. Embassy. In the United States he taught French for twelve years at the secondary and university levels in Cincinnati before receiving a Fulbright Teaching Fellowship in 1981 to teach English in France.

books by Thoreau, Faulkner, and Webster's *New World Dictionary of American English* were among those named (Prendergast 1991). Clearly, one's attitude toward literature conveys something about his or her social class, education, interests, and values.

In a broader sense, literature reflects the culture and the language of a society. The Chinese, for example, value literature in a different way than Americans do. According to Erbaugh (1990), the largest body of writing in China is history; novels and short stories are considered as virtual small talk, while poetry is the most revered genre (p. 17–18). In many Latin American countries as well, poetry is the most valued genre. In the United States, on the other hand, relatively little poetry is read. Changes in society in the Arab countries have brought the various genres of fiction to the forefront in recent years, whereas poetry had previously been the predominant form of literary expression (Allen 1991a and b). In France, Bernard Pivot's television program "Apostrophes," during which he interviewed contemporary authors, was extremely popular for fifteen years, indicating to some degree the important role of literature for the French, or at least for some French. (It is probably safe to say that a program of this nature in the United States would not run for very long.) The average Russian quotes from Russian literary classics in daily conversation, knowing that others will understand (Silbajoris 1991). Although it is difficult to generalize about the importance of literature in the daily lives of a people, it is clear that to truly understand a people, one needs to know something of its view of literature.

To define literature is even more complex, if not impossible. The answer will be sociological, defined by "the disposition adopted by the reader toward the text" (Carter 1986: 124). Therefore, when using literature in a foreign language classroom, we are preparing students for an experience that is not only linguistic, but also cultural. Through reading literary works in a foreign language, the reader learns "the problems, goals, dreams and values of another people as expressed through time and in another language" (Mead 1980: 537). Reading literature, especially in a foreign language, cannot be an isolated activity, but rather one to be viewed in relation to the general cognitive development of the student. "For many, the study of foreign language literatures and cultures is vital to the liberal arts or humanities curriculum, developing critical thinking skills and leading to an understanding of other peoples otherwise unknowable" (Barnett 1989: 150). The ability to read and understand literature in a foreign language is a powerful tool for the enhancement of our students' lives. Reading literature in a foreign language reveals aspects of language, culture, history, and literary convention that are otherwise inaccessible. As Walker (1991b) puts it, literature studies in the foreign language (Lit2 studies) are multicultural: Few fields of study can provide students with so much.

This article will examine a variety of goals and debates surrounding foreign language literature study in a variety of languages. It will attempt to combine a discussion of literary study with language study and pedagogy. In so doing the authors will: (1) review current research on what it means to read a literary text and discuss the various factors that come together in reading literature in a foreign language—language, culture, and history; (2) investigate the curricular arguments for inclusion (or exclusion) of literature, comparing several languages; and (3) provide an overview of current methodological trends for teaching literature and proposals for the training of literature teachers.

Current Research Issues

Definition of Reading Comprehension

During the last five years, several books and numerous articles have appeared on reading comprehension.[2] It is not the purpose of this article to focus on reading comprehension, but it is important to discuss briefly the difficulties that foreign language readers encounter when reading.

Reading has been defined as "the joint construction of a social reality between the reader and the text" (Kramsch 1985: 357). According to Swaffar (1991), studies have shown that (1) regardless of the language level of the learner, "more successful learning outcomes result when assessment measures of reading and writing acknowledge the learners' metacognitive processes" and (2) "regardless of learners' language level—prior knowledge impacts heavily on how well a text is comprehended or presented in a student composition" (p. 253). Therefore, if a text capitalizes on what the students know, thus drawing on familiar schemata, they can understand a text more easily because they also have time to focus on the challenge of the unfamiliar language (Swaffar 1991: 255). Readers must return to their own experience; they must make inferences or predictions based on past experience, which Carrell (1987) calls top-down processing. She says that the reader then checks "the text for confirmation or refutation of those predictions" (p. 147). She defines bottom-up processing as "decoding individual linguistic units" such as the phonemes and graphemes and then revising "preexisting background knowledge and current predictions on the basis of information encountered in the text" (p. 147). Good readers constantly shift their mode of processing and do not overuse either type of processing. Carrell proposes an interactive approach to reading by focusing on building new background knowledge and activating preexisting background knowledge (pp. 153–63). She emphasizes, as have other scholars, that reading is an active process and that many of the techniques proposed for preparing to read expository works are appropriate for the literary text.[3]

From Expository Reading to Literature

Schulz (1981) notes that reading comprehension is at "the base of literary reception and appreciation," which, she continues, we often forget (p. 43). We cannot expect students to take the giant step to literature easily if most of their prior reading has been centered on expository texts read for information (Swaffar et al. 1991: 213; Brumfit and Carter 1986b). (This giant step is, in fact, a major leap for students of Arabic, Asian, and Slavic languages, as we shall see below.) Like expository texts, "light" literature such as a detective or romance novel follows set patterns (Swaffar et al. 1991: 213), while "high-level literature" in the native or foreign language subjects the reader to different perspectives and language; the latter texts contain highly abstract vocabulary, complex syntax, and sophisticated content and style (Schulz 1981: 43). Lit2 studies, then, are extremely complex and demand much from the reader and the instructor. We hypothesize that the greatest difficulties result from native language–target language differences in (1) language and vocabulary, (2) culture, and (3) literary tradition.

Language and Vocabulary.   When asked about the difficulties they encounter in reading literature, students will often complain, first of all, about the vocabulary and idiomatic expressions. They mention the necessity of looking up a great number of unfamiliar words. They search for many words but still have only a vague notion of the literary work. They often refer to the language as "fancy" or archaic.[4] Students have not developed what Culler calls the "grammar of literature," which permits them to change "linguistic sequences into literary structures and meanings" (Jonathan Culler, quoted in Brumfit 1986: 185). Often the basic grammar of the foreign language is still confusing to them, especially in the less commonly taught languages (LCTs) such as Arabic, Chinese, Japanese, and Russian. These students need many more hours of training to develop their reading comprehension (Omaggio 1986: 21; Walker 1991a: 138–39).

An additional issue is that the metalanguage of the classroom discussion of literature is abstract, causing students to miss shades of meaning because they do not have much sense of the technical or figurative expressions of the text. Carrell (1987: 151) and Brumfit and Carter (1986b: 20) point out that to impart knowledge of even a single word is not easy. It may mean teaching a whole new concept because of the "social and cultural associations it can convey" (Brumfit and Carter 1986b: 20).[5] This is especially true of those literatures from societies that are very different from that of the reader.

Cultural Connotations.   Because many of the cultural allusions in a literary text may be totally unfamiliar to students, they can easily misinterpret ideas or characters as they quite naturally draw upon their own background to interpret the target culture. One could argue that the more different the culture, the more difficulty the student will have. Walker (1991a: 135) argues that for students studying cultures of noncognate languages (not related to the Western languages with a family relationship to English), the ability to function in the target culture must necessarily develop over a very long period of time. If, as instructors, we teach general notions about culture, we are in danger of causing our students to overgeneralize (Short and Candlin 1986). Short and Candlin believe that knowledge of the "particular social situation and the particular participants involved" is important because this knowledge reflects the context of events (p. 90). These small-scale social facts need to be understood to avoid misunderstanding. To teach the relevant cultural details needed to make a literary work available and understandable helps instructors choose specific goals for their task. As Swaffar et al. (1991) propose, "an individual who is culturally literate must be capable of reading not only the surface structures and signs of a culture, but also the underlying configurations of meanings from which those surface structures emanate" (p. 216). This implies that Carrell's notion of top-down processing must proceed in a different way when reading in a foreign language than when reading in the native language so that the schematizing can be successful. As teachers we must be prepared to teach our students about different cultural backgrounds if we would have them interact with the text the way a native reader would. Students must read in great quantity and with much frequency to build up a frame of cultural reference. As the literary experience increases, the resources of the individual expand (Brumfit and Carter 1986c: 233), unless, of course, the reader becomes constrained by the literary tradition that instructors often propose (Walker 1991a).

The advanced reader in a foreign language needs to be aware also that texts are configured in the logical thought patterns of different ethnic groups (Kaplan 1987: 9). "Because language, cultural artifacts, and institutions all reflect systems of thought, to become culturally literate L2 students need to be taught to identify and analyze these systems" (Swaffar et al. 1991: 232). For example, Erbaugh (1990) points out that the Chinese find that Americans' thought patterns are like a spiral turning on itself; Chinese students, therefore, have difficulty reading literature in English. Some cultures think in a more linear manner. According to Bernhardt (1991) "If readers can follow an author's structure, their comprehension scores increase" (p. 235). It is therefore important that instructors explore the discourse or rhetorical form of the piece under study with the students before they read a literary passage. Walker (1991a) points out that interpretation of thought patterns is grounded in one's own interpretation, which is culturally biased. But Swaffar et al. (1991) emphasize that educated people can analyze the thought systems of the target culture. This gives them the ability to "interact with, rather than simply react to, cultural messages implied by the written work" (p. 232). The difficulty remains, however, that to achieve this level of understanding may take many years when studying certain languages.

Literary History.   Students must also be taught the constructs of a literary period. This can be done in text-previewing activities during which the genre can be presented together with the historical material and key concepts (Carrell 1987: 155). Artistic categories also need to be taught, because literary concepts vary widely from one culture to another and from one country to another. This implies teaching not only the genre, but also the important social and cultural movements and how they differ from country to country (e.g., romanticism in Germany and France). Students have difficulty "interpreting and understanding the symbolic nature of a literary text and its cultural, social, and historical dimensions"(Kramsch 1985: 357). It is, therefore, the instructor's duty to prepare students for these differences and to place the text in its historical context. By having students compare and contrast literary works, instructors can help students to become more aware of the literary movements. By assigning works that share certain features, the point can be made that literary trends are real.

Definition of the Skilled Reader of Literature

Experienced and skilled readers—i.e. those with literary competence, who read accurately (with careful reading of a text, controlling misunderstanding) and with fluency (rapid and relaxed application of their abilities)—recognize the conventions invoked by the author (Brumfit and Carter 1986c: 235). Such readers are able to interpret these conventions in relation to the world of the writer's experience because they are aware that literature imitates and comments on the writer's world. Furthermore, good readers of literature can generalize from the text to their own lives or to other literary works. In other words, they go beyond the text to interpretation and evaluation. Criteria must be developed to determine what a skilled reader of literature is. Studies must be performed to understand more thoroughly what it means to read and interpret a work of literature. At the present time, instructors seem to have shared goals about what it means to be proficient in a language; there is little agreement, however, about what it means to have literary competence.

Research Needs

Most of the work on teaching literature in the foreign language classroom is experiential and theoretical (Muyskens 1983: 420).[6] Bernhardt (1991) points out that when "L2 researchers begin to use cleaner, more viable research methodologies, procedures, and analytic techniques," instructors will have a better understanding of reading in a foreign language (p. 236). The same is true for Lit2 study. Barnett (1989) suggests several ways to analyze the processes of the reader, mentioning the use of think-aloud or recall protocols (p. 154). Criticism of these protocols has arisen lately, however, because students often report the use of one technique when, upon questioning, they reveal that they were applying a very different process (Bacon 1990). To date, researchers can only hypothesize that it is the difficulty in language and vocabulary, difference in cultural background, and lack of knowledge of the literary tradition that pose the greatest obstacles in understanding a foreign literature. Research will also clarify possible techniques for teaching literature and will help instructors develop curricula in an appropriate way for school and college learners of foreign languages.

Current Curricular Issues

When to Introduce Literature

The difficulties that students have in reading literature cause many scholars to debate at what point in the curriculum literature should be introduced, or if it should hold a privileged place at all. Because the road to literary and cultural competence is long, most scholars believe that students should start down the path as early as possible (Herr 1982). In Arabic and Russian, educators are also beginning to present literature earlier in the curriculum. At the University of Pennsylvania, for example, students read a short story in Arabic shortly after beginning the second semester (Allen 1991a and b). In Russian at The Ohio State University, it is in the second semester of the second year that students begin to read abbreviated, simplified versions of short stories or novels (Silbajoris 1991). In France, students of English read excerpts of literature during the last two years of the *lycée*.

An increasing number of educators are contending that the language skills should not be separated from one another. Literature has often been disengaged from writing and from culture (Swaffar et al. 1991: 231) when, in fact, literature demonstrates writing styles and cultural concepts. Short and Candlin (1986) point out that from the viewpoint of the student, literature is also language (p. 91). In our daily lives, we treat literature as language. Literary study should, therefore, be an integral part of the curriculum from the beginning used to bridge the gap between language and literature classes and the high school and college curricula (Castañeda 1978; Olds 1984; Steiner 1972). Brumfit (1986) contends that literature provides a "convenient source of content" for foreign language courses and asserts that literature plays an important role in the notional syllabus, which is constructed around concepts that develop in complexity (p. 184). Literature should be an integral part of the movement toward the total proficiency of the student.

Other writers believe that because of the complexity of reading literature, its study should wait. Indeed, in the Asian and Slavic languages, study of authentic literary texts is often postponed until the third year of college (Silbajoris 1991; Noble 1991). For Chinese especially, where the spoken language is so very different from the written language, students read spoken texts first. In 1968 Esler and Bolinger published separate articles regarding the difficulties of studying literature. They both implied that students should possess sophisticated reading skills before being introduced to literature. More recently, Brumfit and Carter (1986b) acknowledge that for true literary response, one's reading fluency must be quite well developed (p. 29). It might be naive, in fact, for instructors to assume that students can really be responding to a text using true literary discourse before graduate school. Most scholars believe, however, that literature must be introduced from the beginning of instruction, at least in the Western languages, in order to provide students with the enjoyment and the opportunity to begin early the development of their Lit2 skills. Brumfit and Carter (1986b) contend that if possible, literature should be read "in regular conjunction with other discourse types" (p. 13).

What Type of Literature to Read

Scholars recognize that if texts that are accessible to the students are chosen, literary competence can be slowly, yet surely, developed. Just as works of literature are witness to the values of a culture, the texts that we as instructors choose bear witness to our values. Will we choose texts that are part of the canon of the literature we are teaching? At the beginning, it might be difficult. Authors suggest, in fact, presenting personal narratives before other literature. Vincent (1986) argues for "extensive use of simple texts in the early stages of developing reading skills." She favors simple accounts rather than simplified versions of famous literature (p. 213). At the intermediate level she includes lighter works of fiction from the various series of graded readers to be read rapidly on the students' own time along with a couple of abridged classics. She prefers choosing simple, authentic texts from early on, as do many other scholars as well (Swaffar 1985; McKay 1986): These scholars hold that text simplification in literature may have the same results as in expository texts, destroying cohesion and readability (McKay 1986: 193). A broad range of simple texts and a richer use of language within them may well be a better bridge to works of literature than altered and simplified texts.

In general, scholars acknowledge that if relevant and enjoyable texts are chosen that are within the range of the students' language competence, literature reading will be a motivating experience (Littlewood 1986: 181). He believes that linguistic structures are the gateway to comprehension, stressing that students who cannot understand a text find reading purposeless. Schulz (1981) reviews several methods for objectively gauging readability. Not everyone agrees, however, that readability counts can apply to literary works, because they give "no indication of the complexity of the text in terms of plot, character, or cultural difficulty" (McKay 1986: 194). Skilled instructors who know the backgrounds of their students are often subjectively able to predict the difficulty of a text. The subject matter should be "relevant to the life experiences, emotions, or dreams of the learner" (Collie and Slater 1987: 6). Furthermore, students should have adequate knowledge of the cultural background or instructors should be able to provide it for that specific work. In addition, length is a crucial matter, as can be the status or face validity of the reading. Since interest level is a prime motivator, it is most important to avoid books that the students dislike. If readers do not understand the language or if they misunderstand the conventions or cultural references being used, they will not be interested in reading a book and will not move toward literary competence (Brumfit and Carter 1986b: 16).

Excerpts.   Excerpts from literature are often used in foreign language teaching. Cook (1986) contends that by extracting two or three crucial pages from the middle of a work of literature, instructors are downgrading the superiority of style that they often wish to demonstrate. He points out how literary discourse may "both lose meaning and acquire false meaning when extracted from the full text to which it belongs" (p. 151). If extracts are to be used, he offers several criteria, including the following: Extracts or excerpts chosen should not cause the student to "create false texture by making interpretations"; they should be introductory rather than "continuing or conclusive" (p. 164). One advantage of using excerpts is, of course, the variety of literary styles and vocabulary that students read, which helps to avoid monotony. The satisfaction of reading a whole work of literature, however, is lost. Storme and Siskin (1989) and Collie and Slater (1987) suggest series of extracts when students cannot complete an entire literary work. These extracts should "convey a sense of continuity" in order to gain involvement from the student and the same challenge that reading an entire work can give (Storme and Siskin 1989: 28). In reality, much of literature teaching at the beginning and intermediate levels is approached with extracts. In France, students read many excerpts of English literature until the last year of *lycée* and often until college.

The use of excerpts is especially suited to the Arabic, Asian, and Slavic languages where, because of lexical complexity, the texts can be exceedingly difficult for students. In these curricula students often read excerpts until the third or fourth year of college study.

Poetry.   Some professors of literature believe that some specific genres are more approachable than others. Simple poetry, for example, has been suggested as an effective way to introduce the students to literature because of its suitability to a single class period (Collie and Slater 1987: 227). Poems are often used in the first years of language instruction. Perusal of the literature reveals that some articles have focused on the writing of poetry (Rochette-Ozello 1978; Brod 1983; De Méo 1983); others discuss the study of poetry (Santoni 1979; Creed 1978; Federici 1989; Labonté 1980). Labonté points out the variety that can be found in the study of poetry: *"On peut les écouter, les lire, les mémoriser et les réciter; on peut en parler et surtout les analyser, oralement ou par écrit. On peut aussi partir d'un poème pour écrire un autre texte."* (One can listen to them, read them, memorize and recite them; one can talk about them and especially analyze them orally or in writing. One can also use the poem as a model to write another text.) (Labonté 1980: 686). The videotape shown by Kramsch and Mueller at ACTFL 1989 in Boston during their session entitled "Celebrating, Creating, Understanding Poetry in the Language Classroom" further demonstrates the flexibility of poetry: The viewers saw poems being previewed, students reciting their own poetry, and poetry being taught using a variety of methodologies. Provided that students have the linguistic and cultural background to read a poem, the excitement of reading and reacting to poetry is genuine in any language and at any point in the study of the foreign language.

Drama.   The dramatic quality of the play is an important element for bringing literature alive for the student. Purcell (1988) believes that the genre of drama can hold students' interest through scene changes, character development, action, and the spoken language. Several instructors describe drama production and literature in action courses that build enthusiasm and improve students' fluency through playacting (Tilles 1972; Hunting 1976; Brown 1977). At the graduate level in the Western languages, students can be given part of their final grade in theater classes based on their interpretation and production of a play (O'Connor 1991).

Another positive feature of drama is that the conversational level of the speech may make the reading more understandable. Furthermore, the availability of plays recorded on audio and videotape makes them useful for listening practice and previewing before reading (Collie and Slater 1987: 163). In France, one of the authors asks native speakers of English to present dramatic readings of the play so that his French students can become aware of the subtleties of the spoken word. This helps them read between the lines to draw inferences that may escape them in reading silently.

The use of plays presents different challenges in different languages. In Arabic, for example, the use of drama encounters problems because the spoken language is not considered literary. In addition, governmental censorship has limited the availability of drama (Allen 1991a and b). In Chinese, Walker (1991a) mentions that films based on short stories or novels are a useful way to approach literature. At the present time, narratives of such films are being transcribed and published as they are spoken. These professionally transcribed texts can be studied before the original literary work.

Short Stories.   Short stories are an excellent means to introduce literature to students. Although they are out of the mainstream of the U.S. literary landscape at the present time (Carmody 1991), they have the advantage of brevity, which allows for reading and rereading (Collie and Slater 1987: 196). Because they are short, they can be presented and exploited fully (Leal 1972; Anastos 1981). The novel, on the other hand, is often too long for students who are not advanced undergraduate or graduate students. Only when students are able to understand the underlying themes and can make contact with a work on a deeper level are they ready to study novels. This allows them to go beyond the work to begin understanding a work's place in literary history or the intellectual movements of its time. Dietz (1972) suggests requiring students to keep a diary outlining their experience with the novel. This practice can help them focus on their personal experiences while beginning to understand what Littlewood (1986) describes as the "vision of life or of human nature" that literature embodies (p. 182).

Culture.   Literature is often included in the curriculum as a means to study culture. Several writers have suggested the use of Black francophone and hispanophone literature to acquaint students with traits of other ethnic cultures. Several such programs have been described in the literature (Bostick 1972; Elliott 1977; Brière 1982; Clark 1980). More recently, calls for the use of ethnic literatures in elementary college course sequences have been made in hopes of motivating students to study the target language (Bjornson 1983).

When using texts for cultural description, readers must be reminded that authors use their work for their own purposes. In other words, scenes may be exaggerated or distorted by the writer. As Brumfit and Carter (1986b) state:

> This argument does not prevent us from making use of literary texts; nor does it stop us using them sometimes for linguistic or cultural purposes, as long as we are aware of the risks and feel competent to distinguish the typical native language or culture from the characteristic stylistic or reference features of the writers being used. (pp. 27–28)

In fact, Brumfit and Carter believe that it would be advantageous to read books from other traditions precisely *because* students' assumptions and prejudices will be challenged (p. 34).

The introduction of literature from a variety of ethnic cultures can also be important for addressing the needs of the increasing number of minority students in the language classroom. These texts could be used to contrast with works from the traditional canon of the foreign language literature. They do not need to replace those works, but could be used in conjunction with them.

How to Organize Literature in the Curriculum

Most undergraduate students who are beginning the study of literature in survey courses probably need an overall introduction to the study of literature to become familiar with literary terms and concepts. Several instructors have proposed introduction to literature courses whose level of success has depended on the instruction (Peters 1974; König and Vernon 1980). These courses can meet the needs of students by introducing literary terminology and by considering such issues as the nature of the literary work, the creative process, the possibilities of analyzing and interpreting literature, concepts of literary genre, literary period and history, and criticism.

For students who may eventually become graduate students and scholars, the literary text will almost necessarily be used as a "vehicle for literary criticism" (Harper 1988: 402). Objective knowledge of critical approaches and literary facts have an important place for future scholars (Mead 1980). Literary theory is concerned with why a work is called literature and is defined as "a set of logically consistent concepts and principles for understanding, interpreting, and explaining the object of inquiry—novel, play, poem, story, or any other piece of writing designated as literary by a given society and culture" (Shevtsova 1987: 9).

Theory crosses the boundaries of genre and composition and incorporates sociology, anthropology, linguistics, history, and philosophy. Prince (1983) calls for the study of literary theory in undergraduate education for foreign language students (p. 1). He believes that theory can ground interpretation and that it "constitutes a disciplined space for examining the literature and the conditions of its possibility" (p. 2). He believes that theory should be presented at the beginning of the literary curriculum because it provides a necessary foundation; he proposes a literary theory course for all relevant departments. This course could be team-taught and be part of the core curriculum (p. 4). Of course, not all professors of literature would agree with Prince; many would contend that such a focus on theory removes the reader from the text and the practice of close reading. Here again, we see a demonstration of the lack of agreement on the goals of literary study.

In many universities such introductory theory courses are taught to advanced undergraduates and graduate students. This is often the case in France at the second-year level, while in many U.S. schools it is taught to fourth-year students.

The University of Pennsylvania has a course entitled "Literary Theory and Arabic Literature" that is taught in English using translations so that comparative literature students can be included (Allen 1991a and b). In Chinese at The Ohio State University, there are courses that focus either on Western interpretation of Chinese literature or on Chinese interpretation of their own literature (Walker 1991a). Departments owe it to the future of their literary-scholars-in-training to present various approaches that make use of literary theory whether Western or non-Western. Advanced students must have a thorough understanding of and ability to use several approaches in order to make their own decisions on how they will wish to read literature for personal or professional goals.

Literature-in-translation courses play a specific role in the curriculum, especially at the undergraduate college level. These courses are a means of outreach to students "who otherwise might not appreciate any literature except that written in their native language" (Kolbert 1986: 40). Often courses in translation are taught as interdisciplinary courses. When they do cross to other fields, literature and language departments have the opportunity to share their expertise with others, ranging from political science to art and architecture. Themes as different as war and peace in literature and on the interrelations between literature and the other arts are possible (Kolbert 1986; Barricelli et al. 1990).

Because of the difficulty in understanding some literatures, several authors argue for bilingual readings or comparative readings (Moore 1981; Lindenberger 1986). These texts make students aware of the shades of meaning, the subtleties of language, and the complexities of translation. In France the art of translation is still very important: Students take translation courses for three years leading to the C.A.P.E.S. (*Certificat d'aptitude professionnelle de l'enseignement secondaire*—Certificate for secondary teaching). One section of the C.A.P.E.S. examination requires the candidate to read aloud an 800-word passage, present an oral literary analysis, and translate approximately 250 words in English. In the LCTs, where students' proficiency rates typically develop more slowly, texts may be studied in translation until the final years of undergraduate study. Often undergraduate majors take one or two courses in translation before proceeding to courses in which it is principally the target language that is used. At the University of Pennsylvania, for example, students take a course in Arabic literary history and one in literary theory and Arabic literature; At The Ohio State University, students choose between classical and medieval Arabic literature and modern Arabic literature in translation to acquire an overview of the genres before advancing to authentic literary texts (Noble 1991).

Unfortunately, texts in some of the LCTs abound with improper translations. It is obvious to point out that Westerners may translate using their own value systems, resulting in corruption of the original texts. Furthermore, there is a lack of critical introductions and editions in the Asian languages (Yang 1976). In fact, professors of European languages complain of the difficulty and high cost of editions in their languages as well. These problems will not be alleviated until foreign language instructors can convince publishers to focus on literature and the preparation of texts for their use.[7]

Methodological Concerns ──────────────────────

Materials Available

The publications available on the teaching of literature, such as the MLA series on *Approaches to Teaching Literature* and the special number of *Le Français dans le monde* (février–mars 1988, entitled *"Littérature et enseignement"*), hope to improve the craft (or art) of teaching and present various points of view on specific works of literature or different authors (Gibaldi 1987; Bertrand and Ploquin 1988). There is an excellent handbook prepared by Collie and Slater (1987) that can serve as a guide to any instructor wishing to maximize the benefit of the literary experience. Many practical examples are given for teaching English literature to second language learners, for example, and teachers of other literatures can easily adapt these models for their purposes. In France the *Société des anglicistes de l'enseignement supérieur* publishes a newsletter and sponsors colloquia and seminars on the teaching of English in France. The 1986 book of essays entitled *Literature and Language Teaching* edited by C. J. Brumfit and R. A. Carter contains twenty essays on various aspects of teaching English literature to second language learners. Despite the existence of these resources, there is a continuing need for more publication in the area of reading literature in a foreign language.

Techniques for Teaching Literature

A number of articles have appeared in which authors propose tips on how to approach a specific work of literature. Most of these articles are theoretical and based on the writer's experience, but they are helpful for literature instructors. In general, scholars point out that essential to any approach is to avoid treating the literary text exclusively with discrete-point, comprehension-based activities (Kramsch 1985: 358; Brumfit 1986: 186–88). Most scholars believe that students who "collect" facts from lectures or the text itself are deprived of any active role (Schofer 1984; Mueller and Rehorick 1984; Blackbourn 1986). Too often, literature is presented by the instructor who gives his/her own perspective and the students "interact with the instructor's comprehension of the text rather than their own" (Swaffar et al. 1991: 215). Students listen passively and sometimes realize that they may not even need to read the text in question. In France, where the classes in English literature in the first two years at the university are very large (80–100 students), class discussion is very difficult to generate and maintain. Special efforts must be made to draw out students. It is perhaps because of the special difficulties that we have with developing the literary competence of our students that it is so problematic for us to go beyond lecturing. It is important, however, for Lit2 instructors to focus on what it means to read in order to provide our students the opportunity to participate and grow in the literary tradition.

The process of reading is one of engagement, "a process of meaning-creation by integrating one's own needs, understanding, and expectations with a written text" (Brumfit and Carter 1986b: 23). Each student should have the opportunity to have such an encounter, even though each experience will be different from the other. Students may thus bring different questions to the text and derive different meanings. As instructors, we must be aware of these conditions and develop our classroom techniques and activities accordingly.

Through open discussion, the literary work can be understood and negotiated (Kramsch 1985; Harper 1988). Interactive approaches as described by Swaffar et al. (1991) and Carrell (1987) are appropriate for minimizing difficulties in reading literature. Kramsch (1985), for example, proposes the use of group situations to discuss literature, using the three aptitudes in the construction of discourse: expression, interpretation, and negotiation of meanings. Her goal is to help teachers to "find the discourse context within which the readers' schemata can be discussed in a non-threatening manner" (p. 361).

Harper (1988) suggests communicative approaches that allow for individualization of learning, including the varied perspectives of the students as well as providing a structure that facilitates the reading of a text (p. 403). Her three-step approach is very inclusive and can be used as an outline to summarize the many techniques described by other authors for the teaching of literature at various levels. Her approach begins with a *preinterpretation* stage for establishing a common background and handling linguistic difficulties in order to pave the way for comprehension.[8] The second of Harper's stages is *interpretation,* which takes as its point of departure the assumptions and viewpoints of the reader, with teacher as discussant.[9] Harper's third phase is *synthesis,* which, as the name implies, brings all the parts together. Possible activities at this level include, among others, student-generated reactions to literature or original writing by students, tests, papers, and additional small-group work (Stanislawczyk and Yavener 1976; Schofer 1984; Mead 1980). Although not all Lit2 instructors would agree that these techniques are appropriate (indeed, free writing may be too difficult for students of Chinese and other LCTs), we need to use techniques that will help our students to meet the text first at their own level and then advance to interpretation at a literary level.

Training for Lit2 Instruction

Recent reports in the United States have noted that many college teachers are poorly trained to teach: Elementary and high school teachers are taught pedagogy but not subject matter, while college teachers learn subject matter but not pedagogy. The preliminary report on Competencies of Teachers, presented by the American Association of Teachers of French (AATF) in 1987, emphasized a literary component in the training of high school teachers. For the superior level in French, for example, the report proposed a knowledge of literature to include literary works for each period including texts from the francophone countries.

(These same suggestions would not, of course, be applicable for future instructors of the LCTs.) The report suggested that the teacher at the superior level in French should be able to expose his or her students to a literary experience in which "linguistic, cultural, and cognitive (critical thinking) goals can be achieved indirectly via encounters with literary texts" (Murphy et al. 1987: 16). To teach at the advanced placement level (the equivalent of the third-year college course), the report proposed that the instructor be able to present approaches for textual analysis. It is obvious that courses in content and methodology "which will specifically prepare teachers to be able to deal effectively with literature in the secondary school program" are necessary for teachers of all languages (Murphy et al. 1987: 17).

In France, students who wish to teach attend either an *école normale,* a school specifically for the training of teachers, or the university. Students at the university receive the *licence* to teach in grade schools or junior high schools, or they continue to prepare for the C.A.P.E.S. to teach in the *lycée.* These three groups of teachers do complete internships in the schools; they are not, however, trained with as strong a focus on pedagogy as in the United States. There is a move to eliminate the *écoles normales* and a program entitled *Instituts universitaires de la formation des maîtres* (University Institutes for the formation of teachers) is being initiated in France. The program would bring all training of teachers into the universities. To teach at the university level in France, the *doctorat de troisième cycle* (doctorate of the third cycle, equivalent of the U.S. Ph.D.) must be completed, but it provides no formal training in methodology or pedagogy. Just as in the United States, therefore, French university professors are trained in their content area but not in methods of teaching.

Santoni (1972) and Muyskens (1983) suggest that methodology courses on the teaching of literature are necessary. These preservice courses would include discussion of the major problems that all new teachers have at all levels of literary instruction. Although problems will vary according to the language taught, in general the goals would be similar and could include: (1) helping prospective literature teachers set goals for their courses; (2) presenting methods for presentation, discussion, and testing of literature; and (3) teaching methods of motivating students (Santoni 1972: 433; Muyskens 1983: 419–20). Approaches to teaching literature and the practical application of such approaches would comprise the major segment of the course. Students could peer-teach lessons to colleagues. Discussion of the use of audio and visual materials could bring out their use in the literature classroom. At the conclusion of the course, professional organizations and means for keeping up to date on developments in literary instruction would be addressed (Muyskens 1983: 420).

Rivers (1983) reports from her survey of the preparation of college teachers that at the graduate level, college teachers believed that more "courses in the methodology of language and literature teaching and in psycholinguistics and language acquisition should be regular features of the program" (p. 24).

Bretz and Persin (1987) describe a course entitled "Approaches to the Teaching of Hispanic Literatures." Their goal was to present several critical approaches that offer the possibility of student participation, such as reader response, feminism, contemporary psychoanalytical criticism, and deconstruction. By dividing the course into three distinct components (the study of a specific theory or conceptual literary structure, the application of these theories to specific texts, and the presentation, discussion, and implementation of pre- and postreading activities), they succeeded in making future professors aware of the richness available for the teaching and study of literature.[10]

Such courses are only a beginning. Apprenticeship programs in advanced literature and civilization would be even more beneficial (Lohnes 1972: 99; Rivers 1983: 25–26). Rivers suggests, as a result of her survey, that departments must offer "cooperative, supervised apprenticeships" during which students prepare syllabus, materials, and tests with a master teacher (p. 25). Many U.S. universities, however, do not have the budgets or staffing to provide for such training programs. If the graduate assistants who taught introductory language received an additional stipend to participate in an apprentice program in literature, such programs could be developed. Foreign language and literature departments owe it to their future to press for additional stipends for this initiative.

Muyskens (1983) proposes inservice workshops to revitalize literary instruction among teachers and professors in the field (p. 420). In the United States, the Academic Alliances–National Endowment for the Humanities conferences entitled "Foreign Language Instruction through the Study of Literary Texts" are providing the opportunity for college and school teachers to study literature together. They discuss the timing of literature's use and treatment in the curricula and explore techniques for promoting literature discussion as well (Silber 1990). During these conferences, sessions focus also on how the study of literature can reinforce oral proficiency. These series are "based on the assumption that a relationship between language and literature is at the heart of foreign language instruction" (Silber 1990: 4).

Short and Candlin describe courses on English language and literature teaching overseas that they organized in 1980 and 1981. These courses emphasized the three components of description, interpretation, and evaluation of texts (Short and Candlin 1986: 95). Other programs have been developed in the United States to meet the professional needs of teachers, combining improvement of linguistic skills with graduate courses in literature (R. Smith 1985). Such courses serve to build or rebuild enthusiasm for literature at the school and college levels.

In France, the *recyclage* (reorientation or retraining) programs that exist are meant to help teachers retool. One of the authors is presently teaching an *interne* (inservice) program for teachers who wish to take the *Agrégation* (competitive examination to teach in the *lycée* with higher pay and fewer hours). These classes are arranged at times convenient for inservice teachers and are oriented to prepare them for this very competitive examination by familiarizing them with the requirements and by preparing the texts on which they will be tested.

Whether during pre- or inservice programs, it is crucial that instructors be trained to use literature as an occasion for students to create, question, and investigate the text at hand (Kramsch 1985). If Lit2 instructors can be convinced that literature study is a time for engagement and interaction rather than passive acceptance, students will be motivated to read and study literature. Only then will they reap the benefits of reading literature.

Conclusion

It is perhaps fitting to echo Lohnes's (1972) call for research into the "optimum conditions for the introduction of literature into the language curricula," the ways of teaching literature, and methods of attracting "today's generation of students to literature as a vital and 'relevant' part of the human condition" (p. 103). Much progress has been made in the definition of what it means to read a foreign language; less progress has been made, however, in determining what it means to read *literature* in a foreign language. Investigation must be done through surveys or written protocols into the difficulties that students encounter when reading literature in the foreign language. Instructors still do not agree on when to introduce literature nor on what literature to study in the foreign language. It is our contention that early study will lead to an understanding of the cultural and literary conventions of a society if the instructor proceeds with caution, realizing the gap that exists between the students' background and that of the authors under study. It is crucial to train Lit2 instructors to be aware of the importance of setting clear goals for literature study. Such training would not be prescriptive, but rather would explore problems and approaches.

The future of Lit2 study lies in the exchange of ideas among instructors of different languages and cultures and from countries with different educational traditions and goals. It lies in accepting the importance of reading literature in a second language and the willingness to provide our students with the linguistic and cultural background to make these works truly accessible to them. The ability to read the literature of another culture is one way to truly understand another country, its people, and its past. As the world becomes increasingly international, literary competence is a very desireable quality. As Lit2 instructors, we owe it to our students to help them build this type of competence.

Notes

1. The authors asked several colleagues for comments and reactions. We would like to thank them and ask that they forgive any misinterpretation of their ideas. Thank you especially to Galal Walker, Professor of East Asian Languages and Literatures at The Ohio State University, who read the manuscript and gave suggestions. The following colleagues provided comments through personal communication: Frank Silbajoris, Professor of Slavic Languages and Literatures at The Ohio State University; Stafford Noble, Administrative Assistant in Arabic Languages at The Ohio State University; and Roger Allen, Professor of Arabic Literatures and Languages at the University of Pennsylvania. Professor Allen provided us with two papers he had presented at conferences. They are entitled "The Role of Literature in the Teaching and Learning of Arabic" and "Recent Developments in Arabic Literature Studies: An Overview." These documents were very helpful in clarifying the issues involved in the teaching of Arabic Literature.

2. Two books on reading that we found especially helpful were the following: Marva Barnett, *More than Meets the Eye. Foreign Language Learner Reading: Theory and*

Practice (Englewood Cliffs, NJ: Prentice Hall, 1989); and Janet K. Swaffar, Katherine M. Arens, and Heidi Byrnes, *Reading for Meaning: An Integrated Approach to Language Learning* (Englewood Cliffs, NJ: Prentice Hall, 1991). Both these books address reading comprehension and discuss the reading of literary texts in late chapters.

3. In their recent book about the teaching of reading, Swaffar et al. describe an interactive approach and have examples adapted to literature (1991: 222–30). Thus students, already challenged in reading, may be led gradually and carefully to an interpretive level of reading literature.

4. Muyskens administered a pilot questionnaire asking college students in their first year of literary study to discuss difficulties they have when reading a literary text in a foreign language. The results have not yet been fully analyzed but initial perusal of the responses suggests that students most often mention problems in understanding the language of the literary text as opposed to lack of cultural or historical background.

5. According to Short and Candlin (1986), there is no linguistic distinction between literary language and other kinds of language (p. 91). They know of no "particular linguistic feature or set of linguistic features which are found in literature but not in other kinds of texts" (p. 107) and believe that, as was previously mentioned, what is called literature is named so because of sociocultural reasons rather than linguistic terms. Activating prior experience with native language literature will prepare students to respond to a text as literature; she or he "will attempt to apply a set of special interpretative conventions" (p. 109). These may include rhyme or metaphor or linguistic deviation. This is not a contention based on empirical research but one that they hope will be examined as reader interaction with the literary text is studied.

6. In 1983, Muyskens stressed that many authors suggest directions for research but that few had followed through with such research (1983: 420). At that time, she found only three empirical studies. Young (1963) studied the effect of intensive reading on attitude change; Hooper (1975) researched the reading interest of French college students; Muyskens's (1977) dissertation was a comparative study of the effects of personalizing literature on measures of student achievement and on attitude toward foreign language study and literature study in general.

7. The Modern Language Association recently announced a new publication series that would include texts for the teaching of foreign literatures not available in the United States at an affordable price. It will publish texts aimed at advanced undergraduate or graduate students. Each volume will be composed of the full original text and a short preface. An optional translation of the text will be available. This series could go a long way to providing texts of high quality and at a reasonable price to Lit2 instructors and students.

8. Several authors have discussed the advisability of careful linguistic preparation (Purcell 1985; Spinelli and Williams 1981; A. Smith 1976; Gollert et al. 1989; Storme and Siskin 1989) and of establishing comprehension (Kramsch 1985; Spinelli and Williams 1981; Birckbichler and Muyskens 1980).

9. Other writers have discussed the personal reaction of the reader (Birckbichler and Muyskens 1980; Vande Berg 1990), individual analysis or individualization of literature instruction (Klein 1976; Cummins 1981) as well as open discussion and small-group activities (Blackbourn 1986; Kramsch 1985).

10. Courses for teaching literature in the LCTs would be constructed in a different manner; such courses could be planned when the qualifications for teachers are "agreed upon" (Walker 1991a: 141).

References, Literature in the Foreign Language: A Comparative Study

Allen, Roger. 1991a. "The Role of Literature in the Teaching and Learning of Arabic." Unpublished manuscript.

_____. 1991b. "Recent Developments in Arabic Literature Studies: An Overview." Unpublished manuscript.

Anastos, Perry. 1981. "Probing a Short Story with Language Exercises." *Foreign Language Annals* 14: 127–32.

Bacon, Susan. 1990. Personal Communication.

Barnett, Marva A. 1989. *More than Meets the Eye.* Foreign Language Learner Reading: Theory and Practice. Englewood Cliffs, NJ: Prentice Hall; Washington, DC: Center for Applied Linguistics.

Barricelli, Jean-Pierre, Joseph Gibaldi, and Estella Lauter. 1990. *Teaching Literature and the Other Arts.* New York: MLA.

Berkow, Ira. 1991. "How Bills Build Their Vocabulary." *The New York Times,* January 23, p. B-12.

Bernhardt, Elizabeth B. 1991. "Developments in Second Language Literacy Research: Retrospective and Prospective Views for the Classroom," pp. 221–51 in Barbara F. Freed, ed., *Foreign Language Acquisition Research and the Classroom.* Lexington, MA: Heath.

Bertrand, Denis, and Françoise Ploquin, eds. 1988. "Littérature et enseignement." *Le Français dans le monde* (numéro spécial: février–mars).

Birckbichler, Diane W., and Judith A. Muyskens. 1980. "A Personalized Approach to the Teaching of Literature at the Elementary and Intermediate Levels of Instruction." *Foreign Language Annals* 13: 23–27.

Bjornson, Richard. 1983. "Teaching Third World Literature." *ADFL Bulletin* 15: 8–11.

Blackbourn, Barbara L. 1986. "The Transition for Language Courses to Literature: A Pragmatic Stance." *French Review* 60: 196–202.

Bolinger, Dwight. 1968. "Literature Yes, but When?" *Hispania* 51: 118–19.

Bostick, Herman F. 1972. "Teaching Afro-French Literature in the American Secondary School: A New Dimension." *Foreign Language Annals* 5: 420–31.

Bretz, Mary Lee, and Margaret Persin. 1987. "The Application of Critical Theory to Literature at the Introductory Level: A Working Model for Teacher Preparation." *Modern Language Journal* 71: 165–70.

Brière, Eloise A. 1982. "*L'Enfant noir* by Camara Laye: Strategies in Teaching an African Text." *French Review* 55: 804–10.

Brod, Evelyn F. 1983. "Concrete Poetry: A Linguistic Technique for the Foreign Language Classroom." *Foreign Language Annals* 16: 255–58.

Brown, Valerie P. 1977. "The Dramatic Approach to the Teaching of French." *Foreign Language Annals* 10: 187–89.

Brumfit, Christopher J. 1986. "Reading Skills and the Study of Literature in a Foreign Language," pp. 184–90 in C. J. Brumfit and R. A. Carter, eds., *Literature and Language Teaching.* Oxford, Eng.: Oxford Univ. Press.

————, and Ronald A. Carter, eds. 1986a. *Literature and Language Teaching.* Oxford, Eng.: Oxford Univ. Press.

————. 1986b. "Introduction," pp. 1–36 in C. J. Brumfit and R. A. Carter, eds., *Literature and Language Teaching.* Oxford, Eng.: Oxford Univ. Press.

————. 1986c. "Introduction to Part Three," pp. 233–35 in C. J. Brumfit and R. A. Carter, eds., *Literature and Language Teaching.* Oxford, Eng.: Oxford Univ. Press.

Carmody, Deirdre. 1991. "The Short Story: Out of the Mainstream but Flourishing." *The New York Times,* April 23, p. B-1.

Carrell, Patricia. 1987. "Fostering Interactive Second Language Reading," pp. 145–69 in Sandra J. Savignon and Margie S. Berns, eds., *Initiatives in Communicative Language Teaching II.* Reading, MA: Addison-Wesley.

Carter, Ronald. 1986. "Linguistic Models, Languages, and Literariness: Study Strategies in the Teaching of Literature to Foreign Students," pp. 110–32 in C. J. Brumfit and R. A. Carter, eds., *Literature and Language Teaching.* Oxford, Eng.: Oxford Univ. Press.

Castañeda, James A. 1978. "The Future of Foreign Language Study in American Colleges and Universities." *Profession 1978:* 43–50.

Clark, Beatrice A. 1980. "An Experiment with Ethnicity and Foreign Languages in a Black College." *Foreign Language Annals* 13: 411–14.

Collie, Joanne, and Stephen Slater. 1987. *Literature in the Language Classroom.* Cambridge, Eng.: Cambridge Univ. Press.

Cook, Guy. 1986. "Texts, Extracts, and Stylistic Textures," pp. 150–66 in C. J. Brumfit and R. A. Carter, eds., *Literature and Language Teaching.* Oxford, Eng.: Oxford Univ. Press.

Creed, Carol L. 1978. "Prelude to Poetry." *Foreign Language Annals* 11: 299–303.

Cummins, Patricia W. 1981. "French Literature and the PSI Method." *French Review* 54: 655–60.

De Méo, Patricia P. 1983. "Poetic Games: Fruitful Language Activities for the Intermediate French Class." *Foreign Language Annals* 16: 259–71.

Dietz, Donald T. 1972. "Literature and Relevance: Diary of a Spanish Novel Course." *Modern Language Journal* 56: 296–303.

Elliott, Jacqueline L. 1977. "Poésies et chansons françaises: base pour l'étude de la langue et de la civilisation." *French Review* 50: 401–11.

Erbaugh, Mary S. 1990. "Taking Advantage of China's Literary Tradition in Teaching Chinese Students." *Modern Language Journal* 74: 15–27.

Esler, Richard C. 1968. "The Teaching of Literature: To Whom?" *Hispania* 51: 847–48.

Federici, Carla. 1989. "De la chanson à la poésie." *French Review* 62: 612–22.

Gibaldi, Joseph. 1987. "Preface to Series," pp. viii–x in Renée Waldinger, ed., *Approaches to Teaching Voltaire's* Candide. New York: MLA.

Gollert, Heidi, et al. 1989. "A Touch of. . .Class!" *Canadian Modern Language Review* 45: 362–76.

Harper, Sandra N. 1988. "Strategies for Teaching Literature at the Undergraduate Level." *Modern Language Journal* 72: 402–8.

Herr, Kay. 1982. "The Role of Literature in Secondary and Post-Secondary Language Instruction: Disparity or Unity?" *Foreign Language Annals* 15: 203–7.

Hooper, Ann C. 1975. "Reading Interests of College Students." Unpublished manuscript. [ED 139 250]

Hunting, Claudine. 1976. "Literature in Action: An Undergraduate Course in French." *Foreign Language Annals* 9: 537–41.

Kaplan, Robert B. 1987. "Cultural Thought Patterns Revisited," pp. 9–21 in U. Connor and R. B. Kaplan, eds., *Writing across Languages: Analysis of L2 Text.* Reading, MA: Addison Wesley.

Klein, David J. 1976. "An Individualized Approach to a Literary Text." *Foreign Language Annals* 9,2: 548–50.

Kolbert, Jack. 1986. "The Thematic Approach to Literature in Translation." *ADFL Bulletin* 17: 40–42.

König, Fritz H., and Nile D. Vernon. 1980. "Introduction to Literature: A Stimulant or Depressant?" Unpublished manuscript. [ED 196 288]

Kramsch, Claire J. 1985. "Literary Texts in the Classroom: A Discourse." *Modern Language Journal* 69: 356–66.

————, and Marlies Mueller. 1989. "Celebrating, Creating, Understanding Poetry in the Language Class." Presentation at ACTFL Convention, Boston.

Labonté, René. 1980. "Méthodes d'initiation à la poésie pour jeunes adultes." *French Review* 53: 685–95.

Leal, Luis. 1972. "The Spanish Short Story and Its Potential for the Secondary and College Classroom." *Foreign Language Annals* 5: 442–46.

Lindenberger, Herbert. 1986. "Teaching Literature in the Original or in Translation: An Intellectual or a Political Problem?" *ADFL Bulletin* 17,2: 35–39.

Littlewood, William T. 1986. "Literature in the School Foreign-Language Course", pp. 177–83 in C. J. Brumfit and R. A. Carter, eds., *Literature and Language Teaching.* Oxford, Eng.: Oxford Univ. Press.

Lohnes, Walter F. W. 1972. "Teaching Foreign Literature," pp. 83–103 in Emma M. Birkmaier, ed., *Foreign Language Education: An Overview.* ACTFL Foreign Language Education Series, vol. 1. Lincolnwood, IL: National Textbook Company.

McKay, Sandra. 1986. "Literature in the ESL Classroom," pp. 191–98 in C. J. Brumfit and R. A. Carter eds., *Literature and Language Teaching.* Oxford, Eng.: Oxford Univ. Press.

Mead, Robert G., Jr. 1980. "On Teaching Literature in Today's World." *Hispania* 63: 536–44.

Moore, Roger. 1981. "Introducing Translation: The Comparative Approach." *Canadian Modern Language Review* 38: 10–18.

Mueller, Marlies, and Sally Rehorick. 1984. "Reaching for Caligula's Moon: Teaching Modern Drama in Advanced Language Classes." *French Review* 57: 475–84.

Murphy, Joseph A., et al. 1987. "The Teaching of French: A Syllabus of Competence." The Preliminary Report of the Commission on Professional Standards of the American Association of Teachers of French. *AATF National Bulletin* 13 (special issue).

Muyskens, Judith A. 1977. "Personalized versus Non-Personalized Teaching of Literature: A Study of the Effects of Two Methods of Teaching in Subject Matter Achievement and Attitudes in the Intermediate College French Classroom." Ph.D. diss., Ohio State University.

————. 1983. "Teaching Second-Language Literatures: Past, Present and Future." *Modern Language Journal* 67: 413–23.

Noble, Stafford. 1991. Personal communication.

O'Connor, Patricia. 1991. Personal communication.

Olds, Marshall C. 1984. "French Language Study and the Modern Literary Text." *French Review* 58: 215–22.

Omaggio, Alice C. 1986. *Teaching Language in Context.* Boston: Heinle and Heinle.

Peters, George F. 1974. "Why Introduction to Literature?" *Unterrichtspraxis* 7: 17–25.

Prendergast, Jane. 1991. "Books with Big Words Favored." *Cincinnati Enquirer,* January 3, p. D-1.

Prince, Gerald. 1983. "Literary Theory and the Undergraduate Curriculum." *ADFL Bulletin* 15,2: 1–4.

Purcell, John M. 1985. "Teaching Students to Recognize Literary Style," pp. 90–98 in Patricia B. Westphal, ed., *Strategies for Foreign Language Teaching: Communication, Technology, Culture.* Report of the Central States Conference on the Teaching of Foreign Languages. Lincolnwood, IL: National Textbook Company.

————. 1988. "Using Plays Proficiently in the Foreign Language Class." Unpublished manuscript. [ED 285 421]

Rivers, Wilga M. 1983. "Preparing College and University Instructors for a Lifetime of Teaching: A Luxury or a Necessity?" *ADFL Bulletin* 15,2: 23–29.

Rochette-Ozello, Yvonne. 1978. "Contraintes et créations: pédagogie de la production poétique." *French Review* 51: 626–43.

Santoni, Georges. 1972. "Methods of Teaching Literature." *Foreign Language Annals* 5: 432–51.

————. 1979. "Langues et littérature: poèmes de Desnos et Eluard." *French Review* 52: 690–99.

Schofer, Peter. 1984. "Theoretical Acrobatics: The Student as Author and Teacher in Introductory Literature Classes." *French Review* 57: 463–74.

Schulz, Renate A. 1981. "Literature and Readability: Bridging the Gap in Foreign Language Reading." *Modern Language Journal* 65: 43–53.

Shevtsova, Maria. 1987. "The Case for Theory." *ADFL Bulletin* 18,3: 9–15.

Short, Michael H., and Christopher N. Candlin. 1986. "Teaching Study Skills for English Literature," pp. 89–109 in C. J. Brumfit and R. A. Carter, eds., *Literature and Language Teaching.* Oxford, Eng.: Oxford Univ. Press.

Silbajoris, Frank. 1991. Personal communication.

Silber, Ellen, ed. 1990. "Intellectual Feast Produces Esprit de Corps: School and College Teachers Study Literature Together." *Collaborare* 6: 2–5.

Smith, Alfred N. 1976. "Combining Structure Drills and Reading Comprehension Exercises to Teach Literature." *Foreign Language Annals* 9: 525–29.

Smith, Roch C. 1985. "Meeting the Professional Needs of Teachers: A Graduate-Level Institute in Language and Literature." *ADFL Bulletin* 16,2: 22–24.

Spinelli, Emily, and Shirley A. Williams. 1981. "From Language to Literature: Teaching Figurative Language in the College Foreign Language Classroom." *Foreign Language Annals* 14: 37–43.

Stanislawczyk, Irene E., and Symond Yavener. 1976. *Creativity in the Language Classroom.* New York: Newbury House.

Steiner, Florence. 1972. "Teaching Literature in the Secondary Schools." *Modern Language Journal* 56: 278–84.

Storme, Julie A., and H. Jay Siskin. 1989. "Developing Extensive Reading Skills: The Transition to Literature," pp. 24–39 in Dave McAlpine, ed., *Defining the Essentials for the Foreign Language Classroom.* ACTFL Foreign Language Education Series, vol. 20. Lincolnwood, IL: National Textbook Company.

Swaffar, Janet K. 1985. "Reading Authentic Texts in a Foreign Language: A Cognitive Model." *Modern Language Journal* 69: 15–34.

————. 1991. "Language Learning Is More than Learning Language: Rethinking Reading and Writing Tasks in Textbooks for Beginning Language Study," pp. 252–79 in Barbara F. Freed, ed., *Foreign Language Acquisition Research and the Classroom.* Lexington, MA: Heath.

————, Katherine M. Arens, and Heidi Byrnes. 1991. *Reading for Meaning: An Integrated Approach to Language Learning.* Englewood Cliffs, NJ: Prentice Hall.

Tilles, Solomon. 1972. "An Experimental Approach to the Spanish American Theatre." *Modern Language Journal* 56: 304–5.

Vande Berg, Camille Kennedy. 1990. "Conversation Activities Based on Literary Readings." *French Review* 63: 664–70.

Vincent, Monica. 1986. "Simple Text and Reading Text Part 1: Some General Issues," pp. 208–15 in C. J. Brumfit and R. A. Carter, eds., *Literature and Language Teaching.* Oxford, Eng.: Oxford Univ. Press.

Walker, Galal. 1991a. "Gaining Place: The Less Commonly Taught Languages in American Schools." *Foreign Language Annals* 24: 131–50.

————. 1991b. Personal communication.

Yang, Winston L. Y. 1976. "Teaching Chinese through Chinese Literature." *Modern Language Journal* 60: 31–38.

Young, Eleanor C. 1963. "The Effect of Intensive Reading on Attitude Change." *French Review* 36: 629–32.

12

U.S. and European Perspectives on Language for Specific Purposes

Christine Uber Grosse
Florida International University

Geoffrey Kingscott
Praetorius Limited

For the past thirty years, the language for specific purposes (LSP) movement has offered an alternative to traditional foreign language courses in adult and higher education in the United States and Western Europe. Various acronyms are commonly used to describe specific areas of study in English for Specific (or Special) Purposes such as EAP (English for Academic Purposes), EST (English for Science and Technology), and EOP (English for Occupational Purposes). The willingness of the profession to embrace LSP as an innovative way to expand the foreign language curriculum is evident in the presence of LSP courses at 58 percent of U.S. colleges and universities (Grosse and Voght 1990). Although perceived by many as an innovative approach to teaching foreign languages, LSP is not new, having been used for centuries for maritime, military, medical, and other special purposes.

The development of LSP got a head start in Europe and third-world nations in the 1960s and 1970s primarily outside universities, through large government and private language-training projects. U.S. recognition and development of the field lagged behind that of Western Europe, with major development in this country starting in the late 1970s. The locus of development also differed in the

Christine Uber Grosse (Ph.D., University of North Carolina) is Assistant Professor of TESOL and Modern Language Education at Florida International University. She was recently President of Florida TESOL. Her articles on pedagogy and languages for specific purposes have appeared in the *Modern Language Journal, TESOL Quarterly, Foreign Language Annals, Hispania,* and other professional journals. With Robert Grosse, she coauthored *Case Studies in International Business* (Prentice-Hall, 1988).

Geoffrey Kingscott (BA, MITI, MIL) is Editor of *Praetorius Limited,* a British journal devoted to technical translation, language consultancy, and multilingual documentation.

United States, where universities rather than private corporations or the government took the initiative to institute such courses. In the United States, the popularity of LSP courses at some institutions was born of necessity to save foreign language departments from declining enrollment and to meet economic needs.

Definition of Terms

Language for specific purposes, as we will use the label here, refers to instruction that is primarily based in institutions of higher education and that combines the four skills, culture, and content, with a focus on the language needs of a particular group of learners such as businessmen and women, doctors, nurses, lawyers, engineers, scientists, or tourists. Examples of LSP courses include Business German, Spanish for Medical Personnel, French for Voice Majors, Japanese for Tourism, and English for Academic Purposes. Because of the central role of the learner in LSP, needs assessment is an important element of course design for language use, communicative context, language function, vocabulary, and structures likely to be needed by the group being served.

LSP encompasses all languages for specific purposes, including English for Specific Purposes (ESP), the evolution of which served as a foundation for the development of LSP in other languages. Morrow (1979) asserts that "ESP learners have a very clear idea of why they are studying the language and very low tolerance for studying things which they view as irrelevant" (p. 14).

Geographical and Historical Bounds

The geographical boundaries of this study extend from the United States to Western Europe. Historically, the use of LSP dates from ancient times, for example in seafarers' use of maritime guides in their explorations of the Old and New Worlds. One of the striking examples of the practical use of LSP is the development, by the International Maritime Organisation, of "Seaspeak," essentially a simplified form of English using a restricted but often technical vocabulary that enables those in charge of seagoing vessels to communicate with one another and with shore installations, even when their command of English is comparatively weak.

Military and nautical glossaries and medical and maritime dictionaries have helped language learners to communicate with speakers of other languages over the centuries, and thus could be considered among the earliest forms of LSP literature. Reading courses for specific purposes such as German for Scientists have existed at universities in Europe and the United States since the early part of the twentieth century.

The recent history of LSP begins in Great Britain in the early 1960s with the work of Barber (1988), Herbert (1988), and Higgins (1988), among others, in

English for science and technology (EST). Swales (1984; 1985) presents a useful picture of the development of the field in Europe and the Middle East. For almost three decades, Europe and developing nations have conducted extensive work in LSP. Immigration from the Commonwealth countries to Britain reached a peak in Great Britain in the late 1950s and early 1960s prior to passage of the Commonwealth Immigrants Act in 1962. In response to the need for language training for the immigrants, pilot projects for workers of limited English proficiency were developed for immigrant workers in Great Britain in the late 1960s and 1970s. These programs were company-specific, met daily for ten to twelve weeks on site, closely involved management and workers in the development of course content, and minimized loss of production time. In the 1970s the Council of Europe established a unit credit system to assure transferability of study credits from one nation to another. As part of this work the Council also developed programs and functional/notional materials for forty-four occupational categories of adult LSP.

Brumfit (1979) attributes the evolution of LSP to two recent changes in foreign language education, one theoretical and one pragmatic. The theory-based change occurred in the developments in sociolinguistic theory and practice in the late 1960s and 1970s regarding the relationships between linguistic form and communicative function. The pragmatic impetus behind LSP was the tremendous demand during the same period for ESL courses, with customers willing and able to pay large sums of money for language courses specifically suited to their needs. In such an atmosphere any perceived panacea such as English for Specific Purposes was welcomed.

The increasing use of English as a vehicle of international communication, a phenomenon whose implications are still not fully understood, has meant that on the continent of Europe (in this context we are using *continent* in the British sense of Europe, i.e., not including the British Isles) the study of English—insofar as it relates to the subject—has become a major part of all further professional education courses, for lawyers, accountants, bank staff, computer specialists, aeronautical engineers, and business and management students, to give just a few examples. This phenomenon is farthest advanced in Germany and the Scandinavian countries but is now increasingly being perceived in France, Italy, and Spain.

Because a knowledge of English is becoming a *sine qua non* for professional study in the countries mentioned, there has been in recent years, paradoxically, less demand for specially written training material at the higher levels, since the students are now expected to read authentic texts: business and management students are expected to read publications such as the *Wall Street Journal,* the *Financial Times,* and business magazines published in English; computer specialists soon become so accustomed to working in English that new computer terminology is often not being created in their own languages, preference being given to direct importation of the English terms.

In the countries of the former Eastern bloc (which now no longer like to be thought of as "Eastern Europe"—Hungarians, Czechs, and Poles think of themselves as being "Central Europe") the demand for the learning of English by adults is far outstripping its supply. Teachers of Russian are having to be retrained in these countries to teach English, even though many of them have never been to an English-speaking country.[1]

In Britain an opposite phenomenon is occurring. Until recently foreign language learning for business and professional purposes concentrated on French and German as major international languages, but now there is uncertainty about which foreign language to learn. There has been, for example, a huge growth in the teaching of Japanese for business purposes (Sheffield University has taken the lead in organizing such courses). Previously somewhat disregarded languages, such as Portuguese, are increasingly in demand now that Portugal is part of the European Community.

A pointer in this respect is the BBC, which produces well-regarded multimedia (television, radio, book, and cassette) courses for adults. For many years the BBC produced major courses only in French, German, Spanish, and Italian, renewing them in a nine-year cycle. Sensitive to demand, however, the BBC's senior languages producer, Terry Doyle, was three years ago given the task of producing a major Portuguese course and he is now in the process of producing the first major Japanese course.

Thinking about course content has also changed in recent years, with the move away from teaching the language in general terms to specific context. The BBC's courses, which are of course aimed at the general viewer, reflected this change with the Portuguese course referred to above. There was comparatively little explanation of grammar or stilted and artificial studio conversations; the concentration was on authentic speech recorded on location.

A video course written specifically for English business learners of German, "Making Your Mark"[2] took a similar approach, using only authentic material recorded in actual business situations. The same method has now been applied to French, and the French course "Frank Exchange," was launched in February 1991.

In the United States the pressure of government, educational, and private task forces and the decline of enrollments in foreign languages in the late 1970s helped convince foreign language educators of the need to develop applied language studies: they began to accept that the traditional emphasis on literary studies in upper-level language classes should be expanded to include courses relating languages to a specific subject or professional area. Simultaneously, a slight movement toward interdisciplinary programs helped link foreign language study and other disciplines and professions. In 1979 the President's Commission on Foreign Language and International Studies (1980) published its report, *Strength through Wisdom,* which focused on the decline of foreign language skills in the United States and articulated the need for professionally linked foreign language courses in specific fields such as engineering, business, and nursing.

In the United States most development of LSP has occurred at the university level, while in Western Europe development of language training programs has been concentrated in the private sector. In the late 1960s an association of in-company language-training centers in Germany, Austria, and Switzerland called *Erfahrungsaustauschring Sprachlabor Wirtschaft* (ERFA) was formed with the financial assistance of the Volkswagen Foundation. ERFA holds biannual meetings to address issues in teaching and learning foreign languages in industry and commerce (Freudenstein 1981).

The movement is farthest advanced in Germany, where large companies such as Mannesmann Demag or Krupp have long had what is usually called a *Sprachendienst,* which oversees both the translation of documentation and language training in the company. The tradition of close relations between industry and universities in Germany, and the high status that academics enjoy in that country (even among industrialists, which is not always the case in the United Kingdom or the United States), led not only to the ERFA movement, but also to the *Internationale Vereinigung Sprache und Wirtschaft,* formed in the 1970s as another forum for the exchange of ideas. As a by-product of initiatives like ERFA, terminology and data banks for translation and interpretation are very popular in Western Europe (Brinkman 1981).

Review of Previous Research

A compilation of research publications in LSP of the past twenty-five years yielded over two hundred titles related to French, Spanish, and German for specific purposes (Grosse and Voght 1991). Eight journals (six American, one French, one Canadian) have published two-thirds of the publications on LSP-related subjects. The *ADFL Bulletin* published forty-four articles on LSP between 1973 and 1990, the largest contribution to LSP made by any single publication in a similar period. Johns (1990) reviews the literature in ESP, while Robinson (1980) provides an extensive bibliography for that subject area. Basically the LSP literature can be classified into seven categories: (1) vocabularies and glossaries, (2) career education, (3) curriculum, (4) methods and materials, (5) discourse analysis, (6) proficiency, and (7) integration of language and culture. Honig and Brod (1974) provide one of the most important early U.S. publications in career education; this work establishes a sound basis and rationale for subsequent development of the area.

Most contributions on LSP treat issues in curriculum development: course and program design, needs assessment, and interdisciplinary cooperation. Over fifty papers have been published on the development and implementation of LSP courses and programs in French, German, and Spanish. The language and international trade program at Eastern Michigan University and the Masters in International Business Studies (MIBS) program at the University of South Carolina have received particular attention as models. The place of LSP within the foreign language curriculum also receives attention. Articles on needs assessment typically address the language needs of the workplace, government, corporations, and students in professional schools. Several papers discuss interdisciplinary cooperation between foreign language departments and professional schools or the private sector.

One of the least frequently treated areas in the LSP literature is the integration of language and culture into the LSP program. Some authors have considered the relationship of LSP to the proficiency movement and examined the use of the Spanish, French, and German, "chamber of commerce"-type exams.

Another segment of the literature examines teaching methods and materials for LSP (Drobnic et al. 1988; Allen and Widdowson 1988). Works in discourse analysis have concentrated primarily on scientific and legal texts.

LSP and Foreign Language Education

Influence of Trends in Foreign Language Education on LSP

The most important recent trends in foreign language education to influence LSP are (1) content-based instruction; (2) the learner-centered curriculum (development of focus on the student); (3) critical thinking skills; (4) communicative language teaching; (5) concerns with proficiency and accountability; (6) stress on use of authentic materials; and (7) the use of technology in teaching.

Content-Based Instruction. By definition LSP is content-based instruction, although admittedly not in the purest sense of specific academic content areas such as marketing, finance, biology, or international relations. Instead, the content of LSP courses draws on an interdisciplinary curriculum composed of language and culture and the content areas of a specific profession. For example, a typical business German course might cover aspects of banking, finance, marketing, management, and economics. The target language is taught through the context of a content area, or a professional area of specialization. This trend within the profession derives from the emphasis on teaching language as a vehicle for communication rather than as an end in itself (Snow 1991). Content-based instruction provides a relevant alternative in foreign language instruction to a vast group of students who have an economic foundation for their need to communicate in a second language—to keep or obtain employment. Within the university, new initiatives for interdisciplinary cooperation encourage the combination of foreign language and area studies as well as foreign language and professional studies (business, engineering, medicine, science, nursing). A variation of content-based instruction is foreign languages across the curriculum as related to LSP, where foreign languages are used as the vehicle of instruction rather than as the subject of instruction.

One of the most widely recognized problems inherent in content-based instruction is the lack of training of the language teacher in the content or professional area. In some cases the students know more about the content area than the LSP teacher, which can lead to teacher insecurity. Several models of content-based instruction have been proposed, including the St. Olaf model (in which half the reading material for special history, economics, and sociology courses is in the foreign language and students meet weekly with foreign language faculty to discuss the readings); team teaching by language and content teachers (Johns and Dudley-Evans 1988); the adjunct model, where students are enrolled concurrently in a language and a content-area class (Snow 1991); and content teaching done in the target language by a native speaker content-area professor (Snow 1991).

Learner-Centered Curriculum.   Another basic tenet of LSP is its focus on the learner and the principal importance of needs assessment in designing the LSP curriculum. The subject matter of LSP derives from an identification of the communicative needs of the learner. When the functional–notional approach was developed in the 1970s, the Council of Europe's work on the unit credit system and the development of language programs for specific occupational groups analyzed the language functions and notions needed by each group for communication. Thus, much of the early work in LSP was based on the functional–notional approach to curriculum design. Particularly in ESP, the texts and materials still reflect the functional–notional orientation. The concept of a minimal grammar and threshold level of proficiency needed for survival communication influenced thinking in LSP. Program developers sought to define the threshold level of proficiency in terms of language functions, vocabulary, notions, and structures needed by a certain group of learners in order to streamline instructional programs. This approach works best at the elementary level, helping the learner to reach targeted goals within a designated period of time. Understandably the approach becomes unwieldy and impractical at the intermediate and advanced levels: the difficulty of recycling the same language functions and notions at ever-increasing levels of complexity is implicit. Indeed the teaching of language functions and notions has been recognized as limiting and counterproductive to developing creative users of language and resembles the old structural approach to curriculum design (Krahnke 1987).

Critical Thinking Skills (problem-solving, case analysis).   The push toward development of problem-solving and critical thinking skills permeates education today, not only second language education and LSP. The concentration on developing higher-level cognitive skills is, however, an important consideration in LSP given the triple nature of LSP instruction in language, culture, and content. Using the language to solve problems within the context of the professional area is a powerful component of LSP methodology. The case study approach is an example of a specific means used to promote situational analysis and critical thinking skills in LSP courses, particularly business LSP (Grosse 1988).

Communicative Language Teaching (based on learner needs).   Once again, the trend toward communicative language teaching is at least as influential in LSP as it is in general language courses. Typically, business ESL texts emphasize communicative language teaching more than their counterparts in French and Spanish. According to Schleppegrell and Royster's study (1990), however, the amount of communicative language teaching that actually goes on in the business ESL classes in private language training schools is very limited.

Proficiency and Accountability.   The proficiency movement has had an impact on LSP in the emphasis of many courses and texts on preparing students for the French, German, and Spanish chamber of commerce–type exams. With their clientele of professional students and practitioners, LSP instructors feel pressure to help students attain certain levels of proficiency as measured by performance on these tests. Proponents of ESP, generally far less aware of and influenced by the ACTFL proficiency movement than colleagues in foreign languages for specific purposes, nonetheless are highly motivated by the need to have accountability in LSP programs. LSP students at a university or in the private sector demand results within a limited time for language study, with the result that the trend to accountability in language instruction is especially strong in LSP.

Authentic Materials. LSP courses make extensive use of authentic materials, i.e., materials that consist of real language designed for an audience of native speakers for the purpose of conveying a real message. Some examples of written and oral authentic materials are business correspondence and documents, medical reports, newspapers, advertisements, radio or television shows, movies, videotaped interviews, spontaneous conversations, and a chapter from a college textbook in a content area. The rationale for using authentic materials in LSP as well as in general language classes includes their contextual richness, natural repetition and linguistic redundancy, potentially high interest level of content, and motivational value.

The Use of Technology. Technology has been employed extensively by the British publishers for business ESL (BBC's "Bid for Power" and Longman's "Visitron"). U.S. teachers of business ESL actively use video case studies and simulations in their classroom (Westerfield 1989).

The Foreign Language Curriculum

In the United States, LSP has been gaining ground in the foreign language curriculum of higher education for the past decade. The results of a recent survey of LSP in U.S. higher education (Grosse and Voght 1990) showed that LSP courses are evenly distributed among small, medium, and large private and public institutions of higher education. The percentage of institutions offering LSP has remained fairly constant from 1983 to 1989. In 1983, 280 institutions of 450 responding (62 percent) offered LSP courses (Grosse 1985), while in a 1989 survey (Grosse and Voght 1990), 328 institutions of 569 responding (58 percent) reported LSP in their foreign language departments.

The rationale for the trend toward expanded institutionalization of LSP derives from the national impetus to promote foreign language study and diversify the curriculum, the need to infuse humanistic perspectives into professional education, and the movement to internationalize higher education in the United States.

Department chairs who responded to a 1989 survey (Grosse and Voght 1990) indicated that the most important reasons for including LSP in the curriculum were to promote foreign language study, meet student demand, and diversify the foreign language curriculum. Secondary reasons included the infusion of professional education with humanistic perspectives and meeting the needs of employers. Other chairs cited the following as reasons departments do not offer LSP: low demand, lack of faculty trained to teach LSP, and lack of fit within a liberal arts institution.

The failure of the traditional curriculum to hold student interest in foreign language study beyond the first two years is well documented by the profession as well as national task force reports (Schulz 1979; Brod 1983). Di Pietro et al. (1983) and Woloshin (1983) presented strong arguments in favor of diversification of foreign language course offerings in order to prepare students for a variety of careers in which second language proficiency is needed. In Rivers's (1985) outline of new directions for the curriculum, she emphasizes the need to link foreign languages with international studies and the teaching of LSP to encourage students to stay enrolled in foreign language courses long enough to gain a certain level of proficiency.

Academic professional organizations such as the American Assembly of Collegiate Schools of Business (AACSB) have encouraged their member schools of business to internationalize their curriculum and strongly recommend the study of foreign languages and cultures. The U.S. government through Title VI, U.S. Department of Education, the Fund for the Improvement of Postsecondary Education, and private foundations have funded efforts to link foreign language and professional studies (business and engineering, for example). Kramsch (1989) among others, believes that the initiatives to promote alliances between foreign languages and the professions is motivated more by economic and political pressure than interest in humanistic education. Nevertheless she urges foreign language departments to cooperate with other academic units to offer innovative interdisciplinary courses.

The Content of LSP

How does the content of LSP courses differ from that of traditional language courses? LSP balances instruction in language, culture, and professional content. In first- and second-year LSP courses, the balance of course content tips in favor of language instruction as the student develops linguistic competence. At the intermediate level and beyond, the balance shifts to a more even treatment of language and content.

A major debate within the field, particularly in Great Britain, concerns whether general language courses are more effective than the more narrowly focused LSP curriculum. The point seems moot when authentic materials are extensively used, given their rich linguistic content. Also, Krashen's argument for narrow reading and narrow listening would suggest that concentration on a specific subject area enhances comprehensibility of material and language development. Mohan's (1986) classic work on the power of teaching language through content argues in favor of LSP over the traditional language courses for students with professional interests.

Two of the primary areas of difference between LSP and non-LSP courses are course goals and learner needs. LSP advocates believe that teaching through the context of the content area enhances student motivation, provides focus on specific communicative needs, and is thereby of greater interest and relevance to students than are general language courses. Brumfit (1979) argues that the elements of ESP are present in all good language teaching, specifically with regard to learner needs, focus on language function, register, and sociolinguistic appropriateness of discourse. The virtues of LSP include strong concern for learner needs and purposes for learning the language, the time-saving nature of focusing on the precise linguistic needs of the learner, emphasis on language functions and communicative strategies, cross-cultural understanding, analysis of language interaction, attention to register, communicative context, learner-centeredness, and creation of a humanistic classroom. In Brumfit's opinion the best work in ESP takes into account learner purpose, register, text, and interaction process.

At the beginning and intermediate levels, LSP courses differ from traditional foreign language courses in the context of language learning: Oral and written discourse usually is set within a professional context such as business or medicine; texts introduce specialized vocabulary and authentic materials, such as advertisements and business documents from the profession, as the grammatical structures are presented. In advanced LSP courses, by contrast, a greater emphasis is placed on teaching language through the subject matter: Authentic materials such as readings from newspapers, journals, subject-matter texts, case studies, and business documents are used extensively at this level.

In Great Britain at this very moment (early 1991) the difference between LSP and traditional foreign language courses is having to be faced head-on as a new government organization, called the Languages Lead Body, tackles the whole question of standards and qualifications in the field of languages. The Languages Lead Body is one of a number of organizations created because of the concern about the lack of language training in British industry, which is believed to be seriously affecting Britain's economic competitiveness on the world market. Britain's continental partners in the European Community—particularly its strongest trading rival, Germany—are thought to owe much of their success to the excellence of the language component in their industrial training programs.

Although it has been in existence only for some three months, the Languages Lead Body has already decided that it has to operate in two distinct spheres. One is the laying down of standards and the creation or coordination of qualifications for those using languages as professional linguists—teachers of language to adults (including teachers of LSP), translators and interpreters, etc. The other is where there is a component of language in the training for other professions—accountancy, export management, etc. The organizer of the Languages Lead Body has been instructed to get in touch with similar training bodies for such professions in order to arrange this coordination. This development is likely to accentuate the concept of LSP within language teaching in the United Kingdom.

It is perhaps worth mentioning at this point that a clear distinction is emerging between "language teaching" and "language training" in the United Kingdom. "Language teaching" is the teaching of the language in the traditional manner. "Language training" is where one teaches the language for specific purposes.

Some organizations, especially private language schools, offer both "teaching" and "training," according to whether they are targeting teenagers and the general public on the one hand, or business learners on the other. The distinction was clearly seen in the publicity material available at the London Language Show, which started in 1989 and now looks set to become an annual event.

The London Language Show is specifically targeted at British business (advertising in business publications, minimum age limit for admission, etc.), in sharp contrast to the language shows that now take place in most other European capitals, which are targeted at the general public. It is not thought that the general public in the United Kingdom is interested in learning languages, but that business will have to have a language policy because of the advent of the Single European Market. In the other countries, however, the language shows are dominated by the private English language schools, and young people form the majority of those attending.

Although many LSP instructors may succeed at incorporating the teaching of culture into their courses, an analysis of major business French and Spanish texts revealed a disturbing lack of treatment of cultural topics (Uber and Grosse in press; Grosse and Uber forthcoming). Even business culture topics presented in the texts such as banking, the office, and organizational structure tended to be generic in nature rather than specific to a particular culture. Schleppegrell and Royster's (1990) survey of business ESL in English language training schools around the world makes no mention of cultural goals or content in the 55 programs studied.

The development of cultural understanding was clearly not a priority, nor even a minor issue in the business ESL programs nor in the design of the study about the curriculum. The LSP student has as great a need for cultural instruction as do students in traditional language programs; LSP must be careful not to neglect the treatment of culture. One of the ways to enhance the cultural content in LSP courses is through the use of authentic materials such as videotapes of business news programs, commercials, or company-prepared videos that are inherently rich in the target culture.

As the teaching of language moves away from an academic, often literature-based vacuum, the problems of regional differentiations are arising. In the United Kingdom French was always taught with reference to metropolitan France, and in France and Germany, traditionally, English was taught as if situated in the background solely of the United Kingdom. At the increasing number of conferences of francophone countries, concern is often expressed by French Canadians and representatives of French-speaking African countries of this imbalance, and the growing impact of U.S. cultural norms at the expense of British norms has made many continentals dissatisfied with the traditional teaching they have received.

Methodology

Some controversy exists over whether LSP uses the same teaching methodology as general language classes (Hutchinson and Waters 1988) or whether its methodology is entirely dependent on the content area with which it is linked (Widdowson 1983). Swales (1988) advocates a compromise between these two extremes in recognition of the differences in form and function for language and content classes. Ideally the LSP instructor should use methods for teaching language and culture and content area methodology, as well as generally effective pedagogical techniques that transcend disciplinary lines. As an example of borrowing from the content area methodology, the business ESL teacher can use the case study method, commonly used in business schools, to teach target-language business concepts, communication strategies, and language/culture (Grosse 1988). Drawing from second language pedagogy, the instructor can use an interactive, communicative approach to enhance the presentation of content-area material. Examples of generally effective teaching methods that the LSP teacher can employ are the creation of a learner-centered classroom, promotion of classroom interaction, cooperative learning, peer tutoring, application of schema theory, an integrated skills approach, and a process approach to writing. These methodological approaches are similar to those recommended for many other areas of higher education as well.

Impact on the Profession

LSP has made a considerable impact on the foreign language curriculum in the past decade in the United States; its impact on Western Europe has been felt almost three times as long. Given the recent interest in interdisciplinary cooperation and initiatives to diversify the curriculum with content-based instruction, it is very likely that interest in LSP will continue to grow into the 1990s.

The MLA Job Information List reflects the profession's concern with hiring new faculty who are willing and able to teach LSP: A glance at any recent list of position descriptions shows the widespread interest in finding candidates who can teach or develop a department's LSP offerings.

Spack (1988) has raised the important question of whether language teachers, given their frequently limited expertise in content areas, are qualified to teach content-based ESL courses. She cites as potential problems the inability of untrained language faculty to answer student questions or even correct content-based assignments. In reality the extent of the LSP instructor's training in business or other professions ranges from a general knowledge of the field to experience, coursework, or advanced degrees. Instructors with limited training and experience have several ways to remedy the situation, such as acquiring training in the area through courses offered at the institution or abroad by the French, German, or Spanish chambers of commerce, arranging team teaching with a content-area teacher, or judicious use of students as content-area experts. This problem is, if anything, even more acute in the European context, partly due to the emphasis placed on terminology in LSP by the Europeans.

Conclusion

More research should be devoted to determining what people need to learn languages for, not only among existing business language learners, but also among those who ought to be learning languages but who have ducked the challenge. If the question "Why do people need to learn languages?" were pointedly asked more often, the answer would most likely not be the traditionally vague one about how language study is good for one's general education, but rather would reflect the notion that languages need to be learned for specific purposes. We believe, in fact, that LSP is going to become the core element in adult foreign language instruction.

Toward the goal of strengthening LSP courses, several steps should be taken: the inclusion of more cultural instruction to build cross-cultural awareness and communication strategies, development of course objectives that are not too specific and narrowly focused, strong emphasis on the development of critical thinking and problem-solving skills, and provision of opportunities for the students to internalize the language and culture and to use the language for real communicative purposes in and out of class. In the area of materials development, LSP needs more communicative and culturally oriented texts that are based on authentic materials and technology. Finally, LSP faculty at the university should interact with colleagues in other disciplines to explore areas for cooperation for stronger course development and implementation. Foreign language departments should expand the roles of LSP and content-based instruction in their curriculum, and consider establishing linkages with the community to promote the study of foreign languages for application in specific sectors such as business, health, social services, and engineering.

Notes

1. On 1 June 1991, for example, the United Press reported that the University of Findlay (Ohio) had been selected by three educational institutions in Czechoslovakia to develop a summer English program to retrain some 100 of that country's 40,000 Russian language teachers to become English instructors. Many of Czechoslovakia's Russian instructors, the article reported, have only three years to retrain as English teachers or risk losing their jobs.
2. This course was written by Michael Woodhall, head of languages at the Dorset Business College, and Marianne Howarth, of the Language Centre at Brighton Polytechnic. It was launched in 1988 with the backing of the U.K. Department of Trade and Industry.

References, U.S. and European Perspectives on Language for Specific Purposes

Allen, J. P. B., and H. G. Widdowson. 1988. "Teaching the Communicative Use of English," pp. 69–89 in John Swales, ed., *Episodes in ESP.* Englewood Cliffs, NJ: Prentice Hall.

Barber, C. L. 1988. "Some Measurable Characteristics of Modern Scientific Prose," pp. 1–16 in John Swales, ed., *Episodes in ESP.* Englewood Cliffs, NJ: Prentice Hall.

Brod, Richard I. 1983. "The State of the Profession." *Modern Language Journal* 67: 319–29.

Brinkman, Karl-Heinz. 1981. "The Use of Terminology Data Banks in Solving Problems of Specialist-text Translation," pp. 95–107 in Reinhold Freudenstein et al., eds., *Language Incorporated. Teaching Foreign Languages in Industry.* Oxford, Eng.: Pergamon; Munich, Ger.: Max Hueber Verlag.

Brumfit, Christopher J. 1979. "Commonsense about ESP," pp. 71–72 in Susan Holden, ed., *English for Specific Purposes.* London, Eng.: Modern English Publications.

Di Pietro, Robert J., James P. Lantolf, and Angela Labarca. 1983. "The Graduate Foreign Language Curriculum." *Modern Language Journal* 67: 365–73.

Drobnic, Karl, et al. 1988. "Teaching and Learning Materials," pp. 117–29 in John Swales, ed., *Episodes in ESP.* Englewood Cliffs, NJ: Prentice Hall.

Freudenstein, Reinhold, et al., eds. 1981. *Language Incorporated. Teaching Foreign Languages in Industry.* Oxford, Eng.: Pergamon; Munich, Ger.: Max Hueber Verlag.

Grosse, Christine Uber. 1985. "A Survey of Foreign Languages for Business and the Professions at US Colleges and Universities." *Modern Language Journal* 69: 221–26.

_____. 1988. "The Case Study Approach to Teaching Business English." *English for Specific Purposes* 7: 131–36.

_____, and David M. Uber. Forthcoming. "The Cultural Content of Business Spanish texts." *Hispania* 75.

_____, and Geoffrey M. Voght. 1990. "Foreign Languages for Business and the Professions at U.S. Colleges and Universities." *Modern Language Journal* 74: 36–47.

_____, and Geoffrey M. Voght. 1991. "The Evolution of Languages for Specific Purposes in the United States." *Modern Language Journal* 75: 181–95.

Herbert, A. J. 1988. "The Structure of Technical English," pp. 17–27 in John Swales, ed., *Episodes in ESP.* Englewood Cliffs, NJ: Prentice Hall.

Higgins, John J. 1988. "Hard Facts (Notes on Teaching English to Science Students)," pp. 28–36 in John Swales, ed., *Episodes in ESP.* Englewood Cliffs, NJ: Prentice Hall.

Honig, Lucille J., and Richard I. Brod. 1974. "Foreign Languages and Careers." *Modern Language Journal* 58: 157–85.

Hutchinson, Tom, and Alan Waters. 1988. "ESP at the Crossroads," pp. 174–87 in John Swales, ed., *Episodes in ESP.* Englewood Cliffs, NJ: Prentice Hall.

Johns, Ann M. 1990. "English for Specific Purposes (ESP): Its History, Contributions and Future" pp. 67–77 in Marianne Celce-Murcia, ed., *Teaching English as a Second or Foreign Language.* 2nd ed. New York: Newbury House.

Johns, T. F., and A. Dudley-Evans. 1988. "An Experiment in Team-Teaching of Overseas Postgraduate Students of Transportation and Plant Biology," pp. 137–55 in John Swales, ed., *Episodes in ESP.* Englewood Cliffs, NJ: Prentice Hall.

Krahnke, Karl. 1987. *Approaches to Syllabus Design for Foreign Language Teaching.* Washington, DC: Center for Applied Linguistics.

Kramsch, Claire J. 1989. "New Directions in the Study of Foreign Languages." *ADFL Bulletin* 21,1: 4–11.

Mohan, B. A. 1986. *Language and Content.* Reading, MA: Addison-Wesley.

Morrow, Keith. 1979. "Authentic Texts and ESP," pp. 13–15 in Susan Holden, ed., *English for Specific Purposes.* London, Eng.: Modern English Publications.

President's Commission on Foreign Languages and International Studies. 1980. "Strength through Wisdom: A Critique of U.S. Capability." *Modern Language Journal* 64: 9–57.

Rivers, Wilga M. 1985. "A New Curriculum for New Purposes." *Foreign Language Annals* 18: 37–43.

Robinson, Pauline. 1980. *ESP (English for Specific Purposes).* Oxford, Eng.: Pergamon.

Schleppegrell, Mary, and Linda Royster. 1990. "Business English: An International Survey." *English for Specific Purposes* 9: 3–16.

Schulz, Renate A. 1979. *Options for Undergraduate Foreign Language Programs. Four-Year and Two-Year Colleges.* New York: MLA.

Snow, Marguerite Ann. 1991. "Teaching Language through Content," pp. 315–28 in Marianne Celce-Murcia, ed., *Teaching English as a Second or Foreign Language.* 2nd ed. New York: Newbury House.

Spack, Ruth. 1988. "Initiating ESL Students into the Academic Discourse Community: How Far Should We Go?" *TESOL Quarterly* 22: 29–51.

Swales, John. 1984. "ESP Comes of Age?—21 Years after 'Some Measurable Characteristics of Modern Scientific Prose.'" *AISED-LSP Newsletter* 7: 9–20.

————. 1985. "ESP—The Heart of the Matter or the End of the Affair?" pp. 212–23 in Randolph Quirk and H. G. Widdowson, eds., *English in the World.* Cambridge, Eng.: Cambridge Univ. Press.

————. 1988. *Episodes in ESP.* Englewood Cliffs, NJ: Prentice Hall.

Uber, David M., and Christine Uber Grosse. In press. "The Cultural Content of Business French Texts." *French Review* 65.

Westerfield, Kaye. 1989. "Improved Linguistic Fluency with Case Studies and a Video Method." *English for Specific Purposes* 8: 75–83.

Widdowson, Henry G. 1983. *Learning Purpose and Language Use.* Oxford, Eng.: Oxford Univ. Press.

Woloshin, David J. 1983. "The Undergraduate Curriculum: The Best and the Worst." *Modern Language Journal* 67: 356–64.

APPENDIX 12A:
Sources of Information about
Language for Specific Purposes

I. Annual Conference

Since 1981, Eastern Michigan University has held an annual conference on languages and communication for world business and the professions. For more information contact Geoffrey M. Voght, Associate Director, World College, Eastern Michigan University, Ypsilanti, MI 48197, phone (313) 487-0178.

II. Universities with Integrated LSP Programs

A. Dr. Amelia Chan, Language and World Business Undergraduate Program, College of Business, Eastern Michigan University, Ypsilanti, MI 48197.

Dr. John Hubbard, Language and International Trade Undergraduate and Graduate Programs, Department of Foreign Languages, Eastern Michigan University, Ypsilanti, MI 48197.

See also Ron Cere, "Program Development for Foreign Language Intercultural Courses," *Canadian Modern Language Review* 44,2 (1988): 316–33; Ray Schaub, "International Internship Exchanges for Successful Business Language Programs," pp. 229–34 in Samia I. Spencer, ed., *Foreign Languages and International Trade: A Global Perspective* (Athens, GA: Univ. of Georgia Press, 1987); Ray Schaub, "Language Training for International Business at Eastern Michigan University," *ADFL Bulletin* 14,3 (1983): 51–53.

B. Dr. Bruce Fryer, Master in International Business Studies Program, Department of Foreign Language Studies, University of South Carolina, Columbia, SC 29208.

See also Kate Gillespie and William R. Folks, Jr., "Foreign Language and International Business: The MIBS Program after Ten Years," *Foreign Language Annals* 18 (1985): 47–52; Elizabeth Joiner and Robert Kuhne, "The MIBS Program at South Carolina: An Option for Potential International Business Executives," *Modern Language Journal* 65 (1981): 262–68; Gerda Jordan, "Intensive Language Training for International Business," *Unterrichtspraxis* 10 (1977): 39–43.

C. Dr. Jorge Valdivieso, Modern Languages, American Graduate School of International Management, Glendale, AZ 85308.

D. Dr. José Suarez, Director, Language and International Trade Program, 204 Strode Tower, Clemson University, Clemson, SC 29634-1515.

III. Specialized Programs
  A. German for Business:
    Bettina Cothran, Dept. of Modern Languages, Georgia Institute of Technology, Atlanta, GA 30332-0375.

    Christiane Keck, Department of Foreign Languages and Literature, Stanley Coulter Hall, Purdue University, West Lafayette, IN 47907.

    See also Christiane E. Keck, ed., *Handbook on Business German* (Cherry Hill, NJ: AATG, 1990).

  B. German for Engineering:
    John Grandin, Acting Dean, College of Arts and Sciences, University of Rhode Island, Kingston, RI 02881.

    See also John Grandin, "German and Engineering: An Overdue Alliance," *Unterrichtspraxis* 22 (1989): 146-52.

  C. French for Business:
    Jean-Pierre Cauvin, Chair, French and Italian Dept., University of Texas, Austin, TX 78712.

    See also Eglal Doss-Quinby, "Launching a Business French Course: Networking with New Partners," *ADFL Bulletin* 21,1 (1989): 33-36; Maurice Elton, ed., *French for Business and International Trade* (free newsletter from Maurice Elton, Foreign Languages and Literatures, Southern Methodist University, Dallas, TX 75275-0236).

  D. Spanish for Business:
    Ron Cere, Dept. of Foreign Languages, Eastern Michigan University, Ypsilanti, MI 48197.

    Jorge Valdivieso, Modern Languages, American Graduate School of International Management, Glendale, AZ 85308.

    See also José Reyes, "Commercial Spanish: Instructional Techniques," *Foreign Language Annals* 21,2 (1988): 139-45; Jorge Valdivieso, "Español comercial para estudiantes posgraduados," *Hispania* 70 (1987): 673-78.

13

Current Issues in Distance Language Education and Open Learning: An Overview and an Australian Perspective[1]

Roland Sussex

Centre for Language Teaching and Research
University of Queensland, Australia

Distance education, which used to be considered too complex an undertaking for serious language learning, is making strong progress in Europe,[2] North America,[3] and Australia and New Zealand.[4] The stimulus to add languages to the distance education area has come from policies driving literacy, language education, and further education. The International Literacy Year, 1990, gave strong impetus around the world to mother tongue maintenance. In the European Community many students will be expected to learn two foreign languages beginning in 1992. In North America and in Australia and New Zealand many countries and states have new educational policies, prompted primarily by economic considerations, to put in place significantly wider and more ambitious programs of language learning at all levels than those that have existed heretofore (Stanley et al. 1990). The aim of these initiatives is to integrate language learning

Roland Sussex (Ph.D., University of London) is Professor and Director of the Centre for Language Teaching and Research and Director of the Language and Technology Centre of the National Languages Institute of Australia, both located at the University of Queensland, Brisbane, Australia. He was formerly Professor of Russian and head of the Department of Russian and Language Studies at the University of Melbourne. His teaching and research interests include Slavic linguistics, general and applied linguistics, and computer-aided language learning and artificial intelligence; he has published in these fields in Europe, North America, New Zealand, and Australia. He has just completed a period as Chair of the Cognitive Science panel of the Australian Research Council and is in his last year as coeditor of the *Australian Journal of Linguistics*. He is currently engaged in a research project funded by the Australian Research Council on the application of artificial intelligence and the problem of intelligent help systems in CALL.

into formal educational systems, as well as into broader programs of literacy and language in the workplace.

This expansion has focused attention on a number of problems in language training. In Australia and elsewhere, for example, there is a shortage of teachers of Japanese and other major Asian languages. There are not enough expert centers of instruction, meaning that many would-be learners cannot attend classes. Many other potential learners have full-time employment and thus have no access to traditional instruction. Finally, the ideologies, methodologies, and technologies we are using are not as well suited to the new and more varied context of language learning as they were to the old.

All these factors are focusing attention on distance language education. The British Open University, which has so far avoided language courses, is preparing a full French course for undergraduate study in distance mode (The Open University 1990; Swift 1990). All the European Community countries have open universities, and most are moving into distance language training for both full-degree courses and special-purpose language training (including mother tongue literacy support and second language learning).

These developments have thrown into sharp relief a number of familiar problems, particularly in the cognitive and methodological fields, which successful distance language education will have to master. In addition, there is a revival of interest in open-access learning—the mode of learning that may or may not be proximate, but in which students are able to control much of their own access, pace, and progress through the learning materials, often as an integrated part of a formal course.

The nature and extent of these policy, cognitive, and methodological questions are the focus of this paper. We shall examine a number of parameters in distance and open-access language learning, with the underlying goal of determining key issues that are demanding appropriate answers if applied linguistics is to meet these new challenges. Australia will be used as a case in point, since its National Policy on Languages is giving special impetus to the teaching of languages in a wide range of modes.

The Australian Context

Australia is almost the size of the continental United States, minus Alaska and Hawaii. It has a population of 17 million, or a little more than that of Texas. More than half the population lives in the five major cities, but only Sydney and Melbourne are significantly over the 1 million mark. Australia shares with the United States a dense racial mix, reflecting both indigenous peoples and immigration: in Melbourne, a city of nearly 3 million, one person in four was born overseas and one in four regularly uses a language other than English. Australia also shares with the United States an underlying tendency to monolingualism: Anglophone Australians are not, on the whole, outstanding at learning foreign languages, and in spite of the ethnic mix, much of Australia has been English-oriented and somewhat xenophobic—or merely lazy—about learning other languages.

Some of these factors began a shift about fifteen years ago, when the then-Labor federal government began to implement a policy of multiculturalism. While this change did not radically alter public attitudes toward second language study in Australia, it had a far-reaching effect on language maintenance and on the profile of non-English languages in the Australian educational and social scene. There was a major stimulus for the expansion of ethnic radio and television, ethnic schools, and for general acceptance of non-English languages and cultures as a proper and respected part of Australian society. The movement for language reform culminated in an investigation of the language question by the bipartisan Senate Standing Committee for Education and the Arts, resulting in the National Policy on Languages (Lo Bianco 1987). There followed the establishment of the National Languages Institute of Australia.

The National Languages Institute of Australia has a distributed structure (Sussex 1990) and a mandate to support language and its learning and nurturing in Australia, organized under the following four general headings:

- English for all
- A language other than English for all
- Support for Aboriginal and Torres Strait Islander languages
- Provision of appropriate language support services, including language maintenance

The Institute is composed of a central secretariat in Melbourne; research and development centers in language and society, language and technology, language and testing, and language acquisition; and a growing network of teaching and curriculum centers in major cities. Its goal is to harness Australia's widely distributed linguistic expertise and deliver the benefits of this expertise to the country's widely distributed population.

The Australian National Policy on Languages aroused widespread community discussion and involvement and certainly had a great deal to do with the growing awareness, at both state and federal levels, that Australia's level of language education and skills was significantly below what was required. This perception had to do with an increased awareness of Australia's geopolitical role, economic imperatives involving trade and commerce (partly in the light of the language requirements in the new united Europe of 1992), and the beginnings of a less xenophobic attitude toward the global community of nations and cultures. The immediate result was the designation of nine strategic languages by the federal government, with funding to encourage an expansion of their teaching.[5] The most dramatic effect has been an enormous increase in the number of students learning Japanese: per capita there are more students of Japanese in Australia than in any other country. There has also been a dramatic shortage of qualified teachers of Japanese at all levels, which has been exacerbated by a lack of access to educational facilities, shortages of support services for language teaching and learning, and a heightened tempo in the plans to introduce major changes to the curriculum at all levels from primary to secondary (and perhaps to tertiary), involving the incorporation of language study.

Simultaneously these developments accented the need for improved teacher supply, access to learning, learning support, and means to overcome what Geoffrey Blainey, one of Australia's leading historians, has called "the tyranny of distance" (Blainey 1966). The ground was consequently ripe for the development of distance education; less expected was that language studies would be one of the disciplines in the vanguard.

Language study in Australia is characterized by (1) the presence of expertise at a high level, but unevenly distributed in relation to the nation's need for language education; (2) an excellent technological basis for language-teaching support, including national computer networks and satellite communications, but an insufficient number of teachers skilled in their implementation; (3) a lack of practice in working as teams for planning and delivery of language instruction, largely the product of distance factors; and (4) a sound though numerically small basis of language teaching expertise, which had been nurtured during the preceding decades at least partly by advances in multicultural education (Anderson 1988).

This profile differs from the situation in the United States, where some powerful providers like Pennsylvania State University have long been active in distance education, but where there is little collaboration at a national level; from the situation in Japan, where the Open University of the Air in Tokyo is centrally coordinated and well focused in a homogeneous country and culture; and from that in Europe, where initiatives like the European Open Learning Service (EPOS) are serving to concentrate resources, funding, and goals across national boundaries in a new and powerful way. In many ways Australia has the worst setting, since its geopolitical and economic linguistic needs are particularly pressing while its size and the distribution of expertise conspire against an easy solution (Mageean 1989).

Two Learning Modes for Language: Distance Learning and Open-Access Learning

Distance learning places the problems of language learning in clear perspective. For example, while some aspects of language learning (including linguistic areas and historical/cultural studies) and some aspects of literary studies can certainly be taught effectively in distance mode, the interpersonal and communicative aspects of language acquisition are exceedingly difficult to manage that way. The cognitive language skills and pedagogical issues involved here are not always well understood, and there is unfortunately a widespread and rather simplistic assumption that normal classroom materials can easily lend themselves to transformation into distance-mode learning materials. In reality, such a transformation requires the hands of experts.

Distance education is nevertheless a most powerful medium for the dissemination, updating, and maintaining of knowledge and skills in a country with the geographical and demographic characteristics of Australia, just as it is becoming a key factor in the emerging patterns of teaching and learning in Europe. Distance education offers a vast potential in research, development, and marketing in many areas around the globe. Distance language teaching, which requires a balance of genuine distance-mode and interactive face-to-face learning, presents a particularly challenging test case, but one that is worth tackling. Indeed, it must be tackled because of Australia's National Policy on Languages, which recognizes the need to deploy distance education if second language learning is to be expanded. (Moreover, the lessons learned from developing language programs will be applicable to many other areas of distance learning.)

It goes without saying that significant economies of scale are possible with distance education: The more students that use a course, the more the development costs are amortized and the greater are the possible savings and efficiencies from multiple use of centralized resources. On the other hand, the startup and development costs for such courses are high and the user base is uncertain, since both teachers and students must adopt new techniques of learning in the distance mode.[6] The central question focuses on interaction: What is its source, and how richly can it take place? For computer-aided language learning, for instance, teachers must modify their classroom performance for the new medium. Students, meanwhile, must learn to exploit the new variety of materials and media it offers in spite of the constraints of distance. They must, for example, exercise increased initiative, know when and how to call for help, and generally must take advantage of the democratization of learning that distance learning can provide.

All of this means that distance language learning may not be fully effective for some time, as we learn what kinds of support, interaction, and dialog are needed to address the deficiencies of distance language learning in comparison to face-to-face classroom instruction. It is quite likely that many language skills will not be learnable effectively in distance mode, and that distance learning will have to be supplemented by attendance and learning centers where the interactive face-to-face learning tasks can take place.

Too few educators and learners appreciate the close links between distance education and open-access learning. In the latter mode, students have access to materials to study on their own schedule and at their own pace. In language-teaching terms this often presumes access to a language laboratory, audiovisual and CAL laboratories, and library and other related resources. Both distance education and open-access learning involve high levels of student control and direction, problems of assessment and monitoring, and difficulties of interaction and direction. And both, if well designed and delivered, allow students to learn in ways that make reduced demands on scarce human resources.

For instance, universities everywhere are experiencing reduced staffing and increased student loads. Under these conditions, staff find little time for research or for developing new courses. Open-access learning, even for 20 percent of the course material, can contribute very significantly to making staff teaching loads more manageable. But open-access programs require learning materials of superior quality and design to enable students to achieve levels of learning comparable to those now being attained in regular contact classes. There is a large and significantly unrealized need for the incorporation of open-access learning in non-distance-education language courses. It will be necessary to train language teaching staff in open-access learning techniques if they are to take full advantage of this mode of learning, which is certain to occupy an increasingly prominent place in language teaching in the years to come.

Courses and Resources

The notion of exporting courses is attractive and simple. In a pure distance mode a total, packaged course would seem to have much to recommend it, since in principle the institution managing the course's delivery should have little or no work to do to adapt the course to the conditions of the institution. There are relatively few language courses, however, that lend themselves to instant adaptation to contexts remote from the one where they were developed. Even among cultures as close as those of Britain, the United States, and Australia, foreign language courses do not often transplant well. Computer-based learning materials, for example, are turning out to be significantly culture-specific and some may require rewriting—even in nonlanguage fields—if they are to be successful in different cultures.[7]

A compromise approach that helps to overcome cultural stereotypes as well as the problem of adapting learning materials to the needs of individual learners and groups of learners is to encourage the development of open-access, resource-based materials and curricula: resources rather than courses. With resource-based approaches to curriculum and learning, instructors are able to use collections of modules, materials, and learning-support courseware to construct and tune their own curricula. In some instances, standard packages of resource-based materials may suffice in relatively unchanged form. Where this is not the case, the modular nature of the materials allows a flexible approach, adaptable to the needs of different countries, levels, goals, classes, and individuals.[8] Exportable, exchangeable materials are much easier to conceive and execute in this mode than as self-contained courses.

This issue involves implementation, ideology, educational philosophy, and methodology. Moreover, both course-based and resource-based learning projects (but particularly the latter) depend heavily on the existence of a clearinghouse to facilitate coordination of sourcing of the learning materials. The same can be said of issues of international collaboration in the creation and sharing of data on language-learning materials, research, and support systems: Otherwise it is extremely difficult to find out what work has already been done in this area. While there are important information sources like those for media- and computer-aided language learning,[9] the overall picture of language-learning materials, modes, research, and networking remains obscure. There is a great deal of needless reinventing of the wheel involving the exploration of support services, software, hardware, methodology, learning materials, self-access materials, open-access materials, and so on. There is an urgent and unfulfilled need for a single instrumentality to be entrusted with the collection and dissemination of information relating to these areas.

Advanced Technology and Effective Technology ───────────

Advanced Technology

There are substantial difficulties associated with the creation, delivery, and management of advanced technology-based learning. The most serious of these is cost: Not only is much of the equipment expensive, but also the cost in terms of staff time can be prohibitive, especially in view of the urgent timelines being faced in Australia and elsewhere for the introduction of major expansions of language learning. There are also daunting learning curves for those who wish to become involved in advanced technology and language learning: The whole issue of multimedia and integrated technologies for distance learning and language learning (Plattor and Winn 1983), for example, requires highly specialized skills. This is no less true of interactive videodisc, a specialized area for which developers have to meld a combination of pedagogical expertise with technical video production and editing skills (Castro 1990; Bush et al. 1991). Likewise, the development of "intelligent" computer-aided learning requires the collaboration of a domain specialist in the subject to be taught, an instructional designer, experts in intelligent educational systems, software engineers, and hardware technicians.[10] In sum, our ability to exploit the technology is well behind the potential of that technology, and there are severe and continuing shortages of experts to create, manage, integrate, and deliver high-technology language learning.

This is not to denigrate the high-tech approach to distance language learning. Indeed, not only does advanced technology offer powerful tools for language learning, but also it provides platforms for cognitive research into the kinds of learning that can now be contemplated in a computer-based environment (Last 1989; Lauzon and Moore 1989; Mason and Kay 1989; Phillips et al. 1988; Swartz and Yazdani, in press). The lead time for development of usable learning products in much of the high-technology educational field, however, coupled with the shortage of experts who can implement such teaching and learning, means that we must consider other, shorter-term alternatives as a means of solving some of the pressing needs of language learning, and especially of distance language learning.

Effective Technology

There is a tendency to eschew current technology in language teaching. This is partly due to the perceived inability of much current technology to match the more ambitious pedagogical aims of applied linguistic theory. Rather than regard technological solutions as a replacement for classroom-based language teaching, however, one should creatively investigate ways of exploiting technology-based learning as part of a total integrated learning environment. This approach requires a cadre of teachers and instructional designers with expertise in the exploitation of conventional technology for the purposes of language learning.

While advanced technology is within the budget of research groups in Europe and North America, it is beyond the scope of the majority of countries, whose needs for language teaching are no less pressing but whose budgets and levels of expertise impose severe limitations. (This is true also of many local authorities who are trying to fund new language-learning initiatives on tight budgets.) In these contexts, rather than trying to move directly to the use of advanced technology, which is very expensive and requires advanced skills for its exploitation, it is more effective to consider first the innovative use of more conventional technologies (Bates 1984), such as conferencing (Brochet 1986; Garrison et al. 1987; Wagner and Reddy 1987; Rekkedal 1988; Willis 1987). These options are particularly attractive at a time when, like the present, there is a worldwide shortage of teachers in certain languages.

The familiar telephone can provide one such resource. Though telephone systems in much of Eastern Europe, the Soviet Union, and the Third World remain underdeveloped, most other nations have telephone systems suitable for language teaching and support. The TAMBSPI (Teacher-Assisted, Mastery-Based, Self-Paced Instruction) Project at The Ohio State University has been teaching languages in the distance mode for several years, posting high levels of student achievement (Twarog and Pereszlenyi-Pinter 1988). Schools in Rockhampton, Queensland, Australia, are testing a teaching configuration where a teacher of Japanese uses two telephone lines to deliver simultaneous instruction to a number of classrooms over a distance of about 100 miles: One telephone line carries voice; the second line, using an Australian software package called the Electronic Classroom, connects to Macintosh computers in each classroom, allowing the teacher to run an electronic blackboard at several locations at once. Lesson plans and worksheets are distributed by fax on a weekly basis. This system, which is still under trial, is more efficient and convenient than the peripatetic teacher, especially where long distances are involved. On the evidence so far, the system seems to be very effective, and the students are not inhibited by the technology. Australia has a long tradition of interactive learning by radio for children who live on farms in the Outback, often hundreds of miles from the nearest school. The Rockhampton experiment applies this experience to produce an enriched learning environment at no great cost to the educational system. Mixed technologies are providing even richer potential as language teachers start to exercise their imaginations to find new ways of exploiting these resources. IBM is funding a Foreign Language Multimedia Consortium at Brigham Young University, Smith College, the University of Calgary, the University of Chicago, the University of Illinois at Champaign–Urbana, the University of Iowa, and the University of Pennsylvania to develop multimedia programs for the four skills in French, German, and Spanish. Creighton University, Nebraska, has been experimenting with a program called "Front-Page Sat-Fax," which uses telephone-fax, satellite, and computer technology to transmit front pages of newspapers in various languages to language-teaching sites requiring up-to-the-minute materials in foreign language news and current affairs.

This use of mixed technologies finds a parallel in television teaching. While fully interactive television and teleconferencing are still prohibitively expensive for educational purposes, mixed technologies can overcome some of the costs.[11] The Queensland Education Department, for example, is testing a mixed system in which a teacher is televised from a studio via satellite to a number of school locations, each with a satellite receiving dish; the students, in turn, are linked back to the studio by telephone (Queensland Research Services Branch 1987). Although the channels of interaction are not as rich as in face-to-face contact in the classroom or with full video teleconferencing, the lower-cost solution is viable and effective and can be implemented with a great deal less expense.

Research at the cutting edge of educational technology will continue to provide new initiatives. But in terms of cost and number of educators able to use these initiatives to the best advantage, the most effective way to proceed is to concentrate first on building a sound basis in current technology, generating a significant volume of good-quality teaching and learning materials, and integrating these products and expertise with existing language-teaching expertise. This requires the training of educational technologists, including software engineers; the training or retraining of language teachers in technology-related teaching; and the integration of such technology-based materials into proximate and distance curricula. Finally, it requires a new attitude toward educational networking and the ways in which, without losing the rich initiatives of individual teachers, we use educational networks.

International Communications Media: Radio and Television.   The use of radio and television to support language teaching and language learning has not been implemented in a systematic way in the current language-learning renaissance. The PICS project at the University of Iowa, with funding from the Annenberg Foundation, has been recording satellite television for language learning in the United States and redistributing materials on disk and tape under license. The SCOLA project at Creighton University, Nebraska, arranges for the redistribution of satellite-originating materials to institutions in the United States. The Olympus satellite in Europe broadcasts in five major languages of the EEC (English, French, German, Italian, and Spanish), which brings foreign language television directly to language learners with access to receiving equipment. Even as far away as Australia, dishes of sufficient size—we use 6.5m dishes—are able to provide satellite-based television and radio in a number of languages.[12] With increasing satellite coverage, it would be reassuring to think that some body— perhaps UNESCO—was coordinating international plans for the provisions of radio and television materials for language learners. This is particularly relevant for problems of copyright, which are both complex and often largely untried in the international media. Unfortunately, no such international coordinating authority has yet been established, nor is there an obvious agency to generate the momentum to establish and sustain it.

Electronic Networking: Communication, Information Sharing, and Language Learning Support.   Electronic networks (Lord 1985; Quarterman and Hoskins 1986) have great, and largely unexploited, potential to support language learning in a number of ways. Some of them can provide information collection and dissemination for supporting distance-mode, technology-enhanced language learning. This potential includes the following:

- Teacher support: bulletin boards, advisory services, backup, materials resources, and libraries of computer-aided language learning materials (including digitized speech)
- Student support: communications with instructors and other students, both in Australia and overseas (e.g., electronic mail to students in other countries, as on FrEdMail); backup; submission of assignments; assessment; materials resources; and libraries of computer-aided language-learning materials (including digitized speech)

While working in the context of such a network requires some rethinking of the way one teaches and learns, there are considerable economies of scale to be realized, as well as enhancements of learning modes and flexibility once the networks are integrated into total teaching and learning environments. In particular, networks are able to provide rapid advice, backup, hotlines, and other support for learners who, at certain times, may require urgent attention to learning problems.

International electronic networks like Internet and Bitnet already exist for academics, and language teachers without direct access to Internet and Bitnet can connect to these networks' communications facilities and interest groups through commercial international networks such as CompuServe. The establishment of national language-teaching networks to exploit these communications media is imperative: There are already educational networks in operation in British Columbia (Lange 1986: 3), and the U.S. state of Texas is installing such a network (Stout 1990), as have Queensland and South Australia.

Perhaps the most ambitious initiative in this area, however, is EPOS, the European PTT Open Learning Service network. EPOS is funded under the DELTA (Development of European Learning through Technological Advance) family of research programs of the EEC. EPOS is based in Rome at the Italian telecommunication headquarters, which is coordinating a seven-nation initiative in distance learning. EPOS has a broad and visionary brief centered on the development of an integrated European open-learning system.

Since this is such a fully developed initiative, it is worth presenting the EPOS brief in some detail. Its stated overall goal is:

> to study, define and ultimately to implement a distance learning service aimed at users in many different locations in the partners' respective countries. The service will make it possible to manage, and for users to exchange training and educational information, services and products over the telecommunication network. (EPOS 1990c: 2)

The aim is to exploit Europe's already advanced telecommunications systems to provide a remote-access, self-driven learning environment through which one can gain access to colossal quantities of data, learning environments, and learning materials. The computer basis is to be transparent across a number of standard operating systems and hardware/software platforms. Users will be able to log on to the various data-servers and access the whole data- and learning-base, which will physically be distributed around many parts of Europe. Usage will be charged on a value-added basis, the terms of which are currently being investigated by collaborating companies and research institutes of the EPOS team.

The finer-grained details of the EPOS program include provision of the following:

- Interactive services, such as point-to-point video/audio/text/data transmission
- Background interactive services, including electronic mail, conferencing (audio, video, etc.), and database access
- Directory support: databases of educational materials, educational service providers, and references to other databases and providers
- Tutorial support
- Authoring support
- Assessment/evaluation support
- Electronic library
- Information services

The very scale of the enterprise, and its comprehensive specification, mean that EPOS will potentially provide an interactive network for collaborative work and learning in virtually any field that the EEC chooses to support.

Seen in its broadest terms, EPOS could become a de facto European Operating System, as the EPOS documents frankly state. This goal will put EPOS on a collision course with Friend-21, the collaborative Japanese attempt to preempt the personal computer interface for the next generation of microcomputers, which is being coordinated through the Institute for Personalized Information Environment in Tokyo. Even if EPOS has only relatively minor success, the volume and depth of materials available on and through EPOS will make it a very powerful competitor. Its overt commercial basis and value-added costing philosophy show that the EPOS planners are not in the distance-education business solely in the name of learning and charity, however. It is likely that distance education language planners will have to work with, in parallel to, or in competition with EPOS before the end of the century.

Europe's language needs are probably the most acute of those of any group of countries: The requirements of the EEC include language support for the languages of the EEC, which means massive translating, servicing, and educational commitments for all the member nations. Given the EEC's growing ability to coordinate international projects within programs like DELTA, and given the potential of EPOS to provide learning across national boundaries in an advanced technology environment, it will indeed be a project worth following.

Conclusion: Preparing for Distance Learning _____

On the whole, distance language learning is developing in a bottom-up fashion. Language, however, presents one of the most difficult areas of all to teach in distance mode. For this reason both planning and guidance are needed if the introduction of distance language learning is not to result simply in exaggerated expectations and ultimate disappointment, as happened too often with language laboratories.

Students, Managing Courses, and Learning

Language learning is one of the areas *par excellence* where face-to-face contact between instructor and learner is vital. There are cognitive issues here for distance-education language learning that are relatively unexplored—in particular, what kinds of learning materials, and in what configurations and combinations, will achieve what level of learning, and with what efficiency and retention. Instructors need to understand how to be maximally effective in the distance mode, and students need to know how to get the best out of distance-mode learning; therefore, training programs in the management of distance-mode language learning will be necessary for teachers, students, and policymakers if there is to be success. There is urgent research to be done on distance-mode language learning, in various configurations and with various types of learners and learning domains, in order to establish fundamental principles of learning in this mode, specifically for languages.

Human Capital: Teacher Supply, Training, and Retraining

The current supply of teachers is wholly insufficient, both nationally and internationally, to satisfy the new needs for language learning. If the current goals of Australian language policies are to be achieved, for example, it will be necessary to train new teachers, upgrade the language skills of teachers whose language competence is rusty, and perhaps to cross-train language teachers from less-in-demand to more-in-demand languages. In addition, it will be necessary to train teachers of distance teachers and to train creators of materials for distance learning, so that the distance mode of teaching is properly supported. This is a difficult transition that is widely assumed to be much easier than it is in practice. It will be necessary, therefore, to provide language maintenance support after training, together with a rich collection of teaching- and learning-support materials. Language teachers, already with full teaching and research schedules, will need support and/or relief from their normal duties to tackle the issues of how to encourage a mixture of proximate and self-access learning for language learners.

For this to happen we need both research and coordination, particularly in the area of Asian languages. The European Association of Distance Teaching

Universities model ("EADTU": EADTU Language Programme Committee 1990; EADTU Secretariat 1990; Baissus 1990; Bates 1990; Doerfert et al. 1989), the Centre for Electronic Communications and Open Support Systems in Education (1990) in the U.K., the Commonwealth of Learning (Commonwealth Secretariat 1987), the Open Learning Agency (1989) in Vancouver, and the United Kingdom Council for Educational Technology present useful models of sharing of resources. But a wider forum, particularly for countries of the Third World, would provide a broader base for tackling global problems of language literacy and language competence.

Materials Production

In most languages there is a critical shortage of materials to support distance learning. Distance education, and particularly distance language education, is a highly specialized activity requiring specialized staff, skills, and resources. Instructional design, course structuring, delivery, management, assessment and self-assessment, monitoring, backup and access to help, the combination of distance, indirect-distance, and proximate instruction in language learning, and the use and integration of technology are all factors about which we know relatively little. It is worth considering a means of concentrating and refining existing expertise in the area of materials production, with a view to developing policies for the ongoing supply, training, and retention of expertise.

Accreditation, Portability, and Credit Transfer

A difficult and unresolved issue is the question of credit transfer: how students can gain course credit for units taken in distance mode, or at different institutions. This question is particularly acute with students who are accessing distance learning across national boundaries. If the units are to be accredited nationally or internationally the questions of assessment, evaluation, and accreditation take on major significance. It may well be that existing language tests, including established performers like the TOEFL or IELTS (International English Language Testing System) will need revision, not only to assess language ability acquired in distance mode, but also to make them suitable for ad-ministration in distance mode. These issues should be addressed as part of a coordinated approach to distance language education, since they have a major impact on the portability and exportability of courses.

Distance language learning is not merely a new mode of delivery for language learning. It brings language learning, language teaching, and the planning of language policies into a new cognitive context. Languages are more difficult than most subjects to learn in distance mode because of the complex combination of skills and information required for language mastery. That said, however, distance learning presents a marvelous challenge. Language teachers can either rise to the occasion or can fail to establish a place for languages in what will certainly be a major mode of learning within a decade.

Notes

1. The contents of this paper derive from a 1990 consultancy report that the Language and Technology Centre of the National Languages Institute of Australia submitted to the Australian Department of Employment, Education and Training (Sussex et al. 1990). The other authors of that report all contributed in varying degrees to the ideas presented here. Any remaining infelicities are my responsibility.
2. See, for example, Baissus 1990; Doerfert et al. 1989; EADTU Language Programme Committee 1990; EADTU Secretariat 1990; EPOS 1990a-d; Graff and Holmberg 1988; Holmberg 1985, 1987; Kirkwood 1989.
3. See, for example, Anderson 1988; Davis 1988; Karpiak 1982; Moore 1988, 1990; Russell 1989; Stahmer 1987.
4. See, for example, Evans 1990; Jones 1988; Livingston 1988; South Australian Education Department 1988; Wade 1990; Williams 1988; Williams and Sharma 1988.
5. The nine languages are Japanese, Chinese, Indonesian/Malay, Arabic, French, German, Italian, Greek, and Spanish.
6. These include not only ergonomic mastery of the relevant technologies, but also cognitive mastery, which means reconceptualizing how students, teachers, materials, and resources all interact. Instead of being in the same place at the same time, for example, learners and teachers can be separated by large distances and the lesson can take place synchronously, with students progressing through the same lesson material at different times.
7. For instance, students from many Asian countries are brought up in an educational ethos that does not encourage the vigorous and often aggressive questioning of teachers that is common in North America and parts of Western Europe. Distance learning materials that assume an aggressive independence on the part of the students will be unlikely to succeed in such Asian contexts.
8. Experience in language teaching has shown, for example, that there are many instances where textbooks are not suitable for a given class and require unacceptable levels of supplementation; but modular collections of materials often can be effectively and efficiently developed into a suitable curriculum.
9. For example, the International Association for Learning Laboratories [IALL] and the Computer-Assisted Language Learning and Instruction Consortium [CALICO] organizations, WISC-WARE at the University of Wisconsin, and the journal *ReCall*, the Journal of the CTI Centre for Modern Languages, School of Modern Languages and Cultures, published in connection with the British Computer Teaching Initiative by the Language Centre of the University of Hull, U.K.
10. Most existing intelligent computer-aided language learning is either educationally adequate but not generic, in that it covers a narrow range and cannot be readily adapted to other purposes; or broad but ineffective (or hard to use), since the intelligent tools are not specific enough to given cognitive tasks.
11. This is particularly true of remote locations, where satellites and multiple uplinks make the technology unsuitable for regular teaching purposes.
12. Here, however, there is very little coordination in the area of provision and supply, which means that language learners have to find ways of accessing the material that the satellites provide.

References, Current Issues in Distance Language Education and Open Learning

Anderson, T. 1988. *Trial of Course Delivery by Satellite: The Bar Service and Cellar Operations Courses, via Sky Channel (AUSSAT).* Sydney: New South Wales Department of Technical and Further Education.

Baissus, J. M., ed. 1990. *Report on Language Teaching of the EADTU Programme Committee Language Teaching*. Heerlen, Neth.: European Association of Distance Teaching Universities.

Bates, A. W., ed. 1984. *The Role of Technology in Distance Education*. London and Sydney: Croom Helm.

————, ed. 1990. *Media and Technology in European Distance Education: Proceedings of the EADTU Workshop on Media, Methods and Technology*. Heerlen, Neth.: European Association of Distance Teaching Universities.

Blainey, Geoffrey. 1966. *The Tyranny of Distance*. Melbourne, Vic.: Sun Books.

Brochet, Madge G. 1986. *Effective Moderation of Computer Conferences: Notes and Suggestions*. Papers from the Universities of Ontario Computer Conference. Guelph, Ont.: The Univ. of Guelph.

Bush, Michael D., et al., eds. 1991. *Interactive Videodisc: the "Why" and the "How."* CALICO Monograph series 2. Provo, UT: CALICO.

Castro, Angela S. 1990. "Optical Disks, Multimedia Delivery and Staff Development in Educational Technology." *Distance Education* 11,1: 7–23.

Centre for Electronic Communications and Open Support Systems in Education. 1990. "Elnet. European Business and Languages Learning Network. A summary paper." Southampton, Eng.: The Centre.

Commonwealth Secretariat. 1987. "Towards a Commonwealth of Learning. A Proposal to Create the University of the Commonwealth for Co-operation in Distance Education." Report of the Expert Group. London, Eng.: British Commonwealth Secretariat.

Davis, James N. 1988. "Distance Education and Foreign Language Education: Towards a Coherent Approach." *Foreign Language Annals* 21,6: 547–50.

Doerfert, F., R. Schuemer, and C. Tomaschewski. 1989. "Short Descriptions of Selected Distance Education Institutions." [report.] Hagen, Ger.: Fernuniversität.

EADTU Language Programme Committee. 1990. "Report on the LINGUA Programme." Heerlen, Neth.: European Association of Distance Teaching Universities.

EADTU Secretariat. 1990. *Language Teaching*. [*EADTU News* issue 3, special issue.] Heerlen, Neth.: European Association of Distance Teaching Universities.

EPOS. 1990a. Extracts from WP 2.11: System Architecture. Rome, It.: SIP.

————. 1990b. EPOS Work Packages. Main Goals. Rome, It.: SIP.

————. 1990c. General Technical Issues. Rome, It.: SIP.

————. 1990d. Pedagogic and Didactic Aspects of EPOS. Rome, It.: SIP.

Evans, Terry, ed. 1990. *Research in Distance Education—1*. Geelong, Victoria: Deakin University Institute of Distance Education.

Garrison, D. Randy, Irene Meek, and Ken Adams. 1987. *Enhanced Audio Teleconferencing for University Continuing Education*. Calgary, Alta.: Univ. of Calgary.

Graff, K., and B. Holmberg. 1988. *International Study of Distance Education: A Project Report*. Hagen, Ger.: Fernuniversität.

Holmberg, Borje. 1985. "Teaching Foreign Languages at a Distance." *Distance Education* 6,1: 79–90.

————. 1987. "The Development of Distance Education Research." *American Journal of Distance Education* 1,3.

Jones, N. 1988. *Report of Distance Literacy Projects, July '87–January '88*. Melbourne: Victoria TAFE Off-Campus Network.

Karpiak, Robert. 1982. "Modern Language Teaching by the Correspondence Method: One University's Experience." *The Canadian Modern Language Review* 38: 658–64.

Kirkwood, Adrian. 1989. "Evaluating a Major Innovation in Distance Education: The Home Computing Policy of the U.D. Open University." *Research in Distance Education* 1,2: 4–6.

Lange, James C. 1986. "New Technology and Distance Education: The Case of Australia." *Distance Education* 7,1: 49–67.

Last, R. W. 1989. *Artificial Intelligence Techniques in Language Learning.* Chichester, Eng.: Ellis Horwood; New York: John Wiley.

Lauzon, A. D., and G. A. B. Moore. 1989. "A Fourth Generation Distance Education System: Integrating Computer-Assisted Learning and Computer Conferencing." *American Journal of Distance Education* 3,1: 38–49.

Livingston, K. T. 1988. "Recent Commissioned Reports on Tertiary Distance Education in Australia: Context and Critique." *Distance Education* 9,1: 48–70.

Lo Bianco, Joseph. 1987. *National Policy on Languages.* Canberra, N.S.W.: Commonwealth of Australia Department of Education.

Lord, David. 1985. "Worldwide Networking for Academics." *Computing* 27,5: 27–31.

Mageean, P. 1989. *Overcoming Isolation: Isolated Rural Women's Access to TAFE across Australia.* Melbourne, Vic.: Nelson Wadsworth.

Mason, R., and A. Kay. 1989. *Mindweave: Communication, Computers and Distance Education.* Oxford, Eng.: Pergamon.

Moore, Michael G., ed. 1988. "Telecommunications, Internationalism, and Distance Education." *American Journal of Distance Education* 2,3: 1–7.

————, ed. 1990. *Contemporary Issues in American Distance Education.* Oxford, Eng.: Pergamon.

Open Learning Agency. 1989. *3 Year Strategic Plan 1989–1992.* Vancouver, B.C.: OLA.

The Open University. 1990. "Proposals for the Teaching of Modern Languages." Milton Keynes, Eng.: The Open University.

Phillips, A. F., and P. S. Pease. 1987. "Computer Conferencing and Education: Complementary or Contradictory Concepts?" *American Journal of Distance Education* 1,2: 44–52.

Phillips, G. M., G. M. Santoro, and S. A. Kuehn. 1988. "The Use of Computer-Mediated Communication in Training Students in Group Problem-Solving and Decision-Making Techniques." *American Journal of Distance Education* 2,1: 38–51.

Plattor, Emma, and Bill Winn. 1983. "An Integrated Audio and Graphic Distance Education System, and Its Potential for Teaching Chemistry." *Chemistry in Canada* 35,10 (October): 12–15.

Quarterman, John S., and Josiah Hoskins. 1986. "Notable Computer Networks." *Communications of the ACAM* 29,10: 932–71.

Rekkedal, Torstein. 1988. "The Telephone as a Medium for Instruction and Guidance in Distance Education." Report from an Experiment at NKI, Norway. Stabekk, Nor.: SEFU Norwegian Centre for Distance Education, NKI.

Queensland Department of Education Research Services Branch. 1987. *The Queensland Distance Education by Satellite Trial: Evaluation Report, Year One.* Brisbane, Queensland: Department of Education.

Russell, Thomas L. 1989. "A Study of Foreign Language Instruction via TOTE." *Research in Distance Education* 1,2: 2–4.

South Australian Education Department. 1988. *Distance Learning of Languages in South Australian Schools. A Project of National Significance. Programme Notes and Instructions.* Adelaide, S.A.: South Australian Education Department.

Stahmer, Anna. 1987. *Communications Technology and Distance Learning in Canada: A Survey of Canadian Activities.* Ottawa, Ont.: Social Policy Directorate, Department of Communications, Government of Canada.

Stanley, John, David Ingram, and Gary Chittick. 1990. *The Relationship between International Trade and Linguistic Competence.* Report to the Australian Advisory Council on Languages and Multicultural Education. Canberra, N.S.W.: Australian Government Publishing Service.

Stout, C. 1990. *Electronic Information Transfer System Services.* Austin, TX: State Purchasing and General Services Commission.

Sussex, Roland. 1990. "The Languages Institute of Australia: An Organizational Model for Centralized and Distributed Teaching and Research." *Multilingua* 9,4: 359–75.

_____, et al. 1990. *Report: Australia – UK Educational Exchange Consultancy: Distance Education and Technology in Language Teaching.* Canberra, N.S.W.: NDEC.

Swartz, Merryanna, and Masoud Yazdani, eds. In press. *The Bridge to International Communication: Intelligent Tutoring Systems for Foreign Language Learning.* New York: Springer-Verlag.

Swift, Betty. 1990. *Interest in Open University Modern Languages among Open University Students and Language Students in Colleges of Further Education.* [A report based on surveys carried out in 1988.] Milton Keynes, Eng.: The Open University.

Twarog, Leon I., and Martha Pereszlenyi-Pinter. 1988. "Telephone-Assisted Language Study at Ohio State University: A Report." *Modern Language Journal* 72,4 (Winter): 426–34.

Wade, Mark. 1990. "Distance Education and LOTE in N.S.W." Sydney: New South Wales Department of School Education, Programmes Branch.

Wagner, E. D., and N. L. Reddy. 1987. "Design Considerations in Selecting Teleconferencing for Instructions." *American Journal of Distance Education* 1,3: 49–56.

Williams, S. J., and P. C. Sharma. 1988. "Language Acquisition by Distance Education: An Australian Survey." *Distance Education* 9,1: 127–46.

_____. 1988. *Distance Language Learning: A Survey of Students Enrolled in Language Courses at a Distance in Australian Higher Education Institutions in 1985.* Working Papers in Distance Education No. 12. Brisbane: Univ. of Queensland.

Willis, Barry. 1987. *Teleconference Bridging Options: A Cost / Benefit Analysis.* Anchorage: Univ. of Alaska.

Index to Persons Cited

Index to Topics Cited